T0299281

"International development and cooperation is a profession—like diplomacy and defense. Practitioners all need skills in project design, negotiating, compliance, M&E, and building multi stakeholder alliances. Hats off to Professors Keilson and Gubser for creating a practical set of case studies, 'live' from the real world."

—**William Reese**, *CEO of International Youth Foundation, USA*

"This highly-readable contribution to the development literature eloquently captures what we field practitioners know to be true: that achieving project impact involves dedication to many bureaucratic tasks and distractions that often hinder our ability to serve the beneficiaries of development interventions. The essays in this volume are written by real field professionals who understand, and have lived with and overcome, these challenges."

—**Lee Rosner**, *USAID*

"*The Practice of International Development* is a wonderful resource book to learn the challenges and opportunities that donors, implementing organizations, and governments face when trying to implement successful international development."

—**Byron Radcliffe**, *Radcliffe Global Solutions, USA*

The Practice of International Development

Development analysts tend to give short shrift to the seemingly minor bureaucratic hitches faced by practitioners—those who design, manage, implement, and evaluate aid projects. Often critical of foreign aid either for its apparent ineffectiveness at alleviating poverty or its purported neocolonial implications, the academic literature rarely acknowledges the experiences and pressures faced by practitioners themselves as they implement aid-funded development projects—the meetings, paperwork, negotiations, site visits, financial transactions, logistical arrangements, interviews, program activities, and beneficiary interactions—that keep projects running. And yet the impact of aid projects, and indeed the impact of development itself, often grows out of the daily activities and personal interactions of development practitioners. This unique book considers challenges from the perspective of development practitioners who confront technical, managerial, political, theoretical, and moral quandaries on a daily basis.

With chapters written by expert practitioners on different aspects of design and management of international development activities, this book examines real issues and navigates the often contradictory demands of local development needs, including international donor imperatives; limited financial resources, time, information, and assurance of results; the competing pulls of administrative efficiency; and the desire to alleviate suffering. It also gives readers access to the crucial but little-heard voices of those who spend their professional lives designing and managing foreign aid projects, offering insight into what did or did not work on projects they have managed, implemented, or evaluated. These insights do not seek to identify universally right or wrong ways of doing development; instead, they highlight pros and cons associated with various approaches and decisions. This book provides valuable insights for students and others interested in a development career, encourages practitioners to engage in reflection, and persuades researchers to further consider the influence of practice on project success or failure.

Jerrold Keilson currently serves as AIR Vice President, International Policy, Practice, and Systems Change, and is Adjunct Professor in the School of Public Affairs, American University, USA.

Michael Gubser is Professor of History at James Madison University in Virginia, USA and an aid practitioner with experience in project evaluation and project design. His most recent book is *The Far Reaches: Phenomenology, Ethics, and Social Renewal in Central Europe* (2014).

PUBLIC ADMINISTRATION AND PUBLIC POLICY
A Comprehensive Publication Program

EDITOR-IN-CHIEF
DAVID H. ROSENBLOOM
Distinguished Professor of Public Administration
American University, Washington, DC

Founding Editor
JACK RABIN

RECENTLY PUBLISHED BOOKS

The Practice of
International
Development

Edited by
Jerrold Keilson and
Michael Gubser

Routledge
Taylor & Francis Group

NEW YORK AND LONDON

First published 2018
by Routledge
711 Third Avenue, New York, NY 10017

and by Routledge
2 Park Square, Milton Park, Abingdon, Oxon, OX14 4RN

Routledge is an imprint of the Taylor & Francis Group, an informa business

Library of Congress Cataloging-in-Publication Data
A catalog record for this book has been requested

ISBN: 978-1-4665-8672-7 (hbk)
ISBN: 978-1-315-09843-2 (ebk)

Typeset in Adobe Garamond Pro
by Apex CoVantage, LLC

Contents

Contributors

Abdalla Uba Adamu is Professor of Media and Cultural Communication, as well as Professor of Science Education, at Bayero University in Kano, Nigeria. He is currently Vice-Chancellor of the National Open University of Nigeria, the largest Open and Distance Learning (ODL) institution in West Africa. His research focuses on the transplantation of transnational ideas in developing countries. He is the author of *Reform and Adaptation in Nigerian Higher Education: Living on a Credit Line* (Mellen, 1994). Dr. Adamu also regularly consults on education projects in Nigeria.

Michael Gubser is a professor of history at James Madison University in Virginia and an aid practitioner with experience in project evaluation and project design. His books and articles focus on the history of international development and European intellectual history. His most recent book is *The Far Reaches: Phenomenology, Ethics, and Social Renewal in Central Europe* (Stanford, 2014).

Terrence Jantzi is a scholar/practitioner in International Development and program evaluation. He currently has joint appointments as an associate professor of practice in the Peacebuilding and Development program at Eastern Mennonite University and as Country Representative for the Mennonite Central Committee's programming in Colombia. Since the late 1980s, Dr. Jantzi has worked as a scholar, practitioner, and consultant throughout Latin America, Southern Africa, and Eastern Europe. His research interests revolve around the unintended consequences in development and the construction of community social capital.

Jerrold Keilson is an international development practitioner and academic with more than 35 years of experience in the field. He currently serves as AIR Vice President, International Policy, Practice, & Systems Change. After beginning his career with the State Department as a Foreign Service officer, Mr. Keilson held senior positions with international NGOs such as Creative Associates, the International Youth Foundation, and World Learning. He is also an adjunct professor in American University's School of Public Affairs, where he teaches courses on international development. He has degrees in history from the University of Massachusetts–Amherst and Clark University.

August Longino worked for two years as Medical Programs Coordinator in Ecuador for the medical relief NGO Timmy Global Health. He is currently a medical school student at the University of Washington School of Medicine.

Nathalie Louge has a decade of experience as a Literacy and Learning Advisor providing technical assistance to education programs worldwide in conflict and post-conflict countries. She holds an M.A. in International Education and Development from the University of Sussex, a graduate reading specialist certificate from the University of Virginia, and a Bachelor of Science in Human Development and Early Childhood Education from Cornell. At the time of authorship, she was with Education Development Center (EDC).

Since 1983, **Mark Lynd** has served as a teacher, teacher trainer, instructional materials specialist, project manager, program evaluator, and education policy specialist for USAID, the World Bank, and other organizations in Africa, Latin America, the Pacific, and the United States. Lynd directs School-to-School International (STS), a non-profit organization he co-founded in 2002 with education projects in over 20 countries.

Katherine A. Merseth leads RTI International's practice area in international early childhood development. She builds institutional partnerships, designs programs, and sets the long-term strategic vision for RTI's early childhood work in low- and middle-income countries. She has previously worked for several international development organizations, including Save the Children US, Creative Associates International, and Winrock International.

Joshua A. Muskin is Senior Program Director of Education at Geneva Global. He has over 30 years of experience in international development, working with bilateral, multilateral, and non-governmental organizations and governments in over 50 countries. He has worked especially in the field of education, addressing curriculum and instruction, gender equality, community partnership, assessment, literacy, and vocational training. Most recently, Dr. Muskin was Non-Resident Senior Fellow at the Brookings Institution and Senior Education Officer at the Aga Khan Foundation. He completed his graduate studies at the University of Pennsylvania.

Elizabeth Phelps is a Peruvian-American cultural anthropologist who has worked in international development and non-profit organizations for twenty years. She is currently co-country representative for the Mennonite Central Committee in Bogotá, Colombia.

Carl Stauffer is Associate Professor at the Center for Justice and Peacebuilding, a graduate program of Eastern Mennonite University. He has practiced in the fields of peacebuilding, justice, and development for 26 years. His work has taken him to 35 different countries, and he lived for 16 years in South Africa while training and consulting in 20 other African countries on post-violence reconstruction, transitional justice, and reconciliation.

Anna Vogt is the Latin America and the Caribbean context and advocacy analyst for the Mennonite Central Committee. She is based in Bogotá, Colombia.

Acknowledgments

Jerrold Keilson

The idea for this volume arose from discussions with graduate students at American University, who were eager for careers in international development yet discouraged from pursuing it because much of the literature focuses on what does *not* work in the field. The effort to provide examples of what does work led to this book. My co-editor, Mike Gubser, was instrumental in bringing the concept from idea to finished product. It has been nearly 15 years since we first discussed ideas of development and history, and I appreciate and value every conversation we have. A huge thanks is due to our contributors, many of whom devote their lives to making the world a better place. They did an excellent job sharing what they have learned in these pages. Thank you also to my parents, who never fully understood the nature of international development work but who unfailingly clipped out newspaper articles on anything related to development and mailed the clippings to me. And finally, to Ellen, who gave me the time and support necessary to complete this book, and who keeps me going.

Michael Gubser

I owe my education in international development to many people, but any short list would include Kate Carpenter, Terry Jantzi, Larry Lai, Mark Lynd, and Jon Silverstone. I learned much from all of them. There is one person, however, to whom I am most indebted in this regard, and one of the great joys of doing this book has been the chance to co-edit it with him. Fourteen years ago, Jerrold Keilson hired a complete novice in international development to serve as a proposal coordinator in his new business development unit. Now less green, I want to thank him for the risk he took, the training he patiently offered, and the friendship that he has extended ever since. As always, my deepest debts are the most personal: to my parents and sister, who supported every career turn I made; to my children, Theo and Mira, whose development is miraculous to watch; and to my wife, Elisa, who aids and guides me wherever I go.

Introduction

Jerrold Keilson and Michael Gubser

One rhythm of development practice in the Nigerian city of Kano is the rhythm of heat: the alternation between a pounding sun outside—108°F (42°C) in May—and a cooler but stagnant indoor warmth. In 2011, in a shaded office of the Bayero University Education building, one of this volume's editors (Mike) had a conversation with a consultant for donor education projects in northern Nigeria that encapsulates many of the patterns noted in this book. After completing the interview, the consultant commented that sometimes even seemingly minor project arrangements reveal the gulf between donor expectations and local realities—in this case, the payment schedule for his team of evaluators. Typically, donors do not pay for project activities in one lump sum but, rather, pay in small installments, bit by bit as activities proceed, wiring money to a secure, vetted bank where it must be retrieved in person by the head of the team. For Western project managers, the need for these precautions is obvious: Especially in a country like Nigeria that is so closely associated with financial fraud, limiting the amount of transfers and using a bank with links to Western partners decreases the likelihood of corruption or theft. In addition, splitting payments into small tranches provides an incentive for continued high-quality effort—essentially a salary for ongoing work. This incremental rhythm of payment is such standard practice that it goes largely unquestioned by donors: receive partial payment, do some of the project work, receive more funds, do more.

Yet in Kano, this schedule caused problems. Like many developing country metropolises, Kano has horrible traffic. The recipient bank for fund transfers, complained the consultant, was located across the sprawling city from Bayero University, where he was an education professor. It could take a half day or more—every couple months—just to traverse the clogged urban center to retrieve money needed for activities. In the midst of his various professional duties, each added trip—undertaken in the heat and pollution of Nigeria's second-largest city—was not only a tremendous inconvenience; it conveyed a disregard for local partners, indifference to their time and effort. It could also impede project operation. If the professor's calendar was full, he might not be able to make the trip for several weeks, with resulting delays in the payment of his evaluation team and postponement of planned activities. Why not find a closer bank? Why not wire larger sums less frequently so that activities were not constantly interrupted? Why not recognize that Western practices do not always work well in Nigeria? Why not adjust to realities in the country where a project operates?

This is precisely the kind of practical challenge that is rarely found in the literature on development but that practitioners deal with every day. Indeed, development analysts tend to give short shrift to the seemingly minor bureaucratic hitches faced by practitioners—those who design, manage, implement, and evaluate aid projects. The academic literature on foreign aid concentrates largely on theory, policy, and beneficiary impact—all important themes, but not the only or even the most proximate determinants of project success or failure. Often critical of foreign aid either for its apparent ineffectiveness at alleviating poverty or its purported neocolonial implications, this academic literature rarely acknowledges the experiences and pressures faced by practitioners as they implement aid-funded development projects. There are some important exceptions: The pioneering work of James Ferguson based its critique of a livestock management project in Lesotho on the close analysis of World Bank reports.[1] David Mosse's careful parsing of a decade-long agricultural project in India examined pressures on development workers and the ways they responded.[2] And Mosse's Institute for Development Studies colleague Robert Chambers made a career out of charting the patterns and implications of development practice.[3] The advocates of rigorous impact evaluations, notably Esther Duflo and Abhijit Banerjee, have more recently examined the links between specific activities and desired outcomes, sometimes distinguishing among seemingly slight discrepancies of project application in order to determine if they affect results.[4] It is nonetheless fair to say that development analyses by and large overlook the rhythm of daily practices (the meetings, paperwork, negotiations, site visits, financial transactions, logistical arrangements, interviews, program activities, and beneficiary interactions) that keep projects running and constitute their most obvious face—even though this web of practices stands between policy/planning and outcomes/impact, translating the one, hopefully, into the other.

Since much academic literature ignores these project experiences, it goes unread by many practitioners, who are generally too busy managing projects and meeting deadlines to engage in higher-level debates about the significance of their work. What practitioners do read (and write) constantly are extensive reports and gray literature on project activities and donor trends. These reports contain detailed itineraries of activities undertaken and money spent, yet they are largely ignored in the policy and academic reckoning of aid success or failure. But even this voluminous gray literature, oddly enough, exhibits only a muted concern for the day-to-day practices of aid employees. Instead, project reports concentrate on contractual obligations—summarizing project activities, providing responses to donor requests, or distilling complex problems and challenges into brief 'lessons learned' with proposals for operational adjustment. The often chaotic rhythms of daily implementation are smoothed over to present a clear and positive image of a project's march toward its goals, reassuring donors and politicians alike. As a result, the people who write about development—and shape the aid discourse—are rarely those who 'do' it, and those who 'do' development rarely write about what they do.

Between these two literatures, we are left with a missing middle. It is our contention that the impact of aid projects—in other words, the impact of development itself—often grows out of the daily activities and personal interactions of development practitioners. These can have as much influence on the success and failure of projects as donor policies or cultural expectations. Indeed, as several essays in this volume suggest, an overwhelming focus on the theories, policies, and rhetoric of development can lead us to miss the surprising persistence of many practices across drastically different aid regimes, from modernization and growth with equity to neoliberalism and governance strengthening. These changing paradigms of development might lead us to think that new trends lead to drastic variations on the ground; from a practitioner viewpoint, however, many projects look similar over time despite widely divergent justifications. The same can work in reverse: Changes in hiring practice, report timing, personal interactions, or management styles can radically alter the effectiveness of a program, even if there are no substantial changes in its overarching model. The rhythm of practice, in other words, is different from that of theory and policy, since it involves constant negotiation with administrative duty, contractual detail, and local expectation. This volume highlights these patterns by enabling practitioners to speak about their own experiences and concerns, rather than through donor policy demands or theoretical frameworks.

Both editors of this volume cross frequently between development practice and academics, and they are acutely aware of the paradoxical nature of this border. On the one hand, it is commonly traversed by academic-consultants and practitioner-professors; on the other, it is strangely impervious to the passage of ideas and perspectives, and even those who present one viewpoint in the classroom may practice something quite different on a project. Michael, one of the book's editors, emphasizes the importance of historical analysis in his development research and teaching, but when writing aid proposals or evaluating projects he often finds that he has no time to conduct substantial historical research and thus falls back on more typical presentist or decontextualized modes of project analysis. Part of this accelerated tempo is determined by the constant interplay between planning and improvisation. Development practitioners must adhere to strict overarching goals even while undertaking protean administrative tasks. They must balance the day-to-day negotiations of project management and implementation against the relatively fixed planning and policy documents that frame their work—a near-sighted focus on meeting regular deadlines, interacting with officials, and achieving stated tasks in a particular time and place against the far-sighted concern for programmatic methods and goals. In 1984, the French theorist Michel de Certeau distinguished between two ways of experiencing a city: the "geographical" and the "migratory." The former involves mapping the urban landscape and identifying the direct routes toward various destinations; the latter entails wandering the streets on foot, discovering unexpected neighborhoods and byways.[5] The former requires far-sighted urban planning; the latter, local exploration that does not always have a clear direction or vantage point. In project landscapes across the world, the development practitioner must do both—plan and invent. She must refer to a fixed map yet be ready to improvise and explore the unknown, a combination that is always less precise than it appears in project reports.

It was partly this lack of practical literature on development realities that spurred us to edit this volume. After years of experience teaching international development and working for development NGOs, we were very aware of the dearth of literature related to designing and managing foreign aid programs. Many development analyses written since the late 1980s—even those that address development practice—offer a litany of what does not work and what not to do.[6] It tends to ignore, however, the positive examples of what can work and what should be done. Jerrold, the book's other editor, found that students frequently challenged him in courses on international development management, noting that they were discouraged by literature that portrayed foreign aid projects as poorly designed and ineffective. As a practitioner, he knew of many programs that made a significant difference in their countries and communities of operation. But in the existing literature, it is difficult to find examples of positive change or explanations of what can lead to project success. While this volume offers both positive and negative examples of foreign aid practice, it does so within the broader spirit of trying to improve results and educate future generations of development professionals rather than valorize or condemn the 'aid industry' as such.

One point will be immediately obvious to readers of this volume: There is no single community of development practice or unitary practitioner viewpoint. Indeed, as the reader will find, there are multiple, sometimes overlapping, practitioner communities—and various types of practice that sometimes complement and at other times contradict one another. In this introduction, we would like to distinguish among three divisions or sub-communities of practice. Sometimes practitioners cluster according to geographic focus. While development professionals travel all over the globe, there are subgroups that specialize in certain regions and tend to concentrate there. Some practitioners spend most of their time in Africa or Latin America. In the 1990s, many practitioners developed a focus on Eastern Europe. Unlike academic turfs, these concentrations are rarely exclusive, but experience and language competence do lead to some regional specialization.

More official divisions emerge around development sectors—education, health, civil society, economic growth, poverty alleviation, evaluation, and others. These technical specializations are harder to bridge than those of geography because each sector has its own distinct professional jurisdictions, culture of education, conferences, publications, and required experience. Doctoral degrees are common, for example, among educators and rarer for those engaged in civil society programs. While the two editors of this volume have worked extensively in proposal writing for multiple sectors of development, their background and connections are strongest in education, a fact reflected in many of the contributions to this book.

Finally, development practitioners also form subgroups based on the type of organization they most commonly work for. This volume, for example, highlights a significant divide between those who spend their careers primarily running projects for large bilateral and multilateral donors (sometimes dismissed in the United States as "Beltway bandits" because so many of them cluster in the Washington, DC, area) and those who work for small NGOs, either international or indigenous to the countries of operation. Though by no means universally true, the former are often based around relatively short-term, highly funded projects, whereas the latter often manage longer-term, more inexpensive programs. Some organizations—often those with external religious or child sponsorship monies that do not have to depend on large donor funds—operate in both worlds. A similar divide exists between home office staff (those responsible for managing projects from the United States) and field personnel (who work directly on projects in developing countries). As the contributors to this book reveal, one's assessment of the merits of a development model often depends on the vantage point one typically holds. We do not try to resolve longstanding disputes about the short-term project model of development or the merits of bilateral funding, but the volume does present various perspectives on these debates.

The aim of this volume is not to describe 'what development practitioners do every day'—write reports, attend meetings, visit project sites, make budgets—in any thorough way, although it does touch on many aspects of practitioner life. Instead, the essays address various challenges and dilemmas that practitioners deal with on a regular basis, dilemmas that shape project activities and outcomes in myriad ways but on which practitioners have little time to reflect. These practical challenges rarely enter theoretical discussions about development, perhaps because they often concern seemingly mundane tasks, such as how participants travel to a workshop during rainy season, or how to build a collaborative relationship with a key government official. Yet all of these tasks entail a series of choices—often made by practitioners rather than policymakers—that can make the difference between project success and failure.

The essays in this volume are written by professionals with extensive practical experience designing, managing, implementing, and evaluating development projects; some also have academic experience in research and writing. Among the aims of this volume was to offer them a chance to reflect on aspects of development practice from a more removed vantage than is typically allowed in project settings. It also gives readers access to the crucial but little-heard voices of those who spend their professional lives designing and managing foreign aid projects. Some authors in this volume use theory to shed light on development practice; others provide personal anecdotes or accounts of particular projects that reveal pervasive tendencies; and still others reflect on recent donor emphases such as sustainability, evaluation, and local partnerships. But all of them stress the relation of these themes to the practice and experience of running development projects. And all of them share insights into what did or did not work on projects they have managed, implemented, or evaluated. These insights, it should be emphasized, do not seek to identify universally right or wrong ways of doing development; instead, they highlight advantages and disadvantages associated with various approaches and decisions.

Of the themes that emerge in this collection, we highlight two in the introduction. Perhaps the theme most widely mooted by authors in this volume is the tension between the constraints of following project plans and contractual requirements, on the one hand, and the need for flexibility in order to accommodate local perspectives and changing circumstances, on the other—what Derick Brinkerhoff and Marcus Ingle called the blueprint versus the process model of development management.[7] The blueprint model calls for a clearly articulated program laid out over three to five years, with resources, deliverables, and results specified prior to implementation. The process model stresses that development requires engaging stakeholders in a process of change and local capacity-building, and that this process cannot be fully planned at the outset since it involves working in a fluid environment. The blueprint model frequently prevails with government donors, whereas the process model is often applied on community development programs. Practitioners typically navigate both at the same time, despite the tension between them. As this volume attests, they feel this tension acutely. Some contributors discuss the discrepancy between development as a business dedicated to meeting targets and development as an exercise in social change, with all the implied unevenness; others take up the discrepancy between mandates from donor offices and demands met locally in countries of operation—a widespread mismatch that development professionals, traveling among continents, encounter with great regularity but rarely cite in reports. A related tension is that between the theories and models of development encountered in wealthy countries—often in textbooks or in the halls of the World Bank and other donors—and the practical compromises required in host countries to ensure that a project runs smoothly. The authors do not propose any resolution to this tension between planning and flexibility—both are necessary for a successful project—but they do highlight the quandaries it presents in foreign aid work.

A second theme widely canvassed in this volume does perhaps suggest a wider critique of current development practice. Very often, the local context of a development project—whether regional or national—is given short shrift in planning and design documents. Several contributors highlight the perverse effects of this oversight. Some authors lament the lost political and institutional context of project operation; others, the missing historical background of local cultures and sectors. In either case, they call on managers to cultivate a deeper understanding of local customs, perspectives, and relationships than is typically required in planning documents and project reports—a contextualization, they argue, that can help projects deliver greater success and sustainability. The tension that results from the need to follow decontextualized planning documents while still honoring local norms that may contradict those documents is felt in all aspects of development practice.

The essays in this volume address development practice in many ways. Katherine A. Merseth opens the book by trying to identify the "elusive alchemy of successful development work" in an early childhood education activity in Jordan. According to Merseth, a successful project combines three elements: a proper understanding of the local development problem, a proposed solution that is commensurate with the scope of the problem, and the necessary resources to carry it out. She shows that while these elements may seem straightforward, they are quite challenging to mobilize in practice. Indeed, one of her central messages is the need for projects to be nimble and flexible throughout their implementation. The elements of a good development project are not marshaled once and for all at the start of an activity but must be constantly re-negotiated in response to unforeseen opportunities and challenges. For an industry that places great weight on advance planning, it is often difficult to resolve the tension between the contractual fulfillment of design plans and the frequent need to shift plans as a result of changing circumstances. 'Getting it right' is always an ongoing process.

Mark Lynd addresses similar concerns from a different angle. He reflects on an education project that he managed in Guinea in the 1990s, focusing in particular on the use of radio instruction to improve teaching and learning in remote classrooms. Inverting Merseth's attempt to identify the aspects of successful foreign assistance, Lynd asks what is missing in the standard development template that prevents apparently successful aid projects from building a lasting legacy. He argues that aid projects rely too heavily on the assumption that local problems can be resolved with external project inputs. This self-justifying mandate often leads project designers and managers to disregard or minimize wider contextual factors that external aid alone cannot influence. In addition, the focus on a steady stream of inputs often leaves little time for reflection or course correction during a project. Lynd's essay suggests ways that practitioners can try to improve development impact within the framework of ongoing projects.

In "Balancing the Contradictions," Terrence Jantzi highlights one of the quandaries that makes successful development work so elusive: a resistance to change among many practitioners and organizations. Jantzi notes the surprising persistence of widely accepted critiques of development over many decades. He argues that development projects reproduce the same practices year after year because program managers are caught between two contrasting models: development as social improvement and development as a business. By surveying several "tension points" in modern development practice, he shows how these two models establish incentives that at times complement but often conflict with each other. The result is a frequent inability to implement needed program revisions. While the advocates of rigorous impact evaluation worry that we simply do not know what works in development, Jantzi points out that lack of knowledge is often not the culprit. Development success or failure is also affected by a set of conceptual and organizational impediments to change that prevent the implementation of widely understood principles.

In "Relationships, Emotional Intelligence, and the Management of International Development Programs," Jerrold Keilson presents a practice-based reflection on project management that draws together several themes mooted by other authors in this volume. Directors of foreign aid projects, Keilson notes, are typically recruited for their technical or financial expertise. Yet project management involves first and foremost the management of people in order to encourage new modes of thought and behavior. While all managers motivate people, aid project directors must oversee staff members, beneficiaries, and counterparts across vast gulfs of culture and power. Doing so effectively requires a complex balance of commanding respect and authority while also acknowledging unfamiliarity and the local expertise of others. For Keilson, the ability to "think people, not policies" necessitates a heightened awareness of "intercultural management" principles as well as the cultivation of an emotional intelligence that can span different countries and value systems.

Joshua Muskin's essay homes in on one of the holy grails of recent aid programming: sustainability. Within development, this ubiquitous term means something relatively specific—the ability of project activities to outlast foreign aid funding—though, as Muskin shows, slight differences in definition can lead to real confusion in program goals. Ensuring sustainability may involve locating alternate funding streams; it almost certainly requires embedding activities in local communities and institutions as a way to ensure continued commitment. As Muskin argues, however, sustainability is extraordinarily difficult to achieve. Development activities—even wonderfully successful ones—often dissolve when a project closes, as participants return to old habits. After anatomizing the various dimensions of sustainability, Muskin argues that it depends not simply on operational strategies but also on the cultivation of a shared developmental vision and—paradoxically—on the willingness to change to accommodate new circumstances. A successful project is often one that revises all of its external trappings and activities in order to maintain a core vision as circumstances evolve. This is the paradox of sustainability.

Michael Gubser's essay, "The Walls of Kano," also explores the dilemmas of sustainable programming through the examination of two USAID education projects in northern Nigeria. Gubser argues that one of the fundamental challenges for development planning is to pay greater attention to historical and contextual factors in project design, implementation, and evaluation. Practitioners often pay lip service to the importance of history in shaping the problems of the present, but strict deadlines and funding caps make it far more practical to import models from other countries than to design activities specific to local needs. While these imports may yield a successful aid project in the short run, the failure to accommodate local context and experience means that even successful initiatives, as Muskin noted, do not often survive the end of project funding.

Similar concerns inform Nathalie Louge's essay, "Practitioners Caught in the Middle," about efforts to improve education programming in the Democratic Republic of Congo (DRC). Practitioners working in the DRC are often caught between strict donor timelines and local challenges that inhibit rapid change. Louge argues that practitioners should take an active role in partnering with local organizations and contributing to policy changes as a way to infuse donor plans with local experience and ideas; they should also carefully document challenges and best practices in order to promote more effective development strategies. Louge shows that recent progress in aligning funder goals with Congolese realities has resulted in advancements in local literacy.

In "Participation and Partnership: Power Plays in Lowland Bolivia," Elizabeth Phelps takes a different tack on explaining the success and challenges of community development programming. Examining a small veterinary training project in 1990s Bolivia, she argues that recent emphases on partnership with local NGOs and participation of program beneficiaries in decision-making can enhance the effectiveness and sustainability of development activities. At the same time, however, participation and partnership bring new challenges, setting up conflicts between international and local partner organizations and slowing down the implementation process. Phelps argues that the tradeoffs required to create more "horizontal" (or equal) power relations among local organizations are worth it, since the alternative—relying on a donor—comes with a significant loss of control over project design and direction. While Phelps questions the benefits of external funding more strongly than others in this volume, her local perspective raises a question that all practitioners face: Who is the client—the donor or the beneficiaries?

Anna Vogt takes up a theme that plays a dominant role in recent criticism of foreign aid: the tendency of aid projects to depoliticize local development. Echoing Phelps, she questions externally designed programming and argues instead

for a model of development practice as 'accompaniment': supporting and participating in community initiatives rather than importing project goals and targets.
Based on her work with a small Colombian NGO, she argues that the willingness
of practitioners to subordinate their views to local needs and plans helped the
small community of Mampuján, displaced by Colombia's civil war, to recover
some of its rights and economic base during a lengthy state-mandated legal process. At the same time, Vogt notes shortcomings of the accompaniment model:
It works effectively with well-organized and well-led communities but tends to
marginalize the more remote and fragmented, who form the majority of displaced
persons in times of conflict. As aid practitioners work more and more in conflict
zones, they must effectively balance the needs of long-term development with
threats of violence and insecurity in some of the world's most dangerous locations.

Development practitioners are caught not only between home and abroad or
between donor and beneficiary but also among different communities of practice.
The lines between development and humanitarian interventions, as Vogt's essay suggested, are frequently blurred. So too, as Carl Stauffer shows, are the fields of development and peacebuilding. Since the 1990s, when donors and practitioners turned
to issues of governance, it has become difficult to disentangle these two fields; yet to
conflate them is also disingenuous. Building on a case study from his own project
work, Stauffer explores the progression of these two domains of practice in a South
African township, where a local ecumenical NGO converged on a framework for
the satisfaction of human needs that allowed development and peacebuilding practitioners to promote a shared vision. Stauffer places his analysis within the wider
intellectual history of development programming and peacebuilding theory.

A peculiar version of this tension between sub-communities is a conceptual
dissonance that Abdalla Uba Adamu calls the 'paradigm paradox'—the rhetorical
commitment to a new paradigm of growth and development despite the continued pursuit of old models. He finds this stasis-in-change prevalent in development initiatives in northern Nigeria. A conceptual change in donor approaches to
education in the 1980s did not in fact manifest itself in aid projects. Adamu charts
the shift from an Education for Development paradigm, which used schools to
cultivate 'human capital,' to an Education for Sustainable Development model
that focused on learners and learning outcomes. Despite the changed language in
donor reports and strategies, however, projects in northern Nigeria continued to
emphasize a human capital model. As suggested by Jantzi, the more things change
(apparently), the more they stay the same.

In the volume's final reflection, entitled "Fantasy, Reality, and Illusion in
International Aid," August Longino shifts our focus from institutional and conceptual tensions toward personal factors that both enable and constrain the work
of expatriate development practitioners. As Longino remarks, the rise of development NGOs since the 1970s has broadened the types of people involved in
development practice. Many small NGOs rely on young staff members and volunteers with limited experience. For these new employees, the demands of project

operation are often accompanied by an intense foreign acculturation process in which the line between work-time and off-hours vanishes. Drawing on his experience working for a small American NGO in rural Ecuador, Longino shows that the experiences and relationships forged both in and out of the office can have a crucial impact on the effectiveness of program activities, not to mention the well-being of staff. As Keilson notes in his essay on development management, these personal factors rarely figure into development analyses, though they often shape the fortunes of a project.

The articles in *The Practice of International Development* offer an important but little-heard practitioner perspective on foreign aid programming. It is hoped that they will not only provide valuable insights for students—indeed for anyone interested in making a career of development—but also inspire more practitioners to cross from implementation to reflection and more researchers to consider the influence of practice on project success or failure. The essays are not offered as an attempt to resolve prevalent dilemmas in our understanding of development's impact. Indeed, all of the authors highlight the practitioner's need to be comfortable with tension and ambiguity; to know that there are no sure answers to most development questions; to recognize the importance of thinking through the many possible consequences of any choice; and to be prepared for the unanticipated. Development professionals often embrace their careers with great conviction and clarity, but then confront tremendous uncertainty in practice. It would be easy to dismiss this early conviction as naïve, yet to do so would be a mistake. Indeed, it is precisely the steady belief that alleviating poverty is an essential duty in today's world that enables practitioners of all sorts, including those represented in this volume, to manage the inherent uncertainty of a development career in today's unequal world.

Notes

1. Ferguson (1994).
2. Mossé (2005).
3. See, for example, his well-known Chambers (1983); cf. the little-known but excellent Healy (2001).
4. For a valuable practical guide, see Glennerster and Takavarasha (2013).
5. De Certeau (1984), 91–110.
6. Examples include Dichter (2003) and Guess (2005).
7. Brinkerhoff and Ingle (1989).

Bibliography

Brinkerhoff, D. W., and M. D. Ingle. (1989). Integrating Blueprint and Process: A Structured Flexibility Approach to Development Management. *Public Administration and Development* 9: 487–503.

Chambers, R. (1983). *Rural Development: Putting the Last First*. Essex: Longman Scientific & Technical.

De Certeau, M. (1984). *The Practice of Everyday Life*. Berkeley, CA: University of California Press.

Dichter, T. (2003). *Despite Good Intentions: Why Development Assistance to the Third World Has Failed*. Boston: University of Massachusetts.

Ferguson, J. (1994). *The Anti-Politics Machine: "Development," Depoliticization, and Bureaucratic Power*. Minneapolis, MN: University of Minnesota.

Glennerster, R., and K. Takavarasha. (2013). *Running Randomized Evaluations: A Practical Guide*. Princeton: Princeton University Press.

Guess, G. (2005). *Foreign Aid Safari: Journeys in International Development*. London: Athena.

Healy, K. (2001). *Llamas, Weavings, and Organic Chocolate: Multicultural Grassroots Development in the Andes and Amazon of Bolivia*. Notre Dame: University of Notre Dame.

Mosse, D. (2005). *Cultivating Development: An Ethnography of Aid Policy and Practice*. London: Pluto.

Chapter 1

Children Can't Wait

Effective Development Assistance for School Readiness in Jordan

Katherine A. Merseth[1]

Effective development work happens at the intersection of problems, solutions, and resources. If any of these three elements is missing, the work is ineffective at best and harmful at worst. For example, if one has a brilliant idea (the solution) and donor financing to support it (resources), but has not correctly identified where the idea is needed (the problem), then it will meet with failure. Sometimes we misunderstand the problem or realize too late that it is not the right problem to focus on; a technical solution, for example, will never fix a lack of political will. Conversely, we may have a clear understanding of the problem and a brilliant solution, but lack donor support to fund it, which means an intervention never happens. Finally, we might understand the problem correctly and have resources available to address it, but lack the right solution. Unfortunately, most development work falls into one of those categories, missing one of the essential ingredients that would make it a success.

When these three criteria are met, however, big things can happen. In the Hashemite Kingdom of Jordan, a USAID-funded education program did just that with a small intervention supporting school readiness. This essay describes a case of successful development work at the intersection of an identified problem, a clear solution, and adequate resources. It focuses on one part of a larger USAID-funded project—the Parent-Child Packages activity, which was part of USAID's Education Reform Support Program (ERSP, 2009–2014). The essay explains the

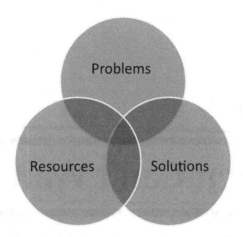

Image 1.1 The intersection of problems, resources, and solutions

particular approaches that resulted in success—namely, pursuing mutual objectives, empowering local leadership, collaborating respectfully, and using data for program improvement. Underlying these approaches is the imperative to be adaptive and nimble—to see opportunities that were not in the original plan and act quickly to seize a moment of prime potential. The nexus of problems, solutions, and resources is never static; it constantly evolves as the momentum of politics and policy shift. Effective development work occurs when practitioners are highly attuned to the context and continually adapt in response.

Understanding the Context

As this case study illustrates, understanding the context in which a development project works forms the essential foundation for all the work that follows. Because any social environment is constantly changing, *situational awareness* is one of the most important skills of a development practitioner. This section describes the case study context, so that the reader is able to understand the intervention.

USAID has had a robust partnership with the government of Jordan for more than 60 years. In 2015, Jordan was the fifth-largest recipient of US-government, non-military foreign assistance,[2] even though its population is barely over 6 million. In the kingdom's rural areas, development indicators are much lower than one might expect when considering Jordan's per capita income. There is high unemployment, particularly among those under age 30, and wide income inequality, with wealth concentrated in parts of the capital, Amman.[3] The socio-political structure is largely governed by tribes who trace their ancestry back to Bedouin nomads who traversed the region for hundreds of years. As a result, the kingdom is torn between tribal social traditions and a conservative interpretation of Islam, on the one hand, and the desire to strengthen a modern democratic monarchy, on the other. This struggle over national identity is particularly manifested in the education system.

During ERSP's five years of implementation (2009–2014), Jordan's Ministry of Education struggled to combat cronyism and patronage in an overgrown bureaucracy. Historically, public sector jobs were awarded based on family or tribal connections rather than an individual's qualifications, and the public education system was no different. As a result, some Ministry employees lacked the essential skills to do their jobs, while Jordan's most talented educators often preferred to work in the private or non-profit sectors, where they found more opportunity and innovation than in public agencies.

Jordan has received many refugees over the years from various neighboring countries, including Palestine, Iraq, and, most recently, Syria. Palestinians who fled or were expelled from their homes in what is now Israel were estimated to make up approximately 60% of the kingdom's population in 2014.[4] Huge numbers of Iraqis fled into Jordan during the Gulf War (1990–1991) and again after the U.S.-led invasion of Iraq (2003–2011). In addition, 300,000 Jordanians who had been living in Kuwait were forced to return home.[5] Although they were not considered refugees because they were Jordanian nationals, they presented a large, unanticipated burden on the kingdom's resources, particularly its public schools. During the Arab Spring in early 2011, peaceful protests against the Assad regime in Syria, Jordan's neighbor to the north, quickly evolved into armed rebellion and full-scale civil war. As of December 2016, the number of Syrian refugees in Jordan was estimated at 655,344, with 514,274 in urban settings and 141,070 in camps.[6] Meanwhile, the Ministry of Education struggles to meet the needs of its own student population, let alone serve the newcomers.

Jordan's education system was once a source of national pride, but its competitiveness, as measured by international test results, has deteriorated in the last two decades. Jordan fell 13 spots in reading and math and 16 spots in science on the Programme for International Student Assessment (PISA) survey between 2006 and 2015.[7] The causes of this decline are difficult to pinpoint but likely include outdated pedagogical practices, a weak pre-service teacher training system, and a curriculum focused on memorization of facts rather than critical thinking. These are longstanding problems, and Jordan has not kept pace with advances made in neighboring countries. In 2002, King Abdullah II bin Al-Hussein laid out a new vision to reform the public education system—the Education Reform for a Knowledge Economy (ERfKE) program, which sought to produce graduates who could succeed in the regional and global marketplace. International donors—including the World Bank, USAID, the Canadian International Development Agency (CIDA), and the European Union—rallied behind this reform effort, providing a combined financial backing of $778 million over 12 years under two phases of support (named ERfKE I and II).[8] The five components of ERfKE II were (1) establishment of a national school-based development system; (2) policy, planning, monitoring and evaluation (M&E), and organizational development; (3) teaching and learning resources; (4) special focus programs (of which early childhood education was one); and (5) quality physical learning environments. Resources were devoted to technical assistance to build the capacity of the Ministry of Education staff in these five reform areas and to direct budgetary support to the Ministry—money given directly to the government to spend as it saw fit.

Thus, the support of USAID to the Ministry of Education was aligned with the King's own vision and with a reform effort designed and managed by Ministry officials. This fact distinguished ERSP from many other development projects funded by external donors, which tend to operate separately from government offices and initiatives, and it was critical to the success of the intervention. At the beginning of ERSP, Ministry counterparts had a relatively high level of commitment to its objectives because they were held mutually. Particularly in the activities related to Early Childhood Education, USAID's ERSP objectives mirrored ERfKE objectives that the Ministry had set for itself in accordance with the King's vision. This does not mean there was agreement between the project and the Ministry about how to achieve those objectives—far from it—but there was a sense of agreement in the direction of ERfKE, which created an enabling environment when ERSP began.

As noted above, one of the special focus areas of the ERfKE reform was investment in Early Childhood Education (ECE).[9] Thanks to a growing body of international research showing the benefits of kindergarten for school readiness[10] and for long-term health and employment outcomes,[11] the Ministry of Education was particularly interested in expanding access to kindergarten. According to Jordanian national law, compulsory schooling began in grade one, and there were only a few public kindergarten classrooms before ERfKE. The vast majority of parents who wanted to send their children to kindergarten had to pay for a private provider, and, as a result, only middle class and wealthy families could do so. The rest of the population had no access to formal education before first grade, exacerbating the socio-economic disparity in school readiness.[12]

During the first and second phases of the ERfKE reform (2003–2009 and 2009–2015), the Ministry slowly opened more kindergarten classes by identifying unused classrooms, refurbishing them to serve as kindergartens, and hiring more kindergarten teachers. By 2012, there were more than 1,000 public kindergartens serving between 21,000 and 25,000 children annually. The dramatic 12-year expansion from just a few public kindergartens to more than 1,000 was largely due to the support of USAID, which had been the lead donor of the ECE component under the ERfKE reform.[13] This is undoubtedly a foreign assistance success story: The Ministry of Education and USAID collaboratively defined a problem, identified solutions, and mobilized financial and human resources to achieve their mutual goal. Yet, the number of kindergartens in the kingdom remained far below what was needed to achieve universal access. There was more work to be done.

It was in this context that the USAID-funded ERSP began its early childhood education activities in 2009. ERSP was a five-year project with a budget of nearly $50 million, and it served as USAID's primary mechanism to provide technical assistance to the ERfKE reform. ERSP aimed to implement and then institutionalize the programs, systems, and capacity to sustain the reforms outlined in ERfKE. It was implemented by a consortium of partners—led by Creative Associates International, a development contractor based in Washington, DC—and included Save the Children US and two Jordanian education training firms. ERSP comprised four components (early childhood education; youth, technology, and careers; teacher professional development; and education management information systems) that supported various aspects of the ERfKE reform. The ECE component's explicit objective was to expand access to quality early childhood education services—in this case, kindergarten.

ERSP employed five strategies to achieve this objective:

1. building the capacity of Ministry of Education policymakers;
2. renovating and furnishing 370 kindergarten classrooms;
3. improving the professional development system for kindergarten teachers and grades 1–3 teachers;
4. expanding parental involvement in kindergarten and grades 1–3 classrooms; and
5. strengthening the Ministry's existing kindergarten quality assurance system.

As is often the case, the activities corresponding to each objective had been written by the consortium partners in a proposal to USAID long before the project began. For ERSP, the competitive proposal process took place almost a year before the project was awarded and activities began. As a result, much of what had been researched and proposed by the winning consortium had to be renegotiated with the Ministry and, in some instances, revised in light of changes that occurred in the intervening year.

In fact, the need to be adaptive would remain important throughout the project. Although the five-year work plan served as a general guide, the project's activities were oriented by an annual work plan, which was drafted at the beginning of each project year and continually revised. The team used monitoring and evaluation to gather feedback about what was working and what could be done better, make data-based decisions, and carry out course corrections when necessary. When it was clear that a particular approach was not working, based on feedback from the field and monitoring reports, a new approach was tried. Similarly, there were continual changes in personnel at the Ministry of Education, which meant that the team often had to change tactics depending on who the decision-maker was at the time. For example, newly appointed senior managers sometimes wanted to make a clean break from the previous leadership and put their mark on ongoing initiatives. The team had to quickly assess the ambitions and motivations of new leaders in key Ministry roles to see how they could be encouraged to support an inherited initiative. In a highly centralized and hierarchical system, success often depended upon gaining the support of influential Ministry officials, as well as being responsive to their changing needs and priorities.

Since ERSP focused on all public schools in Jordan, the Ministry of Education was the project's primary counterpart and collaborator. The Early Childhood Development (ECD) Directorate within the Ministry was responsible for managing the operation of kindergartens. As the institutional home for work related to kindergarten and school readiness, the ECD Directorate played a critical role in shepherding policy changes through the bureaucracy, mobilizing teachers and staff, and advocating for resources within the Ministry. ERSP also collaborated with the Education Training Center (the agency responsible for all Ministry in-service professional development programs, including training programs for kindergarten teachers) and the Quality Assurance Directorate (responsible for internal quality controls, including the kindergarten quality assurance system).

In ERSP's third year, the team responsible for the ECE component developed the Parent-Child Packages initiative. This initiative provides an excellent example of successful development work at the nexus of a problem, solution, and resources. The sections below describe the ideas behind the Parent-Child Packages initiative ("Identifying the Problem"), the obstacles faced and overcome ("Developing the Solution"), and how the resources were secured and sustained ("Marshaling the Resources"). Each section will highlight lessons learned and recommended strategies for development practitioners. We begin by describing the initiative itself.

The Parent-Child Packages Initiative

Kindergarten in Jordan is similar to kindergarten in many parts of the world. Five-year-olds gather with one or two teachers (usually young women) in a classroom equipped with child-sized tables and chairs, low bookcases, and many colorful decorations on the walls. As Jordan is a middle-income country receiving significant international financing, its kindergartens are relatively well furnished and offer sufficient learning and play materials, such as books, puzzles, games, and art supplies. Many kindergartens have a simple playground nearby consisting of a swing set, slide, and monkey bars. The daily routine includes songs and rhymes, reading aloud, learning shapes and counting, snack time, and outdoor play. Depending on the location of the classroom and the population density, class sizes range from about ten students up to 25 (the maximum allowed by Ministry regulations). Kindergarten teachers are usually university graduates who have a degree in early childhood development or education. Additionally, there is a monitoring system in place to ensure that Jordanian kindergartens meet minimum quality standards defined by the Ministry of Education.

However, at the start of ERSP, many children had not attended a public kindergarten. Despite a decade of significant progress in opening new classrooms, demand for quality public kindergarten still far exceeded supply. In 2013, the Ministry of Education estimated that roughly 40% of five-year-olds did not attend kindergarten, either public or private.[14] In some places where a new public kindergarten was opened, more children than could be accommodated tried to enroll, forcing some to be turned away. The Parent-Child Packages initiative was designed to address this gap and increase the school readiness of children who did not have the opportunity to attend kindergarten.

The Parent-Child Packages initiative targeted not only the children themselves but also their mothers.[15] The initiative provided ten three-hour classroom sessions for children and their mothers; they were led by a trained kindergarten teacher and took place outside of school hours. While the children were together in one classroom, their mothers met in a neighboring room and learned about child development and ways to promote school readiness. The central premise of the initiative was that mothers would reinforce their children's learning gains at home and thus expand the impact of the ten sessions by applying what they had learned over an extended period of time leading up to the start of first grade and during the first few months of the school year. The topics included literacy and numeracy skills, social and behavioral skills, health and hygiene, and nutrition and safety. The classes for the mothers were led by Parental Involvement Coordinators (PICs), individuals who were trained and paid by the Ministry to engage parents in volunteer activities in kindergarten and early grade classrooms throughout the country.[16]

Each kindergarten classroom that hosted a Parent-Child Packages intervention received a box of learning materials, all developed and produced locally. The materials included a large floor map of Jordan; puzzles; and books and games to build literacy and numeracy skills, fine and gross motor skills, awareness of friendship and sharing, appropriate classroom behavior, and hygiene. All participating children also received a backpack containing a few books and games, a hygiene kit (which was a big hit with the children), and, most importantly, activity cards suggesting activities that mothers and children could do together using household items.

The Parent-Child Packages initiative was first piloted in Jordan in June 2012 with 450 mothers and 450 children in ten designated "poverty pockets."[17] Anecdotal evidence and feedback received from mothers and teachers suggested that it was successful. This outcome was later assessed through an evaluation, conducted in the fall of 2012, that found a modest positive impact on children's school readiness. As a result of these findings, the Ministry of Education expanded the program the following academic year, with the continued support of USAID. In

2013, the program reached 1,450 mothers and children at 89 training locations throughout the country. Although this was a dramatic expansion, it still represented a small percentage of the total need, and the Ministry planned to continue to expand the initiative in future years.

Identifying the Problem

One of the most common failures of development work is to begin with a misunderstanding of the problem to be addressed. The problem is often defined too broadly to be actionable, or there may be many interlocking problems leading to confusion or disagreement about what is the most important or the initial priority. Sometimes understanding causality can present a challenge: What are the factors underlying the problem, and how can a project ensure that it is treating the cause and not the symptom?

Not having defined the problem clearly enough at the outset, the Parent-Child Packages initiative had to be renegotiated with the Ministry at the beginning of ERSP, setting the stage for an evolution that persisted throughout the five years of implementation. It is a common misconception that development practitioners simply follow a series of steps in a premeditated plan. However, the most successful projects constantly adapt their strategies and activities based on the needs and opportunities they discover. Sometimes, initial plans need to be slightly adjusted, while at other times they need to be entirely discarded. Similarly, an activity that may be impossible to carry out in year one of a project may work splendidly in year four, or vice versa.

The useful insight here is that the definition of the problem is not a one-time occurrence. Successful projects constantly return to their problem definition and pose critical questions: Does this definition still fully capture the problem? It is the right problem to address? Should it be broken down into constituent pieces? Is it within our sphere of influence? This return to the problem definition was employed in ESRP because the needs of children who tried to enroll in kindergarten but were turned away had not been identified when USAID drafted the scope of work or when the consortium partners prepared their work plan. Instead, the need was identified during the course of implementation.

> As projects are implemented and achieve results, it is critical to revisit the assumptions that underlie our understanding of the problem and, therefore, our solution.

Initially, ERSP was designed to continue the approach that both the Ministry of Education and USAID had prioritized: expanding access to quality early childhood education by increasing the number of kindergarten classrooms. Although progress had been made in the previous decade, the pace had slowed, so one of ERSP's major activities was to renovate and furnish 370 kindergartens. However, even with additional classrooms, many children would still be left without any formal schooling before entering grade one, placing them at an extreme disadvantage. The problem of access to school readiness support, in other words, could not be met by classroom expansion alone.

Extensive research in the United States and around the world shows that school readiness preparation is crucial for success in early primary school, which in turn leads to later academic achievement.[18] To assess the quality of ECE, the Ministry adapted a version of the Early Development Instrument (EDI), a population-based tool developed by Canadian researchers at the Offord Centre for Child Studies and applied around the world.[19] The results of a 2010 EDI assessment were dismal. The report showed that many first-graders were unprepared for school across a range of learning readiness measures. Furthermore, results were correlated with mothers' education and family income, as is common throughout the world. Unsurprisingly, those children who had not attended kindergarten were in the worst shape: 49% of children who had not attended kindergarten did not meet the "ready to learn" standard in grade 1, compared to 22% of children who had.[20]

The EDI findings created a sense of urgency in Jordan. Although it was clear that the pace of opening new kindergartens could not be increased, the EDI results confirmed that children who did not attend kindergarten were starting first grade at a disadvantage. These data led to a new characterization of the problem. The most pressing question was no longer how to improve the quality of existing kindergartens, or even how to open more kindergartens (because both of those strategies were already being pursued) but, rather, what could be done to support those children who were not enrolled in kindergarten at that moment? Opening new kindergartens would solve the problem in the long term; but *right then*, out-of-school children would enter first grade that year woefully unprepared. What could be done for them?

Framing the problem in this way had the inherent benefit of narrowing the focus to a smaller population of children. Rather than thinking about all five-year-olds in Jordan, ERSP focused on the roughly 40% who were not enrolled in public or private kindergarten—the lowest performers in the EDI. It also had the benefit of narrowing the timeframe and triggering a sense of urgency. In other words, a fast, temporary solution was needed for an immediate problem while a permanent solution was in the works. When communicating with Ministry of Education officials, the message was clear and compelling: waiting for years while new kindergartens were slowly opened was not acceptable—something needed to be done *right then* for those children who were not receiving services. Children can't wait.

Developing the Solution

One of the difficulties the team immediately faced was how to identify those children who had not attended kindergarten. What were their names, and where did they live? Because these children were not enrolled in school, they were outside the Ministry of Education's database. After contemplating the issue, the team came up with a solution. In schools where demand for kindergarten exceeded the available spaces, the principal determined who would enroll and who was turned away. Further, Ministry staff found that most principals kept lists of applicants from the previous fall. In schools where the information had not been saved, principals could re-create it by making a few phone calls, thanks to the strong family ties and close-knit communities that underpin Jordanian society. Therefore, schools could submit the names of children who had wanted to enroll in kindergarten but had been unable. The ECD Directorate began busily collecting the lists of names.

The development of the intervention (the solution to the problem) was not the work of one practitioner. Instead, it came from the members of the project team, both senior and junior, and from Ministry staff. The old adage that "there is no limit to what you can accomplish if you don't care who gets the credit" was never more true, as various people contributed ideas that became important elements of the Parent-Child Packages design. The ERSP ECE Component Leader, a Jordanian educator with more than 20 years of experience, led the process. Muna Abbas had worked on primary and early education in Jordan for years and was a teacher and a principal before becoming a development program manager, which gave her a substantial historical knowledge of similar efforts aimed at this age group. In projects such as ERSP, where the leadership team is made up of expatriates, it is essential to trust local experts and let them lead the way. Effective development practitioners see their role as enabling the organization and mobilizing local ingredients—leadership, expertise, experience, resources, and opportunities—to come up with a uniquely appropriate solution to a particular, local problem.

The idea for Parent-Child Packages was refined in Ministry committee meetings and discussions over a period of about six months. The project team had a very close relationship with the Ministry staff, in part because the team collaborated with them and regarded them as respected colleagues who had much to contribute—rather than treating them as bureaucrats, as sometimes happens on foreign assistance projects. A spirit of collaboration and a desire for a shared vision propelled all discussions. The project team held informal conversations with the Ministry about the Parent-Child Packages initiative, articulating the problem and getting a sense of the Ministry's level of commitment to addressing it. When the Ministry's interest was clear, the team took firmer steps—first conducting meetings with small groups of key Ministry decision-makers and then slowly engaging a wider circle of stakeholders.

Meanwhile, there was work to do with USAID. ERSP was awarded to Creative Associates using a contractual mechanism called a cooperative agreement. A cooperative agreement is similar to a grant in terms of the relative flexibility permitted to the implementer to make adjustments during the course of the project (as opposed to a standard contract, which is more prescriptive and allows very little flexibility). However, approvals are still required to undertake activities that are not explicitly authorized in the proposal. Since the Parent-Child Packages initiative had not been part of the original project design, USAID managers had to be convinced of its merits. The ERSP team prepared a concept paper outlining the urgent needs of out-of-school children and proposed to reach these children before the beginning of the next school year with a targeted intervention. The team shared this paper with its USAID counterpart (the person responsible for overseeing the cooperative agreement) and revised it several times based on discussions and feedback. Initially the idea was more focused on the packages themselves— i.e., the physical materials children and parents would take home (hence the name "Parent-Child Packages"). But in conversations with USAID and the Ministry, it became clear that the best investment would entail greater focus on skills for children and training for their mothers. Fortunately, USAID agreed that the proposed initiative was well aligned with the objectives of the component and gave approval to proceed.

The best solution is not usually one that is alien to the context in question. The task for development practitioners is not to come up with something out of the blue but to build on what has been done *in situ*. Note that this is not the same as continuing what has already been tried with greater resolve. Rather, it means understanding how and why previous efforts failed, or understanding what made previous interventions work to solve a slightly different problem, and replicating that successful function or mechanism. For example, the successful solution might require taking the kernel of a good idea that was poorly implemented in another project, data from university research that defines the problem in a new way, or a delivery platform from an entirely different sector. For the Parent-Child Packages, the EDI results helped the team redefine the population of interest. The idea of engaging parents in the intervention was not new to Jordan; the Ministry of Education had run a parental involvement program for more than five years, inviting parents to come into kindergarten classrooms to volunteer. In fact, at the time of the Parent-Child Packages initiative, the Ministry was in the process of expanding that volunteer program to grades 1–3 with USAID's support. Moreover, a few years earlier, the World Bank had funded a similar, small intervention that aimed to engage parents in their children's education. Thus, the innovation of the Parent-Child Packages was simply putting existing pieces together in a new way.

> Innovation does not have to be radical; it is often as simple as putting exist-
> ing pieces together in a new way.

Another important element of the Parent-Child Packages was the decision to
use locally developed materials. The team located a Jordanian educator who had left
teaching a few years earlier to start a small business developing and selling educational materials, and it contracted her to develop supplementary program materials.
Using locally developed materials made sense for two reasons. First, it saved time
and resources because no shipping or translation was required. Second, the materials
were context-appropriate and relevant for the target population. In Jordan, political
sensitivities about public school curricula are particularly heightened when USAID
funding is involved. Providing translations or variations of American or other Western early learning products would have been critically regarded and might have been
an obstacle to smooth project implementation. Furthermore, there is long-term benefit for Jordan to have local small businesses with the capacity to make high-quality
learning materials. For these reasons, using local materials was the preferred choice.

The design of the Parent-Child Packages initiative also evolved over time, and
its success in the end was largely due to the team's ability to adapt flexibly to the
obstacles it faced. For example, in the original planning, the ten child/mother classroom sessions were to be spread over a ten-week period (one class per week) based
on the expectation that mothers and children would better absorb and retain information if it was introduced to them slowly and they had time to apply their learning between sessions. However, the Ministry of Education could not accommodate
this schedule. The logistical challenge of delivering the sessions once a week for ten
weeks was too difficult and costly. Therefore, they were delivered on consecutive
days during a two-week period. The project team was disappointed but agreed that
this accommodation should not prevent the program from moving ahead.

There were implementation challenges as well. For example, the Ministry con-
tacted the parents of those children who had tried to enroll in kindergarten and
been turned away, but some of the children had been later enrolled in a low-cost,
community-based (private) kindergarten. This was not a problem, but it meant
that some of the program's resources were spent on students who were not as
needy as those who had no kindergarten experience at all; they were not the target
beneficiaries. It also complicated the data collection for evaluating the initiative's
impact, as described below.

Marshaling the Resources

As noted above, the Parent-Child Packages initiative was developed more than
halfway through the life of ERSP, at a time when donors typically are reluctant to

start new program activities. How then did the project team gain USAID's support for this idea? And how did it find resources in the budget?

During proposal preparation, a project team may have incomplete information about on-the-ground needs and limited time to craft their program responses. The team strives to be specific with targets, activities, and budgets, but inevitably some things must be revised by the implementers once funding is awarded and the project begins. In the case of ERSP, the ECE component work plan had a line referring to "developing and distributing materials to parents," and a modest amount of funds were allocated under the same heading in the budget. The implementing team had to define exactly what they would like that activity to be *in medias res*, based on the evolution of ECE activities during the early phases of the project. As noted above, it would never have been possible to consider the needs of children not in kindergarten if the construction and rehabilitation of kindergartens (an explicit program objective) had not been moving ahead successfully.

Fortunately, the Parent-Child Packages initiative was clearly within the original scope of ERSP's ECE objective: to expand access to high-quality early childhood education services. Although it targeted a slightly different population, the revised target would contribute to the same outcomes. The team funded the intervention from the unelaborated line item in the approved budget and allocated additional resources during a budget realignment. The team did not, however, view USAID simply as a source of money; instead, it treated donor staff as partners in all decision-making. USAID's system of oversight has its own bureaucratic procedures, and successful project teams must anticipate those requirements and have documents ready in advance to help speed the approval of proposed activities. Fortunately, the USAID representative for ERSP was an ECE expert who understood that the approach proposed by Parent-Child Packages—i.e., engaging parents to promote school readiness—was logical and in line with previous efforts, such as the Parental Involvement Program. As the idea evolved through dialogue among stakeholders, USAID and the project team shared a common vision, seeing this initiative as a natural extension of promising work that was already underway. As a result of this shared vision, the details of the intervention (e.g., the number of sessions, kinds of materials, timeframe, etc.) were easily agreed upon.

The first step was a small pilot. The Parent-Child Packages initiative would be implemented in ten locations with 450 children and their mothers to see how well it worked. The team planned to do careful monitoring and evaluation of the pilot and to conduct a rigorous evaluation of its impact on children's school readiness during the next school year. A critical feature of this project's success was using data to reflect on and improve performance. The team focused monitoring efforts on continuous quality control and conducting in-depth analyses in areas of interest. Data were collected, analyzed, and used to inform changes in program design or implementation. During the implementation, the team sent staff with data collection tools out to the various training centers to observe and report on the quality of the delivery and gather feedback from participants. The pilot took place in June 2012 with the objective of increasing participating children's readiness for first grade that September.

The qualitative feedback from the implementation was enthusiastic, and data on students' learning outcomes suggested a modest positive effect of the program. The Ministry of Education, USAID, and the project team decided to invest in the initiative again at a larger scale. After working with the project leadership team for a few years, USAID was confident in the team's abilities and was willing to take risks. The Ministry of Education recommitted itself to allocating budgetary and human resources to the initiative, and promoted the pilot to a World Bank team that visited Amman semiannually to check the progress of the ERfKE reform.[21]

Thus, in 2013, the team turned its attention to expansion and modification of the materials based on feedback from the pilot. For example, participants provided information about the materials in the classroom toolbox (e.g., the cardboard games should be more sturdy). The team also knew it needed to improve facilitator training and materials for both children and mothers in the area of social emotional skills; major improvements in program impact can come from minor adjustments like these. Ultimately, the Ministry trained all of its kindergarten teachers to implement the program and conducted it on a national scale the following summer (2014).

The Ministry gained accolades from the World Bank for the effort to provide services to the most disadvantaged children. At the close of ERSP, the Ministry considered the Parent-Child Packages its own initiative and had an allocated line in its internal budget to fund it in the future. Thus, the initiative evolved from adapting to an ever-changing context to shaping that context.

Bringing the Three Elements Together

The three elements of a successful development intervention—identifying the problem correctly, developing an appropriate solution, and marshaling the necessary resources—are not linear or sequential. They develop simultaneously and through iterative processes. Depending on the situation, the donor, in addition to providing funds, may be intimately involved in the identification of the problem and development of a solution. It is best when the donor is engaged from the beginning because this increases commitment to seeing the project through, in terms of both resources and advocacy with government counterparts. The first definition of the problem may need to be revisited as implementers gather more information about the context. When considering solutions, the first idea is often not the best. The trick is not to impede the brainstorming but to let the idea evolve with input from many perspectives. Every stakeholder has something to contribute, and team leaders should focus on finding the value of each suggestion. The most lasting and effective solutions are those that build on previous experience and put existing pieces together in a new way. Expatriate team leaders must rely on and channel the knowledge of local staff and trust their instincts when making decisions. Similarly, team building and collaboration with government counterparts should begin with a shared vision and mutual objectives. Finally, constant collection and analysis of useful program data helps practitioners make course corrections and scale up their success. Continual adaptation and flexibility are essential.

The success of the Parent-Child Packages initiative is just one part of the larger story of advances in public kindergarten in Jordan and efforts to engage parents in their children's school readiness. As empirical evidence about the return on investment to early education mounts globally, Jordan and many other countries are shifting their focus and resources toward the early childhood years. This case study may provide a useful reflection on the elusive alchemy of successful development work for the next generation of development practitioners.

Notes

1. The author gratefully acknowledges feedback on drafts of this article from Muna Emran Abbas and Eileen St. George. Eileen Dombrowski provided research assistance.
2. Tarnoff and Lawson (2016).
3. United Nations Development Programme (2015).
4. Fine (2014).
5. Hunaidi (2015).
6. UNCHR Jordan (2016).
7. OECD (2007); OECD (2016).
8. World Bank (2011); World Bank (2009).
9. ECE was the terminology used in all Jordan Ministry of Education ERfKE reform documents and in ERSP project reports. Readers may be more familiar with the broader term, Early Childhood Development (ECD), which includes early stimulation, as well as health, nutrition, and other aspects of child development. Early Childhood Care and Development (ECCD) is another related term, emphasizing the role of the parent or primary care-giver in supporting holistic, healthy child development.
10. Berlinski, Galiani, and Gertler (2009).
11. Belfield, Nores, Barnett, and Schweinhart (2006).
12. Reardon (2011).
13. When planning to expand kindergarten access, the Ministry adopted a private sector model, which was relatively expensive in terms of classroom infrastructure, playground equipment, and learning materials. Choosing this model had cost implications for the Ministry's ability to scale up and meant that they had to rely on external funding for their plans.

14. UNICEF (2014).
15. Fathers were also invited, but in Jordan it is usually mothers who engage with their children's schooling, so almost no fathers participated.
16. The PICs were established as part of a separate parental involvement program.
17. The term "poverty pocket" is a Government of Jordan designation for parts of the country with particularly high rates of poverty and unemployment.
18. Although debate continues about the best way to ensure quality in a preschool experience (and quality is often uneven, especially in publicly funded programs), there is consensus about the importance of preschool and the school readiness skills which children need to succeed in grade 1.
19. See www.offordcentre.com for more information.
20. "Study on Early Development Instrument: Measuring Jordanian Children's Readiness to Learn" (2010).
21. In fact, the role of the World Bank in checking up on the Ministry's progress proved to be another point of leverage. Once the World Bank was aware of the promising pilot, it encouraged the Ministry to support it and applied external pressure.

Bibliography

Belfield, C. R., M. Nores, S. Barnett, and L. Schweinhart. (2006). The High/Scope Perry Preschool Program Cost—Benefit Analysis Using Data From the Age-40 Followup. *The Journal of Human Resources* 41(1): 162–90. http://dx.doi.org/10.3368/jhr.XLI.1.162.

Berlinski, S., S. Galiani, and P. Gertler. (2009). The Effect of Pre-Primary Education on Primary School Performance. *Journal of Public Economics* 93(1–2): 219–34. http://dx.doi.org/10.1016/j.jpubeco.2008.09.002.

Fine, J. (2014). The Arab Spring and the Religious Agenda. In G. Ricci (Ed.), *Faith, War, and Violence*. (Ch. 2). Piscataway, NJ: Transaction Publishers.

Hunaidi, R.K. (2015). Reform in Hindsight: Promises and Illusions in Jordan. In *Development Challenges in the 1990s: Leading Policymakers Speak From Experience*. Washington, DC: World Bank.

OECD. (2007). PISA 2006: Science Competencies for Tomorrow's World.

OECD. (2016). PISA 2015 Results: Excellence and Equity in Education, I.

Reardon, S. (2011). The Widening Academic-Achievement Gap Between the Rich and the Poor: New Evidence and Possible Explanations. In G. J. Duncan and R. J. Murnane (Eds.), *Whither Opportunity? Rising Inequality, Schools, and Children's Life Chances*. New York: Russell Sage Foundation and Spencer Foundation.

"Study on Early Development Instrument: Measuring Jordanian Children's Readiness to Learn." Prepared by the National Center for Human Resource Development (NCHRD). Amman Jordan, 2010.

Tarnoff, C., and M. K. L. Lawson. (2016). *Foreign Aid: An Introduction to U.S. Programs and Policy*. Washington, DC: Congressional Research Service.

UNCHR Jordan. (December 31, 2016). Registered Syrians in Jordan.

UNICEF. (2014). *Jordan: Country Report on Out-of-School Children*. Amman: UNICEF Jordan Country Office.

United Nations Development Programme. (2015). Socio-Economic Inequality in Jordan.

World Bank. (2009). *Project Appraisal Document on a Proposed Loan in the Amount of US$60 Million to the Hashemite Kingdom of Jordan for a Second Education Reform for the Knowledge Economy Project*. Washington, DC: World Bank.

World Bank. (2011). *Project Performance Assessment Report, Hashemite Kingdom of Jordan Education Reform for Knowledge Economy I Program*. Washington, DC: World Bank.

Chapter 2

Of High Hopes and Input-Driven Development

Mark Lynd

Introduction

When I stepped off the plane in Conakry, Guinea, in January 1998, the heat and humidity enveloped me like a glove. I had just moved to Guinea from Namibia, where the climate in January was cold and dry, and where you could drive for hours without seeing anyone. After pushing my way through a dark, hectic airport, I braced myself as a car carried me through narrow, winding roads teeming with scenes of local life: welders making huge gates, hawkers selling plastic bags of water, oil barrels with smoke rising around rows of tightly aligned fish tails, a mother pouring water from a plastic bucket over her toddler.

The change from Namibia to Guinea was a jolt, but I was hopeful. I had started doing development work 15 years earlier, when I served as a Peace Corps Volunteer in the Central African Republic teaching English in a secondary school. Since then, I couldn't get the red dust of Africa off my shoulders. I'd gone on to design teacher training programs throughout western and southern Africa, so I felt ready for Guinea. My task: roll out a package of instructional radio programs, teachers' guides, student workbooks, an early grade reading program, and a national in-service teacher training system to reach some 3,000 schools and

20,000 teachers. "Youth is wasted on the young," the adage goes. The development corollary: "Thank goodness such assignments are given to the young."

The assignment was part of the Fundamental Quality and Equity Levels (FQEL) project, an education initiative funded by USAID that ran from 1997–2005. I was there for the first half of the project. This is the story of my experiences there and a few reflections afforded by the passage of time.

Getting to Know You

My first day on the job, a project driver took me through some narrow gates and onto the courtyard of the national curriculum center, called the Institut National de la Recherche et de l'Action Pedagogique (INRAP). This would be my "home" for the next three and a half years. Surrounding me was a large parking lot of broken concrete and weeds flanked on one side by a dilapidated set of brown, two-story, cinder-block buildings. I got out of the car and met the first of many characters I would know over those years: Cellou, the "village griot," who sat on the steps of INRAP's main entrance every morning, shortwave to his ear, listening to Radio France and sharing the news with anyone who would abide. Cellou reached his hand out to me, and we did the famous West African handshake where you extend your hand, pivot to an angle (like the "brother" handshakes of the 1960s), then pull away and catch the tip of the other person's finger and *snap*! Cellou was among dozens of government workers, mostly men, who populated INRAP's courtyard each day, gossiping, greeting those who drove up, and looking for work. Being funded by the U.S. government, FQEL was viewed by locals as an opportunity to make some serious cash.

I entered one of the buildings—a labyrinth of dusty rooms dimly lit by the few fluorescent bulbs that were still functioning—and was shown to an office and seated at a round table, where eight INRAP employees greeted me: Tamsir, Assiatou, Mouctar, El Hassane, Bakary, Becaye, Yaya, Mamounan. These were all seasoned professionals, having worked their way up through the Guinean education system from teachers to principals and eventually to teacher trainers, curriculum developers, and subject specialists. Our meeting was both exhilarating and awkward: exhilarating because we'd been waiting for months to meet one another and the day had finally arrived; awkward because my French was quite rusty and their English virtually nonexistent. We all stumbled through those first few meetings trying to understand one another, figure out what our plan would be, and, most importantly, determine how we would get all this work done. Over time, that group of eight became not only my "team of generals" but also personal friends. (I would later start an NGO in Guinea, and some of them would serve on its founding board.)

Our first order of business was to create a "curriculum user's guide"—a bridge document that took the national curriculum and organized it chronologically so our materials developers would know what needed to be taught each day of the school year as they created radio scripts, lesson plans, teachers' guides, and student workbooks. INRAP didn't have enough usable space, so, each day for two weeks, we piled into cars and headed to our project director's house where we debated the terminology of a curriculum, the sequencing of concepts, and the language, math, and science content that we would deliver over the next three and a half years. After two weeks, we had completed our task. We were ecstatic: our first proof that we could actually create something together as a team.

We recruited more members for the various teams we needed to build, including one that would create guides for the reading and math teachers. Based on the curriculum user's guide, this team designed several prototypes and decided to show them to a few teachers from nearby schools before proceeding further. I remember attending this session at INRAP offices: three women sitting at a small table, leafing through the pages of the draft lesson plans, and quietly speaking amongst themselves. One started asking some questions in very basic French—the language teachers were expected to use with their students starting in grade 1. It immediately became clear that this was a point of difficulty: Though these teachers were certified to teach, their French skills were very basic. And this was the capital city—rural areas would be far worse. We found that when teachers taught, they routinely switched from French to Soso, the local language, partly so the children would understand them, but also partly because their French was too weak to introduce certain concepts. We realized that in order to get feedback from these teachers on our materials, we needed to speak in Soso. And more importantly, if these guides were to be developed for all teachers of Guinea, they needed to be written in the simplest, clearest language possible.

But language wasn't the only challenge. When we developed teachers' guides for math, we did our best to make instructions clear, from the identification of shapes in grade 1 to the measurement of spheres and cones in grade 6. We then "beta tested" these materials, watching teachers using them in real classroom conditions. Frequently, we observed teachers skipping whole sections, even whole lessons. When we asked them why, they sometimes answered, "It wasn't necessary," or "I didn't realize I was skipping something," but, in many instances, they admitted flat out that they did not know the content so they simply didn't teach it. Of course, this happens all over the world, especially in math, where teachers' knowledge starts to get weaker in upper primary and middle school. What struck me in Guinea, however, was that the teachers didn't seem fazed by the fact that they skipped over lessons; apparently, it was their habit. What struck me even more was that there were no consequences for this: Year in and year out, teachers continued to teach the curriculum as they saw fit, and the system allowed them to do it.

One of our biggest challenges was to help teachers move away from rote methods of teaching. Early on in the project, FQEL had found that the dominant mode of instruction in Guinean classrooms was teacher-centered: The teacher dispensed knowledge through questions largely emphasizing recall, and students responded to these questions by repeating key words and sentences and copying it all into their notebooks. This is another worldwide practice, especially in contexts where students don't have textbooks and where teachers have never seen any other way of teaching. The approach is understandable. After all, the teachers grew up in this environment, and this is all *they* had ever seen, so how would they know to teach differently?

Our mandate was to introduce teachers to a variety of student-centered teaching approaches, including using more thoughtful questions, allowing children to work in groups, and employing a "multi-channel approach"—one that engaged children in audio, visual, and tactile/kinesthetic (touching things and moving their bodies) activities to more fully engage them in learning. For example, a teacher might demonstrate a new concept, then ask children to sing, dance, act, play games, manipulate things, or join a group to discuss it. The children could work with their classmates on a structured activity to enable them to discover more about the concept than they might have by just listening to their teacher.

In time, FQEL introduced teachers to methods like positive discipline, gender-equitable teaching, critical thinking, making instructional materials, and using games and songs to teach lessons in all subjects. Teachers also received radios, teachers' guides, posters, and student workbooks to aid in student-centered teaching. To learn about these new methods and materials, they participated in a variety of training activities each year (see box).

Description of FQEL's Teacher Training Program

Each teacher received approximately 13 days of training per school year. Training activities consisted of the following:

- **IRI**: Two to three classroom-based broadcasts per week (total = 33 hours)
- **General methodology broadcasts**: Eight times per year plus teacher discussions and classroom application (total = 16 hours)
- **Week-long workshops**: Held during the school holidays, focused primarily on student-centered teaching methodologies, the use of FQEL materials, and language instruction techniques (total = 30 hours)
- **Bimestrial meetings**: Held once every two months in clusters of schools, helping teachers deepen their understanding of pedagogical approaches and discuss implementation issues (total = 24 hours)

> ■ **Peer observation**: One hour per term, where teachers solicited individualized feedback, support, and encouragement from their colleagues to help them improve their classroom practices (total = 6 hours)
> ■ **Grade 1 and 2 teachers** received an additional week of training in the teaching of reading.

The most well-known feature of our approach was Interactive Radio Instruction (IRI), a method in which a classroom teacher tuned into a 30-minute radio broadcast three times a week and followed the program while teaching. Each IRI program had a "radio teacher"—an actor simulating a real teacher who instructed a "radio class" of simulated students. The radio teacher spoke both to these students and to the real classroom teacher and students, saying things like: "Teacher, draw a triangle on the blackboard and ask your students how many sides the triangle has." The radio class then led the real class in a song: *J'aime le triangle, il a trois côtés* (I like the triangle, it has three sides).

We also developed a second type of radio program addressed directly to the teachers. The design called for them to listen in teacher groups on their day off to learn more about student-centered teaching. Each episode started with a theme song and an introduction followed by a simulated lesson to demonstrate a new teaching approach. After the simulation, a group of radio teachers discussed the new teaching point. The program closed with another song or game teachers could use with their students, and an assignment to apply the new concept in the classroom over the coming week.

To beta-test these programs, we convened groups of teachers to listen to them, then asked the teachers about what they learned and their overall impressions. I remember observing one beta-test on a program introducing the idea of using "realia," or real things such as found objects, in a class. In the simulated lesson, a teacher brought a stuffed bird into the classroom, presented it to her students, and asked what they could say about it. What kind was it? What color was it? How would they describe it? She passed it around, then asked them to think of as many adjectives as possible to describe the bird, discuss these words in groups, and finally share them with the rest of the class. After the lesson, we asked a series of questions to the teachers who had just listened to the program, starting with, "What was the lesson about?" One teacher responded: "First there was an introduction, then there was a lesson, then there was a discussion." We followed up: "Yes, that is what happened in the radio program. In the lesson where the teacher taught the students, can anyone tell us what they talked about?" After a pause, another teacher raised her hand and said: "The program started with a song, then there was a lesson." We tried once more: "What specifically do you remember from the lesson in the radio program?" The same teacher again responded, "There was a bird," but could not say more.

This experience highlighted two important things. The first was that we had to be sure our explanations of new concepts were clear. No doubt some aspects of our radio program were confusing, and the language we used to talk about it equally so. The world over, teachers don't normally use technical language about methods and approaches to talk about their practice. They talk about the activities they use and the notions they are trying to convey to their students. This is the language we needed to use as well. The second realization was that a significant proportion of the Guinean teacher population had limited ability to summarize ideas, especially abstract ones, but were proficient at remembering concrete things. This realization meant that we had to keep our delivery for teachers not only simple and clear but also as concrete as possible. For example, instead of asking a teacher what methods she had used, we should ask: "What activity did you use to introduce the lesson? What materials did you use to teach grouping? Tell me what you did first, second, third. How did the children respond?"

A Few Smiles, a Few Bruises

In time, we observed a mix of results. Some were delightful surprises; others, unexpected catastrophes. Our IRI lessons—punctuated by games, songs, and humor—were always a joy to watch, such as when Safi, the whiz kid "radio student" in reading and math, asked "Bouba," her radio classmate, what answer he'd gotten for a problem. His answer: "Uh, I forgot my notebook at home." In the last lesson of the year, when Safi and Bouba wished the children goodbye for the summer break, some children reportedly broke into tears. In time, we received reports of students complaining to the school principal when their teachers were late: They were missing their Safi and Bouba.

Sometimes during radio broadcasts, merchants around the country shuttered their doors for a half-hour and formed circles to listen to the broadcasts, following the instructions of the radio teacher to learn reading and math. I remember the joyful spirit during radio script-development workshops where we invited local musicians to INRAP to compose, sing, and record songs using local drums, balaphones, violins, and horns. I recall the excitement when our lead trainers—the ones who trained regional trainers who in turn trained the teachers in schools—"got" a new concept like the value of group work, a concept we illustrated by asking a group of them to lift a table together and then do a math problem together.

Part of our teacher training design involved "bimonthly meetings," in which teachers from clusters of three to five schools walked to a central school every two months to learn a new teaching strategy. We always had over 90% attendance at these meetings, even though teachers were not reimbursed for their time or travel.

One of our trainers told me it was "because the teachers knew it was high quality." Trainers had a scripted training session, so there was solid content and teachers always learned something new. And they also received things; we made a point of distributing at least one thing to teachers each training, even if it was only a piece of paper with a summary of the training content. We were surprised to learn that teachers valued these meetings in part because of the opening roundtable: At the beginning of each meeting, teachers discussed business, shared stories, and solved problems. This "check-in time" became as important to the teachers as the new methods they were learning.

Yet in spite of all these inputs—the training, the materials, the radio programs—and in spite of the goodwill we generated, our main objective to improve the quality of teaching and learning was only modestly achieved. While teachers loved the IRI programs, once they turned their radios off, most didn't apply the new teaching approaches to other lessons. Our trainers complained that all these ideas, materials, and methods were sound but that the teachers' French was too weak to understand them and their academic skills too basic to be able to use them. For six years, FQEL conducted annual assessments of students' reading and math ability and found only slight gains. A review conducted in 2004 found that while local education officials were more able to design and deliver training as a result of FQEL inputs, concepts, and strategies, training had not been retained by teachers. In 2007, an evaluation of FQEL found that though IRI had been appreciated by teachers, it was being used less and less, and, in spite of our best efforts to equip every child with a reading and math textbook, only three to five books per class were found in grades 3–6.

By 2006, after nearly two decades of investing in basic education in Guinea ($57 million from 1997 to 2006 alone), a USAID officer told me that literacy rates nationally were still declining. At the same time, USAID concluded that Guinea was a "fragile state" marked by a combination of mismanagement, lack of capacity, and corruption. As a consequence, the donor shifted its focus to a single Strategic Objective (SO): to "Advance Democratic Governance." USAID's new Strategic Statement explained the rationale:

> The hypothesis is that the main blockage to advances in economic growth, agriculture, natural resource management, health, and education is the performance of the government. Before USAID can have an impact on improved service delivery or improved livelihoods, it must first address the governance constraints that impeded development in these areas. By increasing Government of Guinea (GOG) capacity, accountability and efficiency, USAID/Guinea will have a greater, longer lasting effect on its targeted sectors. Thus while the USAID/Guinea program has one SO focused on governance reform, USAID/Guinea will use program components and indicators to demonstrate

that the program addresses fragile governance *and* achieves impact in USAID's respective earmarked sectors.[1]

The net effect: As of 2006—the year of this new strategy—USAID terminated basic education funding for Guinea. And though the strategy intended to advance democratic governance *in order to be able to* support sector-based reform, education funding has not been re-instated to this day.

This sequence of events raises a question for development practitioners: Is it possible to achieve our objectives in a context where local capacity is weak, the government is corrupt, and donor funding may be pulled? The following section explores the evolution of thinking around FQEL and considers alternate routes that might have made some difference in outcomes, even in the context of a dysfunctional government.

Gaps in Thinking

FQEL was designed in response to the state of education in Guinea in the 1990s. As with many countries, Guinea had been struggling through the 1970s and 1980s to enroll all its primary school-aged children, especially girls and rural children. Access became the main focus of the government and donor community, and, by the 1990s, the Net Enrollment Rate (NER)—the percentage of age-appropriate children in school—had increased from 25% to 65%, which was among the highest in Africa. During that period, the primary completion rate—the percentage of children completing all six grades of primary school in Guinea—had more than doubled.

Yet in spite of increased access, gains in the *quality* of education remained elusive. As a result, education funders, while continuing to push increased access, shifted their priority to quality. USAID's strategic objective[2] for education in the 1990s reflected this shift; it called for *a quality basic education provided to a larger percentage of Guinean children, with an emphasis on girls and rural children.* USAID's procedure for designing projects is to first identify a broad strategic objective, then to develop a more focused set of goals, organized in a Results Framework. For Guinea's education objective, the Results Framework consisted of four "intermediate results," or IRs:

- IR1: Improved sectoral strategic planning, management, and decision-making in basic education
- IR2: Improved instruction in basic education
- IR3: Improved community participation in basic education
- IR4: Improved gender and rural/urban equity in basic education.

The U.S.-based firm Education Development Center (EDC) held the contract for the first two IRs and was the lead implementer on the second; Research Triangle

Institute (RTI), also American, was the lead on the first.[3] I was an employee of EDC and the lead coordinator of IR2.

As with all USAID projects, the execution of these IRs was guided by a Logical Framework, or "LogFrame"—a document that specifies the intended outputs, objectively verifiable indicators, means of verification, and assumptions for each IR.[4] For IR2, the LogFrame defined the desired output as *the development of teacher support services and improved instructional design to improve the quality of primary education.* According to the LogFrame, this output could be achieved if the following assumptions proved true:

■ That the Ministry of Education's reorganization does not impede effective coordination of services to improve quality[5]
■ That instructional materials distribution policy issues can be resolved
■ That current teachers' terms of service do not constrain teacher motivation.

In retrospect, two things are striking. First, while I was in Guinea, no one ever mentioned the LogFrame to me, even though I was the main person responsible for making sure it got implemented. Second, had I known about these assumptions at the time, I would have concluded that there was nothing I could do about them. The first assumption simply recognized that the Ministry's recent reorganization could lead to some chaos or, at the very least, a lack of support for FQEL. This clearly was beyond my purview. The second assumption referred to the broken system of distributing materials to Guinean classrooms—i.e., it basically didn't happen—and that measures needed to be taken to resolve this issue. Though this touched on my assignment, as it was a policy issue, it too was beyond my control. Besides, we were going to develop materials and deliver them ourselves directly to districts and schools, so these policy issues were not of direct concern to us. Only the third assumption impacted FQEL's work directly. Teachers' conditions of service were notoriously poor, including inadequate salaries, weak supervision, and little opportunity for promotion. Here again, however, even though these problems directly affected my work, I would have seen them as beyond my control. My job was to provide training opportunities and materials for teachers, not to address structural issues.

When I ask myself then, *Was FQEL's planning sufficient?* I'd say that it was if the goal of planning is to specify an objective, analyze the context, and identify strategies to achieve the objective within that context. And yet, in retrospect, I think there were three gaps.

Gap #1: The Recognition That Inputs Alone Will Not Solve the Problem

In retrospect, it seems that FQEL's design was based on three main ideas: first, that quality, not just access, needed to be addressed if the education system was to adequately meet the needs of Guinea's youth; second, that providing sufficient support for teaching and learning, including instructional materials, would lead to quality learning; and, third, that Ministry policies, procedures, and capacity needed to be reinforced if these improvements were to take root.

The limitation of this view is that training, materials, and capacity building are inputs. Thus, our biggest assumption was that Guinea's educational problems boiled down to a lack of (or insufficient) inputs; if we provide them, the strategic objective would be met. Of course, if the quality of education is to improve, quality teaching and instructional materials must be part of the equation, and the capacity to support these things, at both the government and the community levels, is crucial. In other words, these things were probably necessary, but were they sufficient?

Gap #2: A Recognition of Other Dynamics in Play

While we were busy delivering our inputs, a number of dynamics were at play that affected Guinea's education system, not least of which was the sometimes chaotic nature of Guinea itself in the late 1990s. Economically, the country experienced a period of rapid inflation leading to the devaluation of Guinean currency (the Guinean franc), which in turn led to budget constraints at the national level and reduced purchasing power, particularly for teachers, the poorest paid in the education system. The economic decline was exacerbated by civil wars in neighboring Liberia and Sierra Leone, which forced the government to focus resources on the influx of refugees along its borders. (At the time, Guinea had the largest concentration of refugees in the world in the forest on the border with Liberia.) In response to the crisis, the government provided troops to stabilize these countries to the south, as well as neighboring Guinea Bissau to the north, rocked by a coup in 1998.

These conditions alone would have been sufficient to detract from any effort to bring about full-scale education system reform, as FQEL was attempting to do. But there were others:

- **Teacher quality**: During FQEL, the number of teachers nearly doubled, partly due to a new pre-service teacher training program that reduced the amount of time required of candidates for certification.[6] The influx of these new and often minimally trained teachers at a time of national instability overwhelmed the system. The situation was further aggravated when some teacher training candidates were discovered using fraudulent identities to be admitted—a scam that was resolved during FQEL, but not before an unknown number of candidates were allowed to become teachers.
- **Teachers' academic skills** were extremely weak. In Guinea, the requirement for entry into a teacher training college (TTC) was a secondary school

diploma—hardly a guarantee of minimum skills given the low quality of Guinea's secondary institutions. So low were candidates' skills that donors conducted a "teacher trainability" study and found that grade 4 teachers struggled with grade 2 material. FQEL research found similar patterns. In response, the pre-service program eventually incorporated remedial training in reading, math, and science. The 2006 FQEL evaluation team recognized this problem in its conclusion, stating that "though in-service training is useful and has been generally well implemented in Guinea, it cannot be viewed as a substitute for pre-service training for individuals with the appropriate academic background. In-service training will eventually have an impact on the academic level of students only if a certain number of conditions are met, namely that teachers are able to assimilate new content and classroom practices."

■ **Financial conditions**: Due to historically low pay, many teachers held second jobs or engaged in inappropriate commercial practices at schools, such as extracting fees from children in order to make ends meet.[7] The devaluation of Guinea's currency in the 1990s hit contractual teachers particularly hard, with their purchasing power cut in half. The impact of these conditions on teacher morale and performance cannot be overestimated.

■ **Rewards and sanctions**: During FQEL, outstanding teacher performance was not rewarded, nor was poor performance sanctioned. This creates a dilemma for the system: What to do with underperforming teachers? What to do with teacher absenteeism? It also creates a conundrum for the teacher: Why bother coming to school if I'm going to get paid anyway? Again, the 2006 FQEL evaluation recognized this as one of the key elements that impeded the project: "The success of reforms depends not only on the support provided by the pedagogical supervisors but also on hierarchical authorities at the regional or sub-prefectoral level who have the power to distribute rewards or sanctions to the teachers. As long as neither training nor performance has an impact on career advancement ladders, teacher motivation will remain a constraint to the evolution of the education system."[8]

■ **Grade-appropriate teacher assignment**: The teaching of reading in the early grades requires a specialized set of skills that FQEL imparted to teachers in its training program. Yet during FQEL, no policies existed to ensure that teachers remained in the grades for which they had been trained. As a result, teachers trained to teach reading in grades 1 and 2 could move to another grade the following year. As in most countries, teaching in lower grades has lower status in Guinea, so teachers with higher status were often assigned to higher grades, leaving the lower grades without a sufficiently trained reading instructor.

■ **Corruption**: As indicated in the LogFrame, problems around materials production and distribution did arise during FQEL, though, in our case, policies were not our biggest challenge. It was corruption. This took several forms. One example was contracts. When we needed to award contracts for activities like materials production to local vendors, we vetted our requests with Ministry officials, who often attempted to claim the contracts for themselves. Yet experience had shown that when the Ministry obtained such contracts, it either produced less than what was required and pocketed the difference or produced things that were reported as stolen, only then to appear in local markets. In order to avoid this "leakage," we branded everything we produced—radios, teachers' guides, student books, and readers—with the words "Property of the Ministry of Education: Do not sell." Yet even this did not stop some of our materials from appearing in local markets. No doubt some of these problems resulted from policy issues, since clearer guidelines concerning the awarding of contracts and distribution of materials might have closed some of these "holes in the sieve."

- **Revolving door**: Another problem we faced was the constant replacement of the Minister of Education. Every year or so (and sometimes more frequently), the President appointed a new Minister, a strategy used by many leaders to keep everyone off balance and make the system easier to control. For FQEL, the effect was reduced clarity of direction or strategic support from education officials, many of whom spent their time wondering if they were authorized to make decisions and fearful that the wrong ones would cost them their jobs. In the worst cases, some officials spent their time looking for what they could take before they, too, were shown the door.

- **Cronyism**: Another type of corruption, cronyism manifested itself at all levels, from the least capable teachers being appointed school principal because of connections, to senior educators winning positions that afforded them additional benefits in their more senior years. The FQEL evaluation noted this pattern, citing the regular use of Ministry finance officers[9] whom we had trained to make payments during our training programs: "These officers tended to be teaching staff close to retirement age with no formal credentials in accounting or finance, and are often rotated into other posts in the educational system."

To be sure, many of these problems were known beforehand. Some were made explicit in FQEL planning documents used to inform USAID's education strategy. The FQEL Results Framework was designed, in part, to address them. The main strategy for IR1, for example, was to work with the education system at all levels, from the Minister to schools and communities, to establish standards or "Fundamental Quality Levels" in the major categories of education provision (existence of buildings, books, teachers, data, systems), then to engage officials in their implementation and monitoring. And IR3 was an effort to create demand for education at the community level and build the capacity of communities to address some of the concerns cited above (e.g., rewards and sanctions).

These intentions notwithstanding, the question remains whether FQEL's design was sufficiently robust not only to provide needed inputs but also to confront some of these wider dynamics, so that some elements of the new reform could take root during the life of the project.

Gap #3: The Need to Take Time to Reflect, Experiment, and Adapt

If FQEL's design was overly focused on inputs, and if we didn't sufficiently take larger dynamics into account, what else could we have done? Three thoughts come to mind.

First, societies are dynamic and ever-changing; because of this, no intervention design could ever hope to respond to the needs of a country over an extended period of time. Any analysis, however complete, can be relevant only at the moment it is conducted, and it must constantly be renewed.

Second, implementation itself can be a powerful tool for advancing analysis for two reasons. First, it reveals the degree of *fit* between the intervention and its context; and, second, if it is flexible, it can be altered, thus illuminating options to improve that fit. For example, when we discovered that the teachers we trained for grades 1 and 2 were moving to the upper grades, we might have proposed strategies to the government to change teacher assignment policy to prevent this movement. FQEL did persuade the government to issue instructions suggesting that teachers be kept in training-appropriate grade levels, but these were not systematically enforced, nor did they become policy during my time there. To take another example, once we saw the problems associated with the quality of TTC graduates, we might have offered to pilot an alternative program in one of the TTCs, focusing on reinforcing basic academic skills as well as the teaching of reading. We might have worked out an agreement with schools to keep project-trained teachers at the lower grades for three years, measuring the difference between their effectiveness and that of teachers trained under official programs. Would this have led to an improvement in pre-service teacher training? It is hard to say given the fragile government context, but it may have been worth trying. To do so, however, would have required flexibility in project design and rollout.

Third, in the midst of an ambitious, input-intensive, nationally focused project like FQEL, time needed to be built in for structured reflection that allowed key actors to ask: Are we doing the right thing? Which dynamics are most in play as we try to reach our objective? I had a conversation with a USAID education officer recently in another country. After reviewing the results of a midline evaluation that showed her education project had had little impact, and after thinking of the millions of dollars that had been invested to that point, she asked: "Are we doing more harm than good?" I think she was asking the right question. When a project starts, it often has a clear goal, a strategy for achieving that goal, and an understanding of the contextual factors that may help or hinder that achievement. But as a project proceeds, things change, and a reflection on goals, strategies, and context could—should—shed light on whether the initial path is still appropriate. Time for structured reflection on these matters should also be accompanied by a willingness to make changes based on those reflections, as with the TTC and teacher assignment examples described above. Would such reflection have changed the outcome of FQEL in a context like Guinea? Probably not much. USAID would likely have redirected its funding anyway, perhaps rightly so. Nonetheless, I wonder whether an approach stressing reflection, experimentation, and adjustment might have led to one or two deeper changes *in spite of* the challenges of working in a context like Guinea.

A Final Thought

I first set foot in Guinea almost 20 years ago. Today when I go back and look inside classrooms for my NGO work there,[10] the radios are gone, as are the teachers' guides and student workbooks we developed all those years ago. This should not be a surprise: Most education interventions last only a few years. Textbook life is usually planned for a maximum of three years, and the sustainability of the radio programs— the government's willingness to continue paying for the broadcasts and the associated training and materials accompanying them—was always unsure. What is surprising (and heartwarming) is when people speak wistfully of "the FQEL days"—the buzz at INRAP, the quality of the trainings and materials, the fun of the radio broadcasts. I now know adults who speak enthusiastically about when they went to school as children and remember singing "J'aime le triangle."

If hindsight is 20/20, the present is usually pretty near-sighted. When we worked on FQEL, we were fixated on what was right in front of us. This provides some explanation—and latter-day consolation—for the fact that I spent three and a half years focused on the next "deliverable," believing that if we applied the right number of inputs in the right way, the problem would be solved. Since then, as I've discussed in this essay, I've learned that development is trickier than that. My hope is that this essay will help others think about how to do things a little differently.

Unfortunately, I still hear throughout the development industry the same refrain: "Inputs are the solution." One example is early grade reading. Numerous donors are trying to figure out how to ensure that all children can read by the end of grade 2, but they are finding this goal difficult to achieve. Why? Reasons vary from limited teacher ability to excessive class sizes, a lack of appropriate reading materials, and inappropriate deployment of teachers (many don't speak the local language yet are asked to teach in that language). One of the most common obstacles I hear cited is the "lack of a literate environment"—a type of reasoning that, I fear, will take us back to input-based reasoning, leading ineluctably to solutions like "we need to sensitize communities to the importance of reading" or "we need to provide communities with libraries" without considering the contexts in which they are operating.

Fortunately, there are also signs that this attitude might be changing—this "means-end rationality," as Jürgen Habermas called it, or a focus on controlling the outcome without also negotiating the meanings of situations, people's felt needs, and appropriate strategies. One alternative is flexible program design. For example, rather than relying on a single team to design a project, USAID has begun using a Broad Agency Announcement (BAA) approach, bringing partners together, providing them with information, then asking them to form teams and develop multiple designs to approach a given development challenge. Some DFID-funded projects now call for an inception period, in which a bidder first submits a concept note, and then, if it is found promising, a fuller proposal, and only then, if it meets certain requirements, receives initial funding to test the idea—for example, by conducting a situation analysis or initiating activities. All of these steps occur before the bidder can develop a final design and receive funding for the full project.

One USAID project design, PRIMR/Kenya, follows the reflect/experiment/ adapt approach described above by allowing implementers to test hypotheses as questions emerge.[11] In one instance, PRIMR managers reasoned that even if their intervention design, which focused on mother tongue instruction, led to improved reading outcomes, it might not be adopted locally. Why? Because the government and communities wanted an approach that, without increasing costs, would ensure that children could learn well in *all* subjects. PRIMR conducted a Randomized Controlled Trial (RCT) to see whether support for mother tongue instruction could lead to improvements in several subjects, such as reading (in mother tongue, English, and Swahili) and math. Importantly, this project was implemented without substantially increasing the amount of training or materials the government normally provided for teachers. The study found that when mother tongue instruction was used to teach reading, children's oral reading fluency and comprehension in their mother tongue increased significantly over the control groups; however, no effect was found in English or Swahili reading outcomes, and math outcomes actually declined. This new evidence sheds light on the relative merits of using mother tongue instruction to teach different subjects within a fixed-cost framework. In the context of this essay, it illustrates an approach where project design can be tested and adapted to better meet the needs of governments and communities.[12] Would that these trends continue.

Notes

1. USAID/Guinea (2006), 5 (emphasis in original).
2. Now called "development objectives."
3. World Education implemented IR3. Implementation of the fourth IR began in 2001 as a separate project called Community Participation for Equity and Quality in Basic Education (PACEEQ), also led by World Education/Guinea (prime) with the participation of Save the Children, EDC, RTI, and the Academy for Educational Development (AED).

4. Since FQEL, the definition of LogFrame has changed and now includes inputs and outputs. According to the current USAID project starter website, "A LogFrame validates and potentially updates the Result Framework and includes detail on the inputs and outputs necessary to achieve the intended results or project's purpose as well as project assumptions." Source: http://usaidprojectstarter.org/content/logical-framework-lf.

5. At the time, the Ministry of Education was called the Ministère de l'Education Pré-Universitaire (MEPU).

6. It was called the "sandwich program," and candidates were able to become certified in 15 months: three months at a training college (TTC), nine months of (mostly unsupervised) practice teaching in a school, and three more months of TTC training.

7. One Guinean colleague confessed that when he was a teacher, he had regularly engaged in what we in the West call unethical practices. For example, he told his students: "Tomorrow, we will study fruits. Each of you, bring an orange." The next day, the students brought their oranges; he used one as a teaching aid, then collected the rest and sold them in the market. The following day, the lesson was on how fire works, so each child was to bring a candle.

8. Midling et al. (2006), 49.

9. These officers we called SAAFs, from the Service des affaires adminstratives et financieres.

10. My organization, School-to-School International, has been piloting an initiative called the Whole Child Model in 40 schools since 2002.

11. PRIMR stands for Primary Math and Reading Program. PRIMR is funded by USAID and is managed by Research Triangle Institute.

12. Thanks to Ben Piper, the lead researcher on this RCT, for making this point recently in a webinar on the results of this RCT.

Bibliography

Chapman, D., and J. J. Quijada. (2008). *An Analysis of USAID Assistance to Basic Education in the Developing World, 1990–2005.* Written for the Education Quality Improvement Program (EQUIP2). USAID, Washington, DC.

Creative Associates International, Inc. (June, 1995). *Design of the Fundamental Quality and Equity Levels Project (675–0230).* Prepared for USAID, Human Resources Development Office, Conakry, Guinea.

Midling, M., L. Filion, E. M. David-Gnahoui, M. Gassama-Mbaye, A. T. Diallo, and A. K. Diallo. (2006). *Program Evaluation for USAID/Guinea Basic Education Program Portfolio.* Arlington, VA: DevTech Systems. Written for USAID.

Piper, B. (2016). *Implementing Mother Tongue Instruction in the Real World: Results From a Medium-Scale Randomized Controlled Trial in Kenya.* Research Triangle Park, North Carolina: Research Triangle Institute. November 30. PowerPoint presentation.

USAID. (October, 1998). *USAID's Strategic Framework for Basic Education in Africa.* SD publication series: Technical Paper No. 84.

USAID/Guinea. (February 14, 2006). Strategy Statement.

Chapter 3

Balancing the Contradictions

The Business and the Practice of International Development

Terrence Jantzi

Introduction

The profession of international development has been in existence for more than 60 years, since the initial export of the Marshall Plan to emerging post-colonial nations (Webster 1997). Since its inception, researchers and theorists have generated criticisms of the practice of development. Although the terminology and language of the critiques have changed over the decades, the best practices they recommend for development have remained remarkably consistent.[1] These include:

- A high degree of local ownership
- Decentralization of services
- Broad stakeholder participation in decision making and management
- Negotiated power among all stakeholders
- Flexibility and responsiveness to changes
- An emphasis on developing long-term processes

- Strengthening local social networks with dense and overlapping structures
- Limited dependence on external resources
- An emphasis on citizenship development rather than beneficiary dependence.

Despite these widely touted principles, development practice has been remarkably resistant to change—as suggested by the fact that similar critiques emerge decade after decade. Even a cursory review of contemporary development projects suggests that while these best practices are frequently cited in program documentation, program reality is often quite different. This is not simply a function of lack of expertise: Resistance to change can occur even when practitioners are well aware of the necessary practices for sustainable development (Phelps 2001; Murray and Murray 2007; Flora and Flora 2009). The key question is not, "*Why don't practitioners know the best practices for sustainable development?*" but, "*What are the factors that prevent practitioners from implementing these best practices?*"

The contention of this essay is that program managers operating within organizations—in this case NGOs and international NGOs (iNGOs)—are often caught between two contradictory forces: development as an exercise in improvement and development as a business. When development is articulated as an exercise in improvement, best practices have considerable merit for sustaining long-term change. However, development is also a business that channels the flow of resources from certain sectors and invests them in others. Development as a business focuses on issues related to financial management, accountability, and stewardship of resources. It is not necessarily the case that one mode is preferable to the other. Development as an exercise in improvement would not be possible without the business of development. At the same time, development as a business would be pointless if it had no effect on social improvement.

However, while these two modes may be necessary, they have different emphases and priorities, which can lead to situations where the good business management of development may have the unintended effect of inhibiting good development practice (and vice versa). In those situations, program decision makers are often placed in positions where strategic choices have to be made regarding the balance of interests between the two modes. Three of these tension points are highlighted in this essay:

- Design, Monitoring, and Evaluation (DME) versus Implementation
- Funding Models versus Processes
- Relationships with Local Partners versus Project Cycle Management.

Increasing DME Complexity versus Implementation

Within the last two decades, the field of international development has seen a significant shift in the level of complexity of its Design, Monitoring, and Evaluation activities. This has led to longer, more complex design phases; more sophisticated monitoring requirements with larger numbers of indicators for accountability; and a greater emphasis on attribution and contribution analyses in evaluation (Mayne 2012).[2] There are a number of factors that have contributed to this trend. It should be noted that this phenomenon of increased measurement and account-ability is not endemic to the field of international development alone but reflects larger social trends that have emerged through the advent of globalization and greater inter-connectivity amid reduced resources (Friedman 2005). The trend in development parallels changes in other sectors such as education, where stan-dardized testing and funding restrictions are linked (Linn 2000); social work, where single subject measurements are tied to case management (Rubin and Bab-bie 2010); and even sports, where sabermetric analyses dominate assessments of individual and team performance (Gray 2006).

In development, these changes to DME processes have been linked to renewed criticism in the early 2000s that the development enterprise had failed (Majid and Bawtree 1997). Coupled with the decline in development funding brought about by the end of the Cold War and the reconstruction of Eastern European and post-Soviet societies, this critique prompted a variety of responses, one of which was to contend that the development enterprise was appropriate but had been inconsistently applied (Sachs 2006). Following on this argument, one of the major new aims was to ensure that development practice was applied correctly. This led to greater emphasis on accountability and measurement of results with subsequent implications for all three dimensions of DME.

Design: The research literature is full of descriptions of inappropriate design processes for development interventions (e.g., Plein 2011; Myers 2005; Simpson et al. 2003). Common elements cited in the failure of designs include a lack of contextualization (e.g., Jantzi 2000), insufficient stakeholder participation (e.g., Myers 2005; Phelps 2001; Chambers 1997), a reductionist approach (Brown and Reed 2002), and a lack of strategic thinking (Chambers 1997), all of which lead to the investment of resources in ineffective initiatives or, worse yet, programs that create negative conditions (Uvin 1998).

As a result of these criticisms, NGOs and other development actors strove for increased standardization and control over project design processes to ensure that all appropriate steps were taken to avoid poor design. Each NGO developed its own standardized manuals for design processes that included procedures for Con-text Analysis, Consulting with Stakeholders, Needs Assessment, Partnering, and so forth. While the intention of promoting better design is laudable, the degree of control and standardization has had several unintended consequences, including increased implementation pressures due to long-term design frames and contex-tual rigidity due to long-term planning needs.

Timeframes and Implementation Pressures: The emphasis on appropriate best practices has led to extremely long design timeframes. In some programs, the design process—including both the design development and the feedback and modifications requested by donors—can take over a year to complete. The logic is that taking the necessary time to develop a good design is of paramount importance to ensure the success of a project. However, organizations do not function within a program vacuum: NGOs also need to respond to the business side of development, which focuses on funding cycles and donor disbursement obligations. This pressure can lead to situations where program managers have to balance adherence to an appropriate design process with the demand to finish the design in a set period determined by funding cycles. If the design takes too long, program managers will often feel pressure to "start doing something—even if you haven't finished the design process." Ironically, this can mean the demands of a good design process may actually force managers to make hasty and ill-advised programming decisions.

Long-Term Planning and Contextual Rigidity: Another design pressure involves balancing long-term planning with responsiveness. Development literature continually emphasizes that social processes are complex, changing, and holistic (e.g., Sen 1999; Seligson and Passe-Smith 2008; Easterly 2006). Within this context, program interventions need to be adaptive in order to respond to changing conditions. However, NGOs often require long-term planning and fixed designs that cover multiple years. These strategic designs help organizations plan for future disbursements and projected budgets, allowing for continuity and stability. There is often a tension between responsive programming needs and fixed organizational designs and budgets. While there are usually mechanisms set up in project cycle management to allow for design changes, they are often cumbersome and demand extensive documentation and paperwork. Program managers may find that the time and energy it takes to alter designs is not commensurate with the degree of responsiveness needed in programming, and they may therefore opt for little change even if the context demands it. As a result, design change usually needs to come from the "top down," such as a donor insisting on changing a design or executives at HQ commissioning a re-design. It is relatively rare for program managers themselves to initiate a design change without these external pressures.

Monitoring & Evaluation: The dimensions of monitoring and evaluation are often lumped together in project cycle language as M&E. However, they are distinct systems with different interests (Blue et al. 2009; Mercy Corps 2005; Patton 2001; Chen and Rossi 1989). Monitoring focuses on assessing organizational performance; it is, in other words, an internal accountability mechanism. Key questions for monitoring tend to be ones such as, "*Were the planned activities actually implemented, and were they implemented in a quality manner?*" In contrast, evaluation primarily focuses on assessing program effectiveness and impact: Its key question is, "*Did the implemented interventions lead to the desired individual behavior changes or social changes?*"

It has been a common critique throughout the development decades that practitioners do not hold a clear understanding of the intended changes to be accomplished through their programs. Activities are seen as good in and of themselves (Myers 2005; Chambers 1997; Korten 1990), and the linkages between activities and intended results are often either extremely expansive or vaguely articulated (Jantzi and Jantzi 2002; Phelps 2001). Furthermore, practitioners are often chided for not being able to identify or understand potentially negative consequences of their activities (Flora and Flora 2009; Uvin 1998; Duncan 1996; Ewert et al. 1994). Some researchers have contended that this inability is due not to a lack of intelligence or awareness but rather to the reductionist nature of project design "blinkers" that prevent a good analysis of unintended consequences (Chambers 1993; Phelps 2001; Epp-Weaver 2006).

As a result of these criticisms, development organizations and donors in the late 1990s and early 2000s began to place greater emphasis on developing logical frameworks to articulate the links between planned activities and expected results.[3] Logical Frameworks—or LogFrames—were typically constructed with four layers of effect: activities, outputs, outcomes, and goals. Unfortunately, while there is a standard conceptual framework, organizations have used different variations and definitions of their key terms (Gubser 2012). This can lead to confusion when organizations collaborate. In spite of these variations, a common pattern has been to integrate the monitoring and evaluation functions within the same LogFrame. The frameworks then become both the accountability mechanism for monitoring (usually termed "activity and output indicators") and the guide for measuring effectiveness and impact in evaluations (usually termed "outcome and goal indicators").

Since the mid-point of the last decade (circa 2005), NGOs have noted that the degree of complexity in these logical frameworks has increased. Programs and projects are expected to have more sophisticated indicators, more detailed descriptions of the logical chain, and increasingly ambitious outcome and goal-level results. Some logical frameworks for small projects may now contain more than a hundred indicators to be measured (Ausland 2011). This complexity has forced organizations to divert program resources into acquiring specialized staff with M&E expertise and to allocate more resources for the measurement of indicators. Program decision makers are often caught between investing resources on implementation and investing them in measurement.

A weak or poorly designed M&E system will mean poor monitoring of activities and results, creating situations where the program managers may not be able to determine if their project is effective or to articulate its impact on the larger social context. At the same time, a complex M&E system demands resources that might otherwise go to the interventions themselves—the classic conundrum of "measurement versus saving the hungry."

Highly sophisticated M&E systems can also create excessive programming rigidity. Similar to the design dilemma faced by program managers, over-explicating activity-level actions can lead to situations where flexible responsiveness to changing conditions is impeded because of the need to "stay true to the logical framework"—altering activities or shifting priorities can make indicators irrelevant. If expensive baseline measurements have been carried out prior to implementation, program managers may be reluctant to shift priorities for fear of facing later criticism that they carried out baselines on indicators that are no longer relevant. Of course, a program that changes too often may lose focus and weaken its impact. At the same time, a program that is too rigid can lead to activities being carried out for the sake of a plan rather than because they are truly relevant to the context.

As a consequence, good development programming must balance between insufficient M&E with too much flexibility and excessively complex M&E with too much rigidity. Unfortunately, while managers may feel these tensions, the balance that an organization strikes is often not under its control. Organizational policies regarding DME are often developed at headquarters and then disseminated to field offices to provide a standard organizational approach. Headquarter priorities tend to be focused on internal accountability, donor relations, and funding cycles, while field offices deal with situational complexity and responsiveness.

If DME policies are set by headquarters, it is likely that the "DME pendulum" will shift toward "complex and rigid." If field offices set DME policies, the focus may tilt toward contextual responsiveness and minimal measurements investments, leading the "DME pendulum" toward "flexible and vague." The author's personal experience has been that the more hierarchical and centralized the NGO structure, the more likely it is to develop M&E systems leaning toward "complex and rigid." And the more decentralized and flattened the NGO structure, the more likely it will lean toward the "flexible and vague" side of the spectrum.

While it is not possible to provide a prescriptive set of parameters regarding "how much DME is enough," a good indirect measure is to review the degree of relative power and influence between HQ levels and field levels with respect to the development of the organization's DME system.[4] If an organization wants to determine if its DME system is too vague or too rigid, useful questions might be: "To what degree are organizational structures centralized or decentralized?" or "To what degree was there broad and equally balanced stakeholder inclusion in policy development?" This type of analysis is much easier for an organization to carry out in theory than in practice, but it may nonetheless be worthwhile to attempt (Phelps 2001).

Ideally, a DME system should be designed with equal input from both HQ and field offices. While this ideal is often acknowledged rhetorically, providing feedback on decisions is not the same as actually participating in the development of policies in the first place, and few organizations appear to have truly succeeded in balancing donor, HQ, and field priorities in their M&E systems (Phelps 2001; Uphoff 1998; Chambers 1993).

Funding and Project Cycles (or Structure Pressures and Good Development)

The discerning reader may ask at this point: *"If the trend toward greater M&E complexity is exacerbated by more centralized NGO management structures and a greater focus on donors, does this suggest that something about the nature of donor funding has changed in the last decade and a half?"* Funding sources and project cycles have long been targets for analysts of the tension between development as a business and development as an exercise in improvement (e.g., Drum 2003; Phelps 2001; Chambers 1993; Jantzi 1991). However, significant recent shifts in the nature of funding have heightened this tension, especially the shift toward increased use of dedicated funding and sponsorship-oriented funding models.

In general, there are two archetypes of iNGO funding mechanisms—self-funded and donor-funded. Self-funded NGOs are those that can rely on a source of funding that is not linked to a specific project or program. The actual mechanism can vary from church offerings for denominational iNGOs (e.g., Mennonite Central Committee, World Renew) to some variation of a sponsorship program (World Vision), or individual contributions that are given to the organization as a whole (e.g., Habitat for Humanity, World Neighbors). Donor-funded organizations are those that rely on grants for project implementation (MSI, Creative Associates, DAI, etc.). These are not complete dichotomies as self-funded iNGOs may also access grants from entities such as USAID or CIDA, just as some donor-funded iNGOs develop discretionary reserves. In addition, there are other entities, such as foundations (e.g., Winrock International), that operate within this milieu. However, the primary funding mechanism will influence organizational structures and behaviors. This section is primarily based on reflections from experiences with self-funded iNGOs and the decisions that they take regarding the use of their funding and the development of project cycles for their managements; many of the dynamics, however, will be similar to donor-driven iNGOs even though the relationships are inter-organizational rather than intra-organizational.

Restricted versus Non-Restricted Funding

Within self-funded NGOs, typical funding choices for country offices are either restricted or non-restricted funding. Non-restricted funding supports broad objectives and grants country offices considerable discretionary power in determining where and how to allocate spending. Non-restricted funds can be moved relatively quickly among projects as contexts change, or they can be used for broader institutional initiatives not covered within a specific project LogFrame. By contrast, restricted funds are earmarked to a country office for a specific intervention or set of activities within a LogFrame. In addition, restricted funds tend to operate with tighter reporting and spending requirements, and funds must often be spent within a shorter time frame (usually a project cycle of two to three years, with five years the maximum).

Donors have generally given the vast majority of their funding as restricted funds. However, self-funded NGOs receive the vast majority of their income from non-restricted sources, which have historically provided a significant percentage of their country office budgets. Nevertheless, over the last 15 years, within these self-funded iNGOs, the percentage of funding coming from dedicated sources has increased markedly, with a commensurate decrease in non-restricted lines.

The advantage of restricted funding is that HQ and donors can more easily track their contributions to social improvement. However, restricted funds have limited flexibility and may face delays if a context shifts or initial preconditions at country offices or with local partners cannot be met. Non-restricted funds, by contrast, can be used to support longer-term processes, are flexible for re-allocation, and can finance important initiatives not easily placed within a project timeframe. However, tracking their effectiveness is more difficult.

Best-practice literature concerning development as an improvement exercise has historically encouraged the use of non-restricted funding (Chamber 1993; Chambers 1986; Korten 1990; Phelps 2001; Jantzi and Jantzi 2002). However, the increased interest in tracking and measuring that is part of the business of development has led to an emphasis by donors and HQ offices on disbursing restricted funds. Program managers are often placed in the difficult position of tapping the relatively available supply of restricted development funding even though the community initiatives they wish to support do not align easily with the short cycle and specific LogFrames required for reporting. They have to balance the pressure to spend money quickly in traceable ways with responsiveness to the better principles of long-term development, which require slower and more flexible implementation. Although most managers would prefer to have 100% non-restricted funding, those within self-funded iNGOs have reported a decline in the percentage of non-restricted funds they receive—forcing country managers to shift development activities and approaches in ways that may contradict the best-practice literature.

Funding Models

A variation on the tension discussed above concerns funding models based on individual or corporate sponsorship relationships. Many self-funded iNGOs rely on individual contributions that are essentially unrestricted—the individual simply gives to the organization. While individual contributions can be small, the cumulative effect represents a significant resource. For example, in the United States, the collective contributions of individuals to charity can be up to three times the total of all governmental and foundation sources combined (National Philanthropic Trust 2013). The sponsorship model has proven very effective in accessing this market of concerned individuals. Child sponsorship in particular is an effective funding source for many organizations. There have been significant variations and modifications of the child sponsorship model, but, for the purposes of this section, the general strategy is to solicit individual and corporate funds to improve the life of a specific sponsored child (or the child's larger community). Child sponsorship maintains individual commitment for longer periods of time than other forms of fund-raising models,[5] and it tends to be relatively recession proof—child sponsorship giving doesn't tend to change depending on donor economic conditions. From an organizational perspective and from a development as business perspective, these characteristics make sponsorship highly attractive.

While sponsorship funds can technically be considered non-restricted because they are oriented toward "improving the life of the child," in fact they can generate pressures akin to dedicated funding. While this is not true for all sponsorship iNGOs, a temptation that can occur in some is the pressure to spend money in ways that are directly linked to a specific child within a specific reporting period (usually six months) that can be recounted to the sponsor in order to maintain the sponsor's interest. This pressure can contradict longer-term community-development principles. Some organizations have tried to shift their framing to community-based sponsorship and integrate longer-term processes into their donor messages. While these messages better align with best practices, practitioners involved in child-sponsorship programming have commented that the amount of funding and the degree of recession-proofing tends to be lower in community-based messages than when fundraising targets direct service to specific children.

In some iNGOs, the tension between the funding pressures and best-practice implementation has led to an implicit organizational civil war between the fund-raising departments—who see the value in a constant source of sponsorship income—and professional development staff who are uncomfortable with the charity overtones of sponsorship but who rely on the money to support their community initiatives. These conflicts can absorb an enormous amount of organizational energy and compromise the ability of an NGO to respond to both donors and community beneficiaries.

As a result, program managers may find themselves balancing competing pressures between the type of development practice dictated by models for eliciting individual contributions and the type of development recommended in the best-practices literature. These tensions can also create unintended consequences for the NGO itself.

Relationships with Local Partners

Focus on the business of development can also have negative consequences for how an NGO relates to community partners and other stakeholders. Two examples emerge from conundrums associated with external resources and reporting requirements.

Best Practices versus External Resources

Program managers may experience a tension between the local autonomy advocated by the best-practice literature and the control demanded by external donors. The best-practices literature consistently highlights the importance of community ownership of development processes (e.g., Corbett and Fickert 2009; Sider et al. 2007; Taylor and Taylor 2002; Jantzi and Jantzi 2002; Uphoff 1998; Chambers 1997; Ewert 1997; Korten 1990). In addition, it stresses participatory programming drawing on limited external funding. These goals are espoused by NGOs in their emphasis on community stakeholder participation and their desire to avoid dependency on external funds.

At the same time, billions of dollars are available annually as external resources in the field of international development. Development organizations aim to capture these funds and invest them—ideally for improvement, but not incidentally for organizational survival as well. Program managers therefore face pressures to spend money or to carry out specific types of programming using external resources. A dilemma faced by managers in large NGOs with significant budgets and staff is whether they can actually follow the best practices in community development when their funding sources pressure them to inject as much external funding as possible (Drum 2003; Phelps 2001).

Managers often respond to these tensions by building relational networks and "social capital"[6] with communities and by trying to ensure that all external funds are balanced by internal contributions from local stakeholders and partners. While both relational social capital and internal contributions can help, there are challenges to both approaches. Despite efforts at relational capital, the presence of large amounts of external resources can lead to a "*commodification of the relationship*" (e.g., Corbett and Fickert 2009; Sider et al. 2007; Drum 2003; Phelps 2001).[7] This commodification can actually hurt social capital because it creates vertical relationships oriented toward receiving funding (Jantzi and Jantzi 2002). And while local contributions can mitigate dependency, requiring local partners to provide contributions can also have negative effects if they seem imbalanced with respect to the external resources. For example, regardless of the rhetoric, enormous amounts of external funding can mask or submerge true community priorities, leading to unexpressed frustration (Phelps 2001). In addition, even if external iNGO priorities align with local partners, if an external NGO invests several hundred thousand dollars in an infrastructure improvement project and local partners contribute only a certain amount of manual labor, feelings of tokenism may emerge among community members, leading to diminished local ownership (Rivers and Sider 2007; Taylor and Taylor 2002).

To address this concern, iNGOs currently place high importance on building coalitions among NGOs and engaging in multi-stakeholder collaborations. The theoretical justifications for this collaboration revolve around a set of best-practice assumptions: (a) multiple stakeholder engagement allows for broader ownership of processes; (b) multi-stakeholder coalitions can develop holistic and integrated interventions targeting complex and interconnected social dynamics; (c) coalition building avoids wasteful duplication of effort, as seen when multiple iNGOs engage in similar activities in overlapping regions, and can help improve coordination when donors happen to be in competition; and (d) coalition building allows for small amounts of resources to be pooled and leveraged for greater impact.

However, these same NGOs often work with large budgets from dedicated funding sources and employ large numbers of staff. The tension they face is that while development theory advises coalition building, program managers are accountable to their funding sources rather than local beneficiaries and peer NGOs. As a result, there is little incentive for organizations with large amounts of external funding to invest the necessary time and energy in collaboration—even though their own members may espouse its importance (e.g., Seligson and Passe-Smith 2008; Jantzi et al. 2008; Chambers 1997). Program managers may find themselves caught between a rhetorical commitment to collaborate and a functional disincentive to do so because of dedicated funding silos and large numbers of staff.

Reporting Requirements and Partnering

One response to the dilemma iNGOs face between the importance of local ownership and the demands of external funders has been the widespread promotion of partnering with local NGOs and CBOs (community-based organizations) to carry out programming. This approach is different from the previously mentioned coalition building in that partnering tends to be a one-to-one relationship with a local organization for the implementation of a specific project or sets of activities. The logic is that local organizations are closer to the ground, more aware of ongoing dynamics, and more sustainable than external organizations. Some of this logic has been challenged by theorists (e.g., Jantzi 2011; Myers 2005; Drum 2003), who point out that relatively large amounts of external funding have led to an exponential growth in the numbers of local and national NGOs and that these organizations tend to be at the mercy of external shifts in funding, which may negate their perceived advantages. Many iNGOs argue that shifting from direct programming to "partnering" with local organizations is more sustainable because these organizations have a better understanding of appropriate programming approaches in their local context. However, by becoming subcontractors to iNGO projects, the local organizations lose their independence, and their local knowledge may not be as useful, since the projects that iNGOs fund are often predetermined externally. Nevertheless, this trend toward programming through local partners has achieved widespread prominence in development practice.

Program managers may encourage this type of local support, but because of dedicated funding, reporting requirements, and increasing complexity of DME systems, they may find that the types of community organizations that most deserve support are incapable of providing the reports and M&E data needed by the external agencies. As a consequence, the terms enacted to ensure enhanced accountability may lead to the unintended result of forcing program managers to partner with local organizations that are better at reporting than at implementing activities. The collective shift in project cycle management processes, therefore, has led to a shift in local partners, with a greater percentage now being "Pseudo-NGOs"—organizations set up by entrepreneurial individuals specifically for capturing external resources from iNGOs but no longer locally owned (e.g., Epp-Weaver 2006). The consequences of this shift have not been fully explored, but they will likely include decreased real local ownership, increased resentment by local populations toward development organizations, and decreased effectiveness in terms of long-term sustainable impact—a decrease obscured by improved reporting language.

Summary

For decades, development literature has cited the importance of various best practices, and for just as long development organizations have tended to implement activities that are at odds with these recommendations. While it is tempting to blame a lack of expertise among development organizations, the significant number of internal program documents citing this literature suggests that lack of expertise is not the cause. This essay posits that the mismatch between best-practice literature and development organization practice is due to the tensions inherent in the two forms of development: development as an exercise in improvement and development as a business. Both forms of development may be necessary, but they target different interests and priorities. Program managers and decision makers often find themselves needing to balance the effort to maximize development improvement with the priorities of accountability, management, and reporting required of the business side of development.

These contradictory tensions play out across a gamut of issues, including DME systems, funding sources and obligations, and the inherent tension between external resources and local control. The actual practice of development requires making difficult choices between opposing interests within a dynamic and constantly changing landscape.

One important element for consideration is that effectiveness and accountability may be mutually enhanced if development practitioners are aware that these forces are not automatically aligned. A more deliberate analysis and conversation may allow for a clearer understanding of strategic priorities.

Notes

1. See for example: 1970s—Goulet 1971; Schumacher 1973; 1980s—Bunch 1982; Hope and Kimmel 1983; Chambers 1986; Uphoff 1986; 1990s—Korten 1990; Chambers 1993; Daley 1994; 2000s—Phelps 2001; Jantzi and Jantzi 2002; Myers 2005; Flora and Flora 2009.

2. Contribution and Attribution can be understood as follows: Development organizations strive to produce certain outcomes—increased income, healthier people, etc. Effective projects are those that make a difference in meeting these objectives—they **contribute** to the intended objectives of the organization. In trying to measure the performance of a project, two challenges are present: first, to measure whether or not an outcome is occurring (such as increased income in a household); and second, to measure how much of this outcome can be **attributed** to the project activities.

3. A logical framework is one form of expressing what a project intends to do and what changes it expects to see as a result. A typical logical framework consists of four levels: Activities (actions that the organization or project does), Outputs (changes in knowledge, attitudes, or skills among beneficiaries), Outcomes (changes in individual or collective behavior), and Goals (social change).

4. In some organizations, the Planning (or Design) department is a separate entity from the Monitoring and Evaluation department. Nevertheless, for all organizations in development, the management systems contain a Planning/Design system (D), a Monitoring system (M), and an Evaluation System (E). Thus, for the organization, there is a DME system even if the components are separated into different departments.

5. Such models include general appeals to fund an organization's programming, gift-catalog appeals for specific projects, or community-based sponsorship approaches.

6. The concept of Social Capital has been defined in different ways, but a common factor in all definitions relates to the quality of social networks in a context. Dense and overlapping social networks are usually associated with high social capital and increased effectiveness of development efforts. As such, many development organizations seek to build social networks and relationships among people as part of social capital strengthening and community development.

7. Commodification is the transformation of a non-saleable element into something saleable. The commodification of a relationship means transforming a relationship or friendship into something that can be used to gain money or resources.

Bibliography

Ausland, A. (2011). *Staying for Tea (Internet Blog)*. Bogota, Colombia: World Vision International.

Blue, R., C. Clapp-Wincek, and H. Benner. (2009). *Policy Brief: Monitoring and Evaluation for Results—The Role of M&E in U.S. Foreign Assistance Reform.* Washington, DC: USAID.

Brown, R. E., and C. E. Reed. (2002). An Integral Approach to Evaluating Outcome Evaluation Training. *American Journal of Evaluation* 23(1): 1–17.

Bunch, R. (1982). *Two Ears of Corn: A Guide to People-Centered Agricultural Development.* Oklahoma City, OK: World Neighbors.

Chambers, R. (1986). *Rural Development—Putting the Last First.* Essex: Longmans Scientific and Technical Publishers.

Chambers, R. (1993). *Challenging the Professions: Frontiers for Rural Development.* London, England: Intermediate Technology Publications.

Chambers, R. (1997). *Whose Reality Counts: Putting the Last First.* London: Institute of Development Studies.

Chen, H., and P. Rossi. (1989). Issues in the Theory Driven Perspective. *Evaluation and Program Planning* 11: 179–87.

Corbett, S., and B. Fikkert. (2009). *When Helping Hurts: How to Alleviate Poverty Without Hurting the Poor.* Chicago, IL: Moody Press.

Daley, H. (1994). *For the Common Good.* Boston, MA: Beacon Press.

Drum, P. (2003). *Co-Dependency in Development and Social Work.* Akron, PA: Mennonite Central Committee.

Duncan, C. (1996). Understanding Persistent Poverty: Social Class Context in Rural Communities. *Rural Sociology* 61(1): 103–24.

Easterly, W. (2006). *The White Man's Burden: Why the West's Efforts to Aid the Rest Have Done So Much Ill and So Little Good.* New York: Penguin Press.

Epp-Weaver, A. (2006). A Missiological Shift? Reflections on the Introduction of Results-Based Management within Mennonite Central Committee. *Mission Focus* 14: 27–42.

Ewert, M. (1997). Social Capital and Community Development. *Literacy Practitioner* 4(2): 51–9.

Ewert, M., T. Yaccino, and D. Yaccino. (1994). Cultural Diversity and Self-Sustaining Development: The Effective Facilitator. *Journal of the Community Development Society* 25(1): 45–61.

Flora, C. B. (1995). Social Capital and Sustainability: Agriculture and Communities in the Great Plains and the Corn Belt. *Research in Rural Sociology and Development: A Research Annual* 6: 227–46.

Flora, J. (1998). Social Capital and Communities of Place. *Rural Sociology* 63(4): 481–506.

Flora, C. B., and J. Flora. (2009). *Rural Communities: Legacy and Change.* Westview Press. Boulder, CO.

Friedman, T. (2005). *The World is Flat: A Brief History of the 21st Century.* New York: Farrar, Straus, and Giroux.

Goulet, D. (1971). *The Cruel Choice: A New Concept in the Theory of Development.* New York: Athenaeum Press.

Gray, S. (2006). *The Mind of Bill James: How a Complete Outsider Changed Baseball.* New York: Doubleday Press.

Gubser, M. (2012). What Do We Mean When We Talk About Impact? *Monday Developments* 30(9): 5–6.

Hoksbergen, R., and L. Ewert (eds.). (2002). *Local Ownership and Global Change: Will Civil Society Save the World?* Monrovia, CA: World Vision International.

Hope, S., and A. Kimmel. (1983). *Training for Transformation: A Handbook for Community Workers*. London: Practical Action Publishing.

Jantzi, T. (2000). *Local Program Theories and Social Capital: A Case Study of a Non-Governmental Organization in Eastern Bolivia*. Doctoral Thesis, Cornell University.

Jantzi, T. (2011). Towards Developing a Theoretical Framework for Relationships in Community Development. In A.E. Weaver (Ed.), *A Table of Sharing: Mennonite Central Committee and the Expanding Networks of Mennonite Identity*. Telford, PA: Cascadia and Herald Press.

Jantzi, T., and V. Jantzi. (2002). Strengthening Civil Society for Rural Development: An Analysis of Social Capital Formation by a Christian NGO in Bolivia. In R. Hoksbergen and L. Ewert (Eds.), *Local Ownership, Global Change: Will Civil Society Save the World?* Monrovia, CA: World Vision Publications.

Jantzi, T., and V. Jantzi. (2009). Development Paradigms and Peacebuilding Theories of Change: Analyzing Embedded Assumptions in Development and Peacebuilding. *Journal of Development and Peacebuilding* 5(1): 24–51.

Jantzi, T., F. Rojas, and C. Falconi. (2008). Volunteerism and NGOs in Latin America: Elements that Enhanced Long-Term Retention. In *Center for Social Development Research Report—08–01*. St. Louis: Washington University, Center for Social Development.

Jantzi, V. E. (1991). Socio-Political Paradigms of Development and Underdevelopment. In C. De Santo, G. Zondra and M. Poloma (Eds.), *Christian Perspectives on Social Problems*. Indianapolis, IN: Wesley Press, 60–79.

Korten, D. C. (1990). *Getting to the 21st Century*. West Hartford, CT: Kumarian Press Inc.

Linn, R. (2000). Accountability and Assessment. *Educational Researcher* 29(2): 4–16.

Majid, R., and V. Bawtree (eds.). (1997). *The Post-Development Reader*. London: Zed Books.

Mayne, J. (2012). Contribution Analysis: Coming of Age? *Evaluation* 18(3): 270–80.

Mercy Corps. (2005). *Design, Monitoring and Evaluation: Guidebook*. Portland, OR: Mercy Corps.

Murray, P., and S. Murray. (2007). Promoting Sustainability Values Within Career-Oriented Degree Programmes: A Case Study Analysis. *International Journal of Sustainability in Higher Education* 8(3): 285–300.

Myers, B. (2005). *Walking with the Poor*. Maryknoll, NY: Orbis Books.

National Philanthropic Trust. (2013). *Donor Advised Fund Market Report*. Jenkintown, PA: National Philanthropic Trust.

Patton, M. (2001). *Qualitative Research and Evaluation Methods*. Thousand Oaks, CA: Sage.

Phelps, E. (2001). *Participation and Power in Community Development Program Planning: A Study of a Process in the Bolivian Lowlands*. Master's Thesis. Cornell University.

Plein, C. (2011). Place, Purpose and Role in Rural Community Development Outreach: Lessons From the West Virginia Community Design Team. *Journal of Higher Education Outreach and Engagement* 15(2): 59–81.

Rubin, A., and E. Babbie. (2010). *Research Methods for Social Work* (6th ed.). Pacific Grove, CA: Books & Cole Publishing.

Sachs, J. (2006). *The End of Poverty: Economic Possibilities for Our Time*. New York: Penguin Press.

Schelhas, J., T. Jantzi, C. Kleppner, K. O'Connor, and T. Thacher. (1997). Meeting Farmers' Needs Through Forest Stewardship. *Journal of Forestry* 95(2): 33–7.

Seligson, M., and J. Passe-Smith. (2008). *Development and Underdevelopment: The Political Economy of Global Inequality.* Boulder, CO: Lynne Reiner Publishers.

Sen, A. (1999). *Development as Freedom.* New York: Random House.

Schumacher, E. F. (1973). *Small is Beautiful: Economics as if People Mattered.* London: Harper & Row.

Sider, R. (2007). *Just Generosity: A New Vision for Overcoming Poverty in America.* Grand Rapids, MI: Baker Publishing.

Simpson, L., L. Wood, and L. Daws. (2003). Community Capacity Building: Starting with People Not Projects. *Community Development Journal* 38(4): 277–86.

Taylor, D., and C. Taylor. (2002). *Just and Lasting Change: When Communities Own Their Futures.* Baltimore, MD: John Hopkins Press.

Uphoff, N. (1986). *Local Institutional Development: An Analytical Sourcebook with Cases.* West Hartford, CT: Kumarian Press.

Uphoff, N., M. Esman, and A. Krishna (eds.). (1998). *Reasons for Success: Learning from Instructive Experiences in Rural Development.* West Hartford, CT: Kumarian Press.

Uvin, P. (1998). *Aiding Violence: The Development Enterprise in Rwanda.* West Hartford, CT: Kumarian Press.

Vergara, R. (1994). NGOs: Help or Hindrance for Community Development in Latin America? *Community Development Journal* 29(4): 322–28.

Webster, A. (1997). *Introduction to the Sociology of Development* (2nd ed.). New York: Palgrave Macmillan.

Chapter 4

Relationships, Emotional Intelligence, and the Management of International Development Programs

Jerrold Keilson

The design and implementation of successful foreign aid projects is more of an art than a science. Practitioners have discovered some key principles based on program evidence over time, but how they are combined and who implements them makes the difference between project success and failure. Some of these principles are operational—how to work in remote or conflict environments; whether to rely on external experts or local know-how. Others are technical—what activities will address extant problems; what is the proper sequence of activities; and what is their appropriate reach and intensity. But all of them must be combined in ways unique to each project.

The question of what contributes to the design and implementation of a successful foreign aid project is not trivial. Since the launch of major foreign assistance programs in the late 1940s, the global community has spent trillions of dollars on development aid.[1] The value of aid, however, should be measured in more than just monetary terms. The work that donors and NGOs undertake is often a matter of life and death for beneficiary communities. Foreign aid programs heal the sick, educate children, and provide a voice to the disenfranchised. They give people hope for the future. Foreign aid's effectiveness, in other words, goes far beyond cost-effectiveness, and doing development 'right' is therefore crucially important.

Regardless of the sector of operation, a foreign aid program is designed to change how individuals and institutions work. It aims, in other words, to change human behavior in order to alter the functioning of an economic, social, or political system. Aid brings new knowledge, skills, and attitudes designed to address a problem that, for whatever reason, cannot be resolved with domestic resources alone. To be effective, these new approaches must be relevant to the local environment in which they are implemented and acceptable to those in local positions of authority.[2]

In order to accomplish these aims, development professionals typically deploy a range of tools to design and manage an aid program. Most commonly, the development challenge is conceived as a technical one. Donors start from the assumption that the project's host country lacks an understanding of one or more issues related to the proper functioning of a social sector (e.g., health or education), and they provide advice based on research and experience from similar situations elsewhere. This inclination toward technical approaches masks certain key assumptions: First, it often subordinates cultural or social factors that may have a direct influence on the relevance of particular development strategies. Second, it reflects a tacit view of local attitudes and aptitudes. Project designers may assume, for example, that host country citizens either are not entrepreneurial or tend to refrain from risk-taking, attitudes ingrained by local history or culture that may impede development. Alternatively, it may be supposed that local experts lack planning, management, and budgeting skills; appropriate technology; access to recent research; or supportive institutions and policies—all inputs needed to effect change.

In trying to understand why foreign aid programs succeed or fail, development scholars have typically adopted a systems or policy perspective, analyzing whether the most important technical problems have been prioritized and whether solutions were provided in the right order. They devote only limited discussion to strategies for managing and motivating people. This essay argues, in contrast, that discussions of program success or failure should focus less on the technical intervention and more on how to facilitate clear, forthright, honest human interaction—on how to work with people.

Think People, Not Policies

Good management concerns not only interventions, physical assets, and money. It is also—perhaps primarily—about managing people. This should be true of all management tasks in which motivating employees is critical to success. But supervising a foreign assistance project poses unique challenges. Aid projects are typically led by an expatriate project director who must manage an array of factors to be successful. The legal representative of a project in its country of operation, she is usually responsible for its overall technical direction, personnel, financial management, and public relations. Balancing these demands can be difficult, and it is hard to find a director who is strong in all areas. Project directors must oversee multiple organizational and stakeholder relationships, including relations with the donor/client, the home office, organizational partners, local government counterparts, community leaders, community beneficiaries, and project staff. Each group has its own agenda, so conflict is almost inevitable. Donors support foreign aid projects for complex reasons. Official government donors, such as USAID, provide foreign assistance to support policy objectives such as promoting stability, creating market opportunities, or encouraging democratic institutions. In recent years, U.S. foreign aid goals have been explicitly tied to national security concerns. There is nothing inherently wrong with this tendency, but it is important for managers to keep in mind that much foreign aid is not driven by the charitable motives that inspire staff, and that a project's goals may be different from what the donor country itself prioritizes.

In the host country, project directors tend to focus on the needs of their ministerial counterparts because these are the people with whom they work most closely. But this is not a simple one-to-one relationship, since there is often little uniformity within local government agencies about the goals of the project or the best ways to achieve them. Since development projects promote change, their results can be unsettling to entrenched interests, undercutting the credibility of officials who are unwilling or unable to provide the project services themselves. Some governments—such as Russia, Egypt, Ethiopia, and Zimbabwe—either place restrictions on foreign aid projects or do not permit certain types of projects to operate.

Similar tensions can exist with local officials or community leaders. Some leaders in project communities may feel disempowered by receiving charity. A local agency or community group charged with delivering a service to their constituents may consider it a failure to accept external aid and may fear a growing dependency on outside support. Alternately, local service providers may abdicate their responsibilities by ceding them—along with the blame for failure—to a foreign implementer that is not accountable to constituents. Some leaders, in fact, see foreign assistance as an opportunity to direct country resources to pet projects, such as military buildup, making up the difference with aid monies. In the worst cases, they may siphon off foreign aid funds for personal use, thus contributing to increased corruption and lack of transparency.

Project community beneficiaries also have their own interests and agendas, which often do not align with those of local or national officials. This mismatch is often noted in the case of women or youth, who face unique challenges that many governments do not address. But it is also true for any marginalized group that lacks representation or is perceived as a threat. Donor agencies as well, seeking the greatest impact for their projects, may ignore the disenfranchised or assume that they will benefit from the same approach that works for other groups.

Project directors must navigate this maze of competing interests from various 'clients.' The term itself is ambiguous in a foreign aid context. Unlike in most businesses, where keeping the client happy means responding to the customer, it is not clear on aid projects who the client (or customer) is. Is it the donor agency that provides the funds, contracts the implementer, and pays for the work? Or is it the host country for whose benefit the project is run and which otherwise lacks influence? If the latter, which host government or host society constituency should be the primary client? Should it be the national government ministry that oversees the project sector? Local officials or community leaders in regions where the project operates? Or the people themselves, the ultimate beneficiaries of project activities? It is difficult to answer the question definitively. The best project directors understand that they are successful when they meet the needs of all of the above-mentioned groups. In order to accomplish this, though, the director must understand what motivates each constituency, develop open relationships with all of them, and negotiate among their competing needs. Since most project directors are selected for their technical expertise or their experience managing budgets and material, there is often a mismatch between the technical skills a director brings and the 'people skills' that occupy the bulk of her time.

In addition to this complex ecosystem of 'clients,' there are two other constituencies internal to the project that must be acknowledged. One is local staff. Nearly all foreign aid projects have a very small number of international employees and a much larger number of staff from the host country. These country nationals have typically worked on predecessor projects, and they have preexisting relationships with relevant government agencies and communities. Taking smart advantage of those connections can provide a boost for a new project. But often there is conflict between country nationals and the expatriates leading the project. In some cases, expatriates subtly denigrate the skills of national staff, or, vice versa, local employees express skepticism of the way expatriates understand their country. There may also be tension around compensation: Expatriates nearly always receive far higher salaries than locals, even though the latter do most of the work. The two groups often do not socialize after work, and they frequently have different motivations for the work they do. For an expatriate manager, a foreign aid assignment is a job lasting two to five years before a move to a new post. For local employees, however, a project concerns their country, and they have a different level of investment in its success. A director must always be attuned to these motivational discrepancies among project staff.

Both expatriate and local staff in project countries also have to foster another non-client relationship: with employees of the implementer's home office. Although part of the same organization, the international home office and the national project office are driven by different motivations and face different pressures, which may lead to clashes. National staff, led by a project director, work directly and daily with the local donor, government counterparts, community leaders, and individual beneficiaries. They often operate with a strong 'can-do' attitude, in which the focus is on getting work done within a time frame and keeping local stakeholders happy. The home office confronts a different reality. As a corporate headquarters, the home office is of course interested in the success of the project, but its staff has other interests as well that field staff may consider secondary. Often, a major divergence surrounds compliance with donor rules and regulations. All donors, for example, have requirements designed to ensure open and transparent procurement. Sometimes meeting these requirements means that activities occur more slowly than field staff would like, prompting complaints that home office staff do not support project activities. Another area of potential conflict is the time, attention, and resources devoted to new business development. For the home office to raise funds, it often needs support from field staff, even though fundraising is rarely an explicit part of their job. In some instances, field staff have little time or incentive to help with new business development: Since they frequently shift organizations when a project ends, they may see little need to raise funds for what is, after all, only their temporary employer.

Effective Management of People

What makes one person more effective than another in managing people? Let me illustrate the importance of management by describing a USAID-funded education project in the Middle East for which I provided home office oversight.[3] The project was well funded and well designed, incorporating industry-standard approaches to promoting safe schools and increased community engagement in education. The host country had a strong relationship with the United States, and its Ministry of Education had been actively involved in the project design, proposal review, and selection of contractors, ensuring that activities were aligned with the national education strategy and interests. Despite these advantages, however, the project floundered because its director, an American, was not respected by his staff. He did not speak Arabic and had to rely on advice from deputies. Cliques developed among the staff, and a conflict with a local partner had gotten so aggravated that the partner circumvented the director to talk directly to the home office vice-president and donor, undercutting the director's authority and creating a perception that the organization was unable to manage its staff. Not only did these breakdowns threaten project activities, but they ran the risk of tainting the organization's reputation and its ability to win future work.

After two years trying to fix the problem through increased home office oversight, extensive conversation with the protagonists, and a management compliance audit, the organization finally replaced the director with a new head who had similar technical expertise, a few years more management experience, and a different personality. The first project director was a consensus-builder; his replacement listened carefully but then determined what to do on his own. He quickly developed better relations with staff by taking them to lunch, listening to their concerns, and either acting on them or explaining why he was not. He met regularly with donor officials and created clear guidelines for subcontractors, with explicit threats of cancellation for non-compliance. Within a few months, the project was achieving its targets, and at closure both the donor and stakeholders felt it had turned itself around and become successful. This is not an isolated occurrence. Any experienced international development professional can describe projects that flagged under one management but flourished under new direction. The same can happen in reverse: A successful project can decline if new leaders do not mesh with the team.[4]

There are two large baskets of skills that are necessary to manage people successfully on international development projects. One is intercultural skills; the other, emotional intelligence. What does it mean to have intercultural management skills, to be able to work effectively across cultures? There is a story sometimes told of an American businessman overseas who comes to a meeting with foreign counterparts loudly and with lots of energy. He has an agenda for the meeting and is eager to start quickly, since he has another meeting after this one and, after all, time is money. After quick, cursory introductions, he starts on his agenda, leaning forward in his seat as he talks and gesticulating broadly. When he finishes speaking, he leans back and crosses one leg over the other, eager to get a response to his propositions. When, after a little while, he realizes no decision will be immediately forthcoming, he ends the meeting. He has some hope that his counterparts will get back to him, since they had not rejected his ideas, but of course they never do, and ultimately he writes the whole experience off as a problem of foreigners not knowing how to do business 'the American way.'

From the perspective of the host country team, the American violated numerous taboos that made them believe that he was unsophisticated or unreliable—and certainly not someone with whom they wanted to do business. Speaking loudly and directly can sound angry. Not giving the other party time to think and react can come across as rude. The businessman's behavior, in other words, while it might have achieved results at home, stood in the way of his success in another culture. Someone with greater sensitivity might have adopted a few of the following principles.

All business is personal: In many cultures, business is not simply transactional but part of a long-term relationship. One has to establish a common ground that is personal in nature, not based on the desire to do business. When I worked in

Mauritania in the mid-1980s, every meeting with a government official began with 20 minutes of personal ritual. We introduced ourselves, and the host offered me mint tea or water. I could not refuse, despite worrying constantly that I might get sick from unclean water. The host poured the tea himself into a very small cup, took a sip, determined that it was well prepared, poured it back into the pot, let the pot simmer for a few minutes, then finally poured me a cup before taking one himself. After that, we talked. He asked how I was enjoying my stay in his country; we discussed our families, the number of children we had, and how many were sons. The discussion was not one-sided: I often asked if he had been to the United States and what he thought about it. We typically passed 15–20 minutes in this way before even beginning to talk about business. The importance of this interchange must not be dismissed. We were establishing a personal rapport that would help our professional collaboration advance, sharing private information and food in order to cultivate a sense of trust and a common ground for a working relationship. It worked. Some months later, I had a problem obtaining customs clearance for furniture being trucked in from Senegal. I visited my official contact to discuss the problem (the phone system did not function), and by the next day the items had received their clearance and were on their way to the capital, Nouakchott.

We don't know everything. There is a tendency among successful people to believe that they know more than others. On a development project, this attitude can be exacerbated by the view that technical experts are there to help locals deal with a problem they cannot overcome themselves. Yet despite the impoverishment of many developing countries, it is important to remember that their citizens understand the country better than we do, and they will live in it after we leave. As foreigners, we are temporary residents; we go home at the project's end and do not have to live with its consequences. While it is professionally important for expatriates to succeed, they have less invested in the project than people from the country. An alert manager should recognize this dynamic in her relations with staff and counterparts and remember that the local staff have extensive experience and a personal investment in project success. Moreover, expatriates need the local staff, since they are the ones with relevant connections.

Values matter and values differ. Development is about changing people's knowledge, skills, attitudes, and behaviors. In order to do so, a manager must know something about the people she is trying to influence. One way to find out what motivates them is to understand their values in relation to our own. This requires two sorts of awareness. First, expatriate staff need a basic understanding of the history, culture, and values that shape their own attitudes and behavior. At the same time, a good manager must be attuned to the values and experiences of the culture in which she works. Development projects play out in the nexus between these two sets of values.

We see this play out, for instance, when the U.S. government frames detailed processes for reducing corruption. Other cultures place different importance on taking care of family, which can lead to national staff hiring relatives or giving contract work to companies owned by friends. For American managers, this smacks of nepotism; for nationals, it is normal operation. Of course, the distinction is not that binary: Most Westerners can think of instances where we shopped at a store or hired a contractor because we knew the company owner. Nonetheless, understanding these value differences is essential if one is to know what is feasible and expected in a foreign development project.

One area where the clash of values frequently arises is in gender relations. The international development field employs many women, often in leadership roles and overseas as project directors. This can create challenges when working with national staff, who may be conflicted about men working with and taking direction from women. While it is important for American development professionals to promote gender equality, other cultural beliefs must be carefully understood if a project is to effect change.

Be a role model and a mentor. Americans running development projects overseas typically do not think of themselves as diplomats, but that is just what they are to their staff and to most host country nationals they meet. This is even more true when traveling outside a capital city, where he or she may be the first American that people ever see. This role demands careful attention to behavior, dress, and discourse so as to be taken seriously and not give offense. When you visit a friend's house, you do not criticize the decorating scheme, furnishings, or food. The same graciousness applies to an even greater degree when living or working in another country.[5]

As one of the only Americans your staff knows, you must act as if you represent the United States. In practice, this means acting in accord with the values you want to inculcate. Regardless of the project, development practitioners should model transparency and equity, effectiveness in service delivery, honesty, and free speech. Management behaviors should align with core values. In addition, expatriates are often called on to mentor local staff, providing technical or managerial training, offering professional opportunities, counseling employees, and grooming them for promotion. These efforts are not simply the personal byproducts of a larger project; they build critical local expertise so that vital activities may continue after a project concludes. If, as noted earlier, development is about changing individual attitudes, then mentoring is a crucial strategy for success.

Communicate clearly. Clear communications are not easy in the best of circumstances. Linguists and psychologists have written extensively about the importance of communications and about the difficulty of understanding what another person is saying.[6] If communication is difficult for people from the same country, it is even more so across cultures and languages. In some countries, men will rarely take advice from women; in others, only the leader is authorized to speak on behalf of a group. These differences exist atop the very real confusion or lack of clarity that arises when speaking a different language or communicating through an interpreter. A further obstacle to clear communication on development projects is power dynamics. A donor or NGO representative is in a much more powerful position than a beneficiary organization, which may defer to what it thinks the donor wants in hopes of receiving future funding or services. This imbalance can have a major impact on the willingness of stakeholders to speak honestly with international development professionals. Development practitioners encounter these challenges frequently, and they demand great patience to navigate.

Listen to constituents and stakeholders: A development professional can learn a great deal about a country by asking questions and listening to the responses. This sounds easier than it is, because consultation is time-consuming and potentially destabilizing. It might uncover perspectives that are different from what the donor wants to hear, and it can raise expectations that go unfulfilled. Moreover, consultation yields divergent opinions and points of view, and decisions will necessarily affirm the perspectives of some people and not others.

As the following account illustrates, good consultation is considerably harder than it appears. In the 1990s, the World Bank and USAID advanced a new commitment to participation, insisting program planners must consult with stakeholders as part of their design process. A colleague described for me a consultative process he used for a rural development project in Bolivia. The World Bank and Bolivian officials organized a series of town hall meetings with local people in order to introduce the project. They explained that they were there to engage the affected communities in a participatory, consultative process. After they described the project, they opened the floor to questions. There were none. The World Bank interlocutor asked a community leader what he thought of the project. The leader responded, in halting Spanish, that he and the community were glad that the government was taking an interest in their needs, and that they thanked officials for their efforts. Nobody else said a word. After a while, the consultants left, satisfied that they had engaged in true participation and that they had the community feedback they needed. My colleague, however, found a great deal wrong with the process. First, even a cursory knowledge of regional history would have told consultants that the Bolivian government convened communities only when they intended to exploit them. Second, most of the region's residents did not speak Spanish and therefore did not understand what the consultants were saying. Third, greater social awareness would have reminded consultants that these communities held to a strict hierarchy in which the leader of the community spoke first, then other community members—and never women or youth. In sum, the bank designed a consultative process that the audience did not understand or participate in. There are solutions to these problems: Practitioners can use the language of people with whom they wish to speak, and they should recognize the value of smaller discussions and focus groups that separate distinct constituencies so they can speak freely. These approaches might have yielded more genuine consultation.

Emotional Intelligence

The first basket of skills needed for foreign aid management, discussed above, involves cultural competency. The second, emotional intelligence, is equally crucial. Daniel Goleman has written extensively on emotional intelligence and its importance for good management. His hypothesis, backed by behavioral and brain research, is that there is a set of emotional skills—such as self-awareness, self-discipline, and empathy—that contributes to managerial success as much if not more than intellectual ability or technical knowledge. Recent research shows that successful managers often score very high on measures of emotional intelligence and competence.[7]

Applying Goleman's paradigm of emotional intelligence provides important insight into what makes a strong manager in an international development context. One key principle in emotional intelligence is being self-aware. Goleman defines self-awareness as knowing your emotions as they happen. A manager should be able to identify her feelings about a particular situation as they occur and understand what situations—or emotional triggers—set off certain feelings. Everyone has circumstances that consistently make us happy, sad, or frustrated. People who are self-aware know what those triggers are. This knowledge does not always allow us to avoid awkward situations, but it does help to manage them.

A second trait in Goleman's framework is self-discipline, which flows from self-awareness. Having self-discipline means that once you have identified your typical emotional responses, you can keep them under control. We all experience intense emotions such as sadness or anger, but, in a professional environment, anger toward a co-worker can be disruptive. A manager must learn to treat employees honestly and fairly whether or not she likes them, avoiding signs of favoritism or dislike. Cultivating self-discipline helps to prevent intense emotions from interfering with managerial judgment.

According to Goleman, self-awareness and self-discipline not only help to keep impulsiveness at bay. They also allow a manager to marshal her emotions for personal motivation, to focus on long-term rather than short-term goals. In addition, heightened emotional intelligence helps a manager become more aware of emotions in others; it helps her, in other words, cultivate empathy. But empathy alone is not sufficient in a managerial situation. The goal should be to use empathy to manage and motivate a person more effectively, to guide the person toward greater productivity and professional self-realization. The purpose of this effort is not to be manipulative but to help an employee to achieve a desired outcome, whether it is fostering the employee's own professional development or fulfilling a greater social end to which he or she has expressed commitment.

Since development management involves changing human behavior and building human capacity as much as it does technical work, having the skills to understand yourself, understand others, motivate others, develop trust in relationships, and use those relationships to create change stands at its heart. Cultivating these skills is difficult even in a workplace where employees share a similar social background. It is much harder when staff have diverse cultural values and experiences and is more challenging still when you as a manager are in the minority, when the rest of the staff has cultural expectations that differ from your own, and when systems and infrastructure that you take for granted do not function as you anticipate.

To illustrate the situation, imagine an expatriate who has managed a mid-sized foreign aid project for six months. She is the only American on the staff and has had to move from home, pack up her house, ship her goods overseas, find and set up a house, buy a car, and otherwise get settled. There are lots of choices associated with this process, each of which entails effort and stress. There are also security concerns; the country is generally safe, but she stands out because she looks different and because she is a Western woman wearing Western clothes. Amenities taken for granted in the United States may not exist in her new country. Water may need boiling to be potable. Electricity may be unreliable, roads poorly maintained, and the internet spotty. One must take precautions against diseases such as malaria or intestinal bacteria. If our aid worker has a family, she has to make sure that her children are enrolled in good schools, that her spouse has something to do so that he does not become frustrated. If she is single, there are different pressures: isolation, distance from friends. In particularly insecure countries, aid workers' families may have to remain home, adding another set of emotional pressures: missing the family, feeling guilty about being away.

We can see, in other words, that our project director is dealing with a lot of emotional stress unrelated to her job. Yet work adds further pressures: systems that don't function properly; poor traffic that delays appointments and lengthens the time it takes to accomplish things. If our aid worker does not speak the local language, she will miss a great deal of discussion and nuance at the office and in meetings. While project staff generally speak English, their casual banter will most likely be in their home language, and they may even resent speaking English to accommodate one foreign project director. Gender roles may add additional stress. Senior national staff may not be used to working for a woman and may resist in subtle or obvious ways. Age also is a factor; if the project director is younger than staff members or government officials, she may not command great respect. What can be done in such a daunting situation? My experience is that traditional tools of command and control or management approaches that focus on technical interventions are not as effective as working to understand the underlying socio-cultural dynamics and developing strategies that make use of emotional intelligence.

Following Goleman's framework, the first thing for a manager to do is recognize what causes her own anxiety. She is most likely stressed by the myriad day-to-day challenges of moving to a foreign country. Accepting the stress inherent to this situation might help to reduce her anger when the water is shut off or the internet fails. While these frustrations remain, a self-aware, self-disciplined manager can strive to isolate them from activities at work. This is not easy to do and requires sturdy coping mechanisms. Some people throw themselves into work so as not to think about the anxieties of daily life. Others try to see as much of the new country as possible, using travel as a form of release. Still others exercise, learn the local language, take up photography, or paint. Whatever the choice, a good manager develops robust mechanisms for channeling and coping with stress. When I lived overseas, for example, I used physical activity not only to reduce anxiety but also to build relationships with local employees and partners. At the U.S. Consulate in Tijuana, Mexico, an American co-worker and I played weekly basketball and bicycled with the administrative staff. While posted to Mauritania, I joined the Hash House Harriers and took part in weekly runs.

A director who is sensitive to intercultural emotional dynamics can also take many seemingly incidental steps to cultivate greater trust and build social relationships with local staff and host country partners. Office culture often inhibits this process, so regular lunches or other get-togethers can be extremely valuable, building trust by enabling managers and staff to discuss non-work topics and learn about each other's interests and motivations. External gatherings also provide valuable insight into local culture that has myriad payoffs in project implementation. The layout of a manager's office can also make a surprising difference in her ability to communicate with staff. While an expatriate director typically has the nicest office in order to hold formal meetings, the difference can be galling to local staff.[8] Foreign aid projects already have a built-in hierarchy, with the expatriate paid more in both salary and perquisites than local employees. Physical structures can intensify this divide, as can an open- or closed-door policy. Another example, seemingly trivial but actually quite important, is where a manager sits in a car. An expatriate who always takes the back seat relegates her driver to the subservient role of chauffeur. If she sits in the front with the driver, or simply wherever there is space, it creates a different dynamic, often one that is more equitable. All of these examples make an apt point about managing with emotional intelligence: How an expatriate manager treats the driver, the tea lady, or the char force sends crucial signals to the entire staff. A warm, open manner helps to build the kind of trust that contributes to program success.

As a project director learns more about her national staff, she will gain insight into what motivates and troubles them. This empathy, in turn, can help her become a more effective intercultural manager. Typically well-educated and experienced, national staff often have sound ideas about technical innovations and local attitudes that managers should tap. While they may lack the breadth of global experience brought by expatriates, they have an invaluable depth of understanding regarding their home country. If project directors grant staff the opportunity to take risks and innovate, they will generally win local trust, promote local expertise, and improve project performance.

Conclusion

International development work is about more than just government contracting or technical innovation. It is about saving and improving lives. A good manager will be comfortable saying this clearly. If, as Alan Thomas noted, development is about changing how human beings think about their position in life and what they can do about it, then the focus of development work should be on people. Development, after all, is not simply a technical problem that requires a technical solution. It is a human problem that requires human understanding and human resolve. A developed country, in this regard, is not one where the trains run on time, though that may be an indicator of advancement. Rather, it is a country in which its citizens have the opportunity to live their lives to the fullest.[9]

Notes

1. According to Easterly (2006), 4, the figure stood at $2.3 trillion over five decades.
2. Thomas (1999).
3. Identifying information has been removed to protect the individuals and organizations involved.
4. This phenomenon is not limited to foreign assistance projects. It is very noticeable in sports when a team owner changes the coach or manager in an effort to reverse the fortunes of a losing team.
5. See Keilson (2006).
6. Deborah Tannen (1991), for example, highlights the difficulty men and women have in understanding each other. Women, to use one of her examples, tend to discuss challenges at work as a way of sharing emotions. Men hear these discussions as a request for advice. Both parties end up frustrated: The woman feels the man does not understand what she is saying; the man does not understand why his advice is rejected.
7. Goleman (1995). The framework presented in this article can be found in Part II, "The Nature of Emotional Intelligence," 33–126. Research on emotional intelligence as a management skill is presented on 35–40. See as well Gardner (1983), which presents the concept of multiple intelligences, the idea that people learn differently based on different orientations, and that their ability to manage and motivate depends on their capacity to uncover the different learning styles of subordinates, peers, and supervisors.
8. This issue is not limited to overseas projects. I once worked for an organization where the VP created an environment in which all staff felt empowered to talk with him, to have spontaneous meetings, to discuss frankly whatever concerns arose. He had a large office with two doors, one near his executive assistant and the other opening onto the hallway. The second door meant that staff could talk with him without having to request an appointment from his assistant. After his retirement, his replacement also espoused an open-door policy, but closed the door to the hallway, requiring staff to request an appointment from the assistant. That simple signal sent the message that truly open communication was not as valued as before.

9. Maslow's Hierarchy of Needs, first published in 1943, hypothesizes that humans proceed through a series of five steps or levels of meeting their needs, from basic biological needs (food, clothing, shelter), through emotional needs (love, self-esteem) to human fulfilment (self-actualization). To be fully human, according to Maslow, requires meeting needs on all five levels. Decades later, economist Amartya Sen (1999) applied an economic analysis to similar questions and reached a similar conclusion: that people require more than their basic needs to live fully human lives, to be fully 'developed.' Thus, development work, by helping people meet their basic needs, is a precursor to their fuller human development.

Bibliography

Easterly, W. (2006). *The White Man's Burden: Why the West's Efforts to Aid the Rest Have Done So Much Ill and So Little Good.* New York: Oxford.

Gardner, H. (1983). *Frames of Mind: The Theory of Multiple Intelligences.* New York: Basic Books.

Goleman, D. (1995). *Emotional Intelligence: Why It Can Matter More than IQ.* New York: Bantam.

Keilson, J. (2006). Opportunities for Public Diplomacy Programs in USAID and the Peace Corps. In William Kiehl (Ed.), *America's Dialogue with the World.* Washington, DC: Public Diplomacy Council.

Sen, A. (1999). *Development as Freedom.* New York: Random House.

Tannen, D. (1991). *You Just Don't Understand: Women and Men in Conversation.* New York: Ballantine.

Thomas, A. (1999). What Makes Good Development Management. *Development in Practice* 9(1–2): 9–17.

Chapter 5

Sustainability in Development Projects

How Do We Do It, and Do We Really Want To?

Joshua A. Muskin

The goal of sustainability has challenged development practitioners since the start of the modern development era over half a century ago. Given the massive commitment of funds, materials, time, and intellect put into the promotion of development, it is wholly reasonable to expect models and benefits that will endure beyond the life of an aid-funded project. The aim of a project, after all, is to be the start of a long story of change, not the front and back covers of a slim volume.

It is hardly news, however, that true sustainability remains exceptional in projects implemented across the globe. As a rule, the impact of development initiatives is relatively limited in time and space, either stalling, dissipating, or completely disintegrating shortly after project funding ends. The reasons for this repeated disappointment—evoked in the literature and evident to this researcher over three decades of field-based practice—are myriad. This essay attempts to illuminate some of these reasons and indicate promising pathways to sustainability by relating a set of useful strategies illustrated with concrete experiences. Most of the notions shared below derive from the areas of education and training, reflecting the major domains of my professional activity, but the expectation is that they are transferrable across sectors.

What Precisely Are We Trying to Sustain

The first and perhaps the most important insight concerning sustainability in international development projects is to be clear and modest about what exactly we are trying to sustain. Certainly the aim is not to extend a precise facsimile of the models that operated under a funded project. After all, as a model reaches new geographies and endures into the future, many, if not most, of its original design elements will change. Prominent among these are the needs and capacities of the beneficiary populations, the abilities and mindset of the implementers, the plans and resources of the local supervisory institutions, the technological context, and the range of alternative models.

In fact, circumstances can change so dramatically and quickly that sustainability might prove wholly undesirable. Such was the case, for example, with a USAID-funded education project in Mali on which the author worked in the mid-1990s. For over a year, project consultants collaborated with senior officials from the Ministry of Education to prepare a strategy to introduce local languages in early primary grade classrooms that teach French to children. The project developed guidelines and instructional materials to support teachers in their efforts to improve French language learning by referring to local mother tongues. On the day before the project began to introduce the model, the ministry announced a new policy of full mother-tongue instruction in early primary school. French language was now simply a subject in the curriculum, and the project's relevance vanished. Yet even in this extreme example, the original model included elements of language instruction and learning that remained relevant under the new policy. There was much to sustain.

Decades of practice, along with a substantial literature, reveal six elements that are vital to project sustainability; paradoxically, these are precisely those aspects that enable a project to change when expectations and conditions alter. The first is the initiative's fundamental vision and goal. Attainment of positive outcomes and impact will often require revisions to an original plan over a project's lifespan. The longer a project lasts, the more likely it is that conditions will change. In such circumstances, adhering to a project's original design will likely result in a deviation from core aims. Put more bluntly, if you reach the end of a project having done exactly what you said you would in the original plan, you were clearly not paying attention. Because of this, it is crucial to have a core vision that is broad enough to offer precise orientation and flexible enough to accommodate dramatic shifts. Without this, a project can go adrift.

Second, it is vital that the intended beneficiaries, responsible technical agents, and local authorities understand and embrace the project's vision. This matters most critically because it is they who will ultimately live with its consequences and be responsible for sustaining its operations. If they do not perceive the project as responding to their own priorities, prospects are poor that they will invest in it once outside funding disappears. A common trap for donor projects is that host-country partners view their role as helping a donor implement its own initiative. For them to sustain the effort, however, partners must instead see the initiative as theirs. In other words, host country partners should not view themselves as helping a donor succeed, but the other way around.

Third, the full understanding of a project by host-country stakeholders must extend to its underlying logic and technical dimensions. As the ultimate guarantors of sustainability, host-country partners must possess all the knowledge and skills needed to operate a project. They must also have the authority to perpetuate it and to undertake any necessary modifications. Summoning a time-honored adage, this is not just a matter of teaching folks to fish instead of giving them a fish; it involves teaching them to choose the correct bait, adjust the tension of the reel, and select the rod and line. Further, it equips them to repair their tackle and even opt for a completely different technology, such as a seine, in the event that fishing conditions change. Achieving this level of mastery often requires that stakeholders participate in a project from the time of conception, engaging equally in its design and choice of techniques as in all the stages of reflection, revision, and validation. This mastery certainly is not attainable using a classic "turn-key" handover process in which project implementers pass their activities to new local managers with only minimal orientation once a project is completed.

Fourth, responsible technical agents should be able to communicate to beneficiaries the purpose, relevance, component parts, and implementation strategy of the project. Since sustainability frequently entails expansion, host-country authorities must be able to attract adherents and train them in various aspects of implementation.

Fifth, host-country managers and authorities must possess the tools, skills, and resources to monitor and evaluate the project—both its operation and its impact—in order to inform future modification and expansion. It is critical to note here that the indicators applicable to the sustained and expanded version of a project may differ from those used in the funding phase.[1]

Sixth, it is essential to look beyond the technical dimensions of a project to the institutional structures, strategies, plans, budgets, and responsibilities associated with its operation. The responsible host institutions must be able to manage and revise the project as needed. Unfortunately, the classic delimited project approach—what might be characterized as a greenhouse or a laboratory approach to project implementation—often undermines these institutional features of sustainability by maintaining tight internal control over a project's operational systems. Host-country structures are frequently viewed as impediments to success and are therefore ignored or sidelined—an attitude that effectively imperils a project when external funding ends and local structures must carry it forward.

Too often, projects feature conditions that only minimally reflect those of the country as a whole. The beneficiaries of an intervention commonly number in the hundreds rather than tens of thousands; and foreign aid projects generally have more resources, technical expertise, logistical means, and time than are available to host jurisdictions. Under these privileged conditions, a project develops as a sort of hothouse flower, blooming beautifully in conditions in which the temperature, humidity, nutrition, and other key factors are ideally managed. At the end of the project, however, managers must hand these plants over to host partners to sustain and spread. Local implementers must now cultivate them in the metaphorically arid, saline, hardscrabble, resource poor, technologically barren, pest- and disease-ridden settings that prevail across the real landscapes for which they are responsible.

Viewed through these six lenses, the challenge of sustainability concerns much more than a simple perpetuation of what a project launches. Indeed, project sustainability may be little concerned with perpetuating a core model itself. As the Mali language of instruction project illustrated, a project's lasting impact is secured by an officially designated cadre of technical agents who are committed to a core vision and shape a project model to reflect that vision even as the context evolves. The Mali project built the agents' capacity to support the continued implementation and revision of basic educational goals. These agents were committed to the project because they had been instrumental in its conception, ensuring its technical integrity as well as its continued relevance to national priorities. Described in this way, sustainability is much more a matter of establishing an enduring *process* than of perpetuating a technical *product*.

Defining Sustainability

Various definitions of sustainability appear in the development literature as well as the policy, program, and evaluation documents of international organizations. Some of the definitions are as follows:

- "The ability of a project to maintain its operations, services and benefits during its projected life time"—United Nations Development Program (UNDP) (Khan 2000: 3);
- "The ability of a project to maintain an acceptable level of benefit flows through its economic life"—World Bank (ibid.);
- "Ensuring that the institutions supported through projects and the benefits realized are maintained and continue after the end of the project"—International Fund for Agricultural Development (IFAD) (Tango International 2009: 8);

- "The capacity of a host country entity to achieve long-term success and stability and to serve its clients and consumers without interruption and without reducing the quality of services after external assistance ends"—United States Agency for International Development (USAID 2015);
- "The continuation of benefits after the end of an intervention. The probability of obtaining these benefits over the long-term. The situation by which the net gains are likely to resist any risks"—Agence Française de Développement (attributed to the United Kingdom Department for International Development, DfID) (Agence Française de Développement 2015; translation by the author);
- "The continuation of benefits after major assistance from a donor has been completed"—Australian Agency for International Development (AUSAID 2000: 4);
- "The continuation or maintenance of structures or initiatives created, or benefits of inputs distributed, beyond the lifetime of the project and . . . key to whether a project will achieve a wider and longer-term impact"—Action Contre la Faim (ACF) International Network (Solomon 2015: 9).

Consistent across these definitions is a focus on perpetuating the "products" of an intervention, whether these take the form of a model or strategy, outcome, benefit, or implementing structure. The main difference among the references concerns duration. For some, the time horizon of sustainability is the "lifetime" of the intervention; for others, it is survival beyond the project's end.

Projects by the organizations cited above are commonly time-bound initiatives in which the organization provides technical expertise, logistical support, material resources, and funding. These initiatives are conceived, designed, and operated to address a particular problem at a particular time under particular conditions. They can range from less than a year to several years, though it is rare that they extend beyond five. Often they occur at a relatively modest scale, suited to a discrete time span and budget, though the actual size may vary considerably. A project might involve a few dozen schools, villages, families, or entrepreneurs; or it could reach thousands.

The aim of many projects is to test and validate at a small or medium scale a solution to a problem that pertains at the system level. In this regard, sustainability is also linked with potential expansion. Indeed, the goal often conflates the notions of scalability (expanding activities in space) and sustainability (extending them in time). By project-testing a model on a small scale, the hope is that it (or its component parts) will be effective across diverse settings in the country in the future. Yet such transferability cannot be assumed. As Rodrik (2008) explains in his critical analysis of randomized controlled trials, a project's success in one location offers no guarantee of similar outcomes elsewhere or at a different time.

In undertaking a project with the aspiration of continued applicability and broad adoption, institutions might endeavor to conduct the experimentation and validation phase in a wide range of settings, hoping to capture the diversity that characterizes a full population. Few projects, however, actually do this.

There are understandable reasons why projects overlook the wider complexities of sustainability, particularly when pressed to favor short-term results. For one, there are practical business concerns. Donors routinely count companies' "past performance" as a factor in deciding whether to award a new contract or grant. As impressive performance must occur in the short time-frame of a funded project, it behooves an implementer to do everything in its power to garner the greatest measurable success possible. The relatively new formula of payment by results, which some donors are now using, puts even more pressure on firms to maximize evidence of short-term success. Otherwise, not just future but even present revenues are in jeopardy.

Similarly, the exorbitant targets that some international agencies set for their core strategies—e.g., USAID's ten-year goal of 100,000,000 new children reading—might compel project implementers to favor product over process and short-term gains over long. Such targets may be morally and politically defensible, but they can also incentivize short-sighted strategic decisions at the expense of long-term goals. In the same vein, the expectation of reaching high targets with modest resources can induce projects to work with populations that are geographically and socio-culturally accessible, leaving the neediest to fend for themselves. Although it is not automatic that such pressures yield models that undermine sustainability, the potential is considerable and the anecdotal evidence widespread.

Even when a project is designed and operated with an eye toward sustainability, truly sustainable outcomes are likely to be more aspirational than guaranteed. This is so for at least two reasons. First, the differences among distinct project locations—including the knowledge base of the local population, available resources, the precise nature of the problem, local perceptions, physical access, and institutional commitment—is often great. These factors may appear in abundant permutations. In addition, the effects of time and place on sustainability and scalability are compounded by the tendency of institutions to produce homogenized models for universal dissemination, such as uniform curricula, standardized medical protocols, or common criteria for micro-lending. 'One-size-fits-all' approaches emerge from a legitimate concern to ensure quality programs with equitable coverage, yet crafting singular strategies to suit disparate contexts is illogical. The poor record of sustainability and scalability throughout development history heightens this concern. As the cartoon on this page illustrates, equality in the treatment of different groups does not always result in equal outcomes; indeed, quite the contrary is often true.

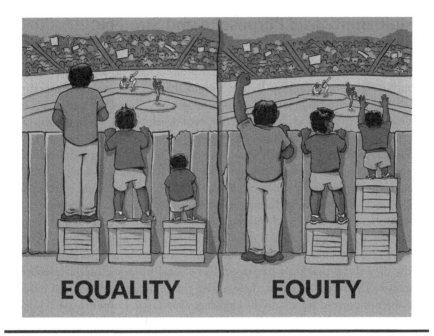

Image 5.1 Equality vs equity

Certainly, most development organizations understand that one size does not fit all. Yet, they also cannot realistically customize all aspects of their initiatives to the unique conditions of every setting. Instead, they frequently shoot for a "sweet spot" of relevance and efficacy, endeavoring to disseminate models that merge the strengths of different pilot efforts. The expectation is that the resulting "mash-up" will be at least approximately relevant in all locations and generate an acceptable level of results that are comparable to those of the original project. This approach suggests that implementers believe not only that the project is universally appropriate but also that conditions after the project ends will be adequate to sustain it.

In reality, implementers often recognize that this assumption is not guaranteed, accepting that its core model will not be suited to every setting. They may invite representatives from regions considering the project to adapt it to their own characteristics. In practice, however, this adaptation rarely happens, whether due to lack of authority, resources, or familiarity with the project model. And even if implementation is adapted, many of the conditions of success from the externally supported phase may be absent, dooming the initiative's new version from the start. Simply put, delivering a project 'as is' for replication in a different place and time is often an invitation to failure, even for the most well-structured efforts.

Sustainability as a Purposeful and Strategic Aim from the Start

The main lesson of this analysis is not that projects have no legitimate prospect for sustainability or scalability. Rather, I argue that for sustainability to occur, it must constitute a prominent and purposeful objective from the start, built into all dimensions of a project. In the international development sector, considerable research, analysis, and negotiation precede final project design and approval. This preliminary work must similarly account for sustainability and scalability, or else it may be difficult to capture these aims later on. Sustainability is most likely to ensue if a project wins the full commitment of local authorities and beneficiaries, an allegiance usually gained during the earliest stages of project conception.

Too often, a fundamental hubris leads to the overly precise definition of a final product. Implementers and their partners take great pride in their successes, but they often mistake these accomplishments as linear and inevitable. In other words, they think that they have found in a local project a uniquely effective solution to a universal problem, disregarding the abundant learning that resulted from the full process. Rarely do the challenges and failures experienced along the way factor into final reports, leading new fishermen to believe they have identified a universally valid angling rod. But there is no guarantee that a rod that serves superbly in the original project is appropriate for a new context. And what if the rod breaks? In both cases, the new users will need to react accordingly. Such eventualities are almost assured. Yet without intimate experience and knowledge of the project—and most especially of the steps that produced the final "rod"—new implementers will struggle to adapt or repair it to meet new needs. They will, in other words, struggle to sustain it.

The following case study illustrates some of these risks. Around 2000, the director of a highly successful and renowned women's literacy program in Africa came to Central America to share her experience with a group of USAID beneficiaries. The program had achieved spectacular gains in raising women's literacy, and the model was of great interest to her hosts. It had also led to remarkable changes in some widespread and deeply entrenched negative practices while elevating the socio-economic status of several African villages. The representatives of the women's organizations were highly impressed by the model and keen to explore how they might replicate it in their own communities. During a question-and-answer session, one woman asked the director: "What do you propose we do to adapt the model to the context of our own communities?" The response was striking. "Adapt?" she asked. "There is no adapting. The model is exactly as it must be. We have spent 20 years working on it to get it just right. There is nothing to change."

Nothing to adapt?! Did the director have no sense of the degree to which her process of experimentation and revision contributed to the successful model, of how much she and her colleagues had learned from their failures? Was there no appreciation of how the local context had influenced project methods and materials as well as their effectiveness and relevance? This director was asserting that her 20 years of labor in Africa had led to the discovery of a universally applicable formula for women's literacy. Instead, I argue, she had toiled to find the correct formula for that time and place. The successful results cannot be attributed to the strategic model alone; they depended on the hard-earned time spent adjusting to ever-changing conditions and needs. And surely her revisions never ceased. Much as the sustainability of Canon Corporation is not due to the continued production of its successful film-based SLR cameras, the sustainability of an aid project cannot depend on wholesale allegiance to a product model that brought initial success. Canon's durability may be traced to its processes of continuous innovation designed to capitalize on ever-new technologies and demand. This is the core lesson of sustainability.

Re-Defining Sustainability as a Goal and an Outcome

What is not evident in the above definitions—and what is argued here—is that true sustainability implies an enduring impact that transcends a project's benefits, strategies, and structures. In fact, there is often little reason to sustain many successful interventions. When a community has successfully eliminated the practice of female genital mutilation (FGM), the original project is no longer pertinent. But attainment of a project's goals certainly doesn't signify that the need for related development disappears. The eradication of FGM might inspire a community or organization to tackle a wider range of gender-related concerns such as domestic violence or women's economic rights. Supporting a community to launch an effective early childhood development program is not necessarily a stopping point; it may serve as a catalyst to strengthen the quality and relevance of other levels of education.

If a project is truly sustainable, it should be a natural consequence of the capacities established during its operation. This does not mean that responsible local systems, institutions, or beneficiaries will not need further support. What a sustainable project can provide, however, is the insight and initiative to articulate a new set of ambitions and new processes aimed at their attainment.

Khan (2000: 3), a senior monitoring and evaluation advisor to the UNDP, seems to acknowledge this definition when he writes that "sustainability should . . . be seen within time and changing social, economic, and political contexts." It is concerned not solely with the continued "delivery of project goods and services" but also with any "changes stimulated [or] caused by the project" and "new initiatives" that the project helped to spawn. Similarly, Ingle (2005: 2) notes that impact tends to be "measured in terms of benefits at the end of the project funding cycle." Yet,

> research has shown that this definition of 'end' is too short-sighted. Projects frequently stop delivering the desired benefits as soon as the money runs out because benchmarks were defined only in terms of effectiveness, *neglecting institutional aspects concerning the capacity to sustain the delivery of benefits after donor funding ends.*
>
> (italics added)

A similar concern may be inferred from USAID's 2015 definition of sustainability as "the capacity of a host country entity to achieve long-term success and stability and to serve its clients and consumers without interruption and without reducing the quality of services after external assistance ends" (USAID 2015).

The benefits of sustainability, then, are not simply those captured in a project's strategic objectives and operational indicators. Rather, they should be those embodied in a project's vision statement, goals, and higher objectives; or, in the language of the conventional LogFrame, sustainability should apply to impacts and outcomes, not just outputs. In this sense, the benefits to sustain are not just the elimination of FGM or the creation of Early Childhood Care and Education (ECCE) centers. They also comprise broader protection and enforcement of women's rights and greater improvement across the whole educational system—goals that might not fall within the purview of project objectives but may ultimately be influenced by them.

Viewed in this way, all the technical and strategic aspects of a project might change without undermining its essential sustainability. In fact, the core of this essay's argument is that achieving true sustainability requires that these aspects do change as new efforts embrace new goals. When sustainability is defined as process rather than product, four basic dimensions prevail:

- the effective, flexible, and evolving use by "front-line" implementers;
- clear and committed institutional structures and systems to support these actors and activities;
- the availability of adequate financial and material resources; and
- a supportive policy environment that translates into appropriate decisions, plans, and budgets.

These are discussed more fully below.

Effective and Flexible Use by Front-Line Operators

The different techniques a project introduces must be understandable and manageable by the main "front-line" practitioners who both implement and benefit from them. These might include teachers, farmers, or micro-credit officers, depending on the project. Full commitment to these innovations—and ability to manage them—implies that these operators:

- understand project concepts, motivations, techniques, and strategies;
- use project innovations routinely in appropriate circumstances to generate results;
- use them flexibly in order to suit new circumstances;
- integrate them appropriately into other practices; and
- modify them as needed for new applications.

There should be little expectation that front-line actors will demonstrate these abilities at the start of a project. And they may never achieve full technical mastery. But there is also little prospect that local expertise will develop unless a project incorporates strategies for building its capacity. Project designers and implementers often talk about the need to "scaffold" the performance of the front-line operators, buttressing their use of project innovations with tightly scripted or circumscribed inputs and strategies. Admittedly, many of these actors require precise guidance. But not all do. Nor do many who require instruction at the project's start need it for very long. Unfortunately, the time-bound, results-focused nature of many projects can encourage designers to use scaffolded methods with little idea of what the activity will look like once the scaffolding is removed.

Clear and Committed Institutional Structures and Systems

The second dimension requires that there be a formal operational system in place to train new adopters in project techniques and then monitor and support those who use them. It is commonly accepted that projects should cooperate with host country institutions. While this cooperation helps to avoid redundancy and rivalries, sometimes a new structure must be created when no adequate institution exists to carry out project activities.

To help facilitate successful institutionalization, a project must:

- be integrated into official priorities, policies, and programs at all levels;
- have sufficient numbers of well-qualified, committed personnel assigned to it;
- have an adequate budget to perform its functions;
- incorporate relevant models and strategies into official pre-service and in-service training programs; and
- introduce relevant criteria into personnel and program evaluation protocols.

None of these factors is necessary for most donor-funded projects to meet their targets. However, it is unlikely that activities will outlast external funding unless these measures are taken. If sustainability is indeed a goal, a project should embrace these objectives and work with the host system to achieve them over the course of the project.

This requires collaborating on all key project elements. First, the project must create training and support materials that are manageable technically, logistically, and financially by host country institutions. Second, it must strengthen the capacity of host-country personnel to understand the technical dimensions of the project and manage the associated strategies. Third, it must ensure that associated costs are not beyond the system's capacity to maintain. This does not necessarily mean that a project should have no budgetary costs but rather means that additional expenses should be feasible for the host country and defensible based on project impact. Finally, all persons involved in the project must have both the professional and the personal motivation to promote it. This motivation may be partly pecuniary, but it should also tap a person's sense of autonomy, mastery, and purpose—what Daniel Pink (2009) calls "Motivation 2.0."

Secure Availability of the Material Requirements

Sustainability and scalability also depend upon having sufficient resources for successful dissemination. Most obvious among these are:

- practitioner manuals, guides, and technical documentation to support project strategies;
- relevant forms and tools to support implementation, monitoring, and communication with beneficiaries;
- material tools or other objects, such as laboratory equipment for agriculture extension units or refrigeration for vaccination campaigns; and
- suitable physical space for replicating project innovations.

Access to these resources can depend upon a wide range of factors. Most obvious is cost. Quite simply, a donor project can usually afford far more material inputs than can host institutions, at least on a per user or beneficiary basis. Another concern is language. Project materials may need to be in multiple languages, and illiterate populations may require alternative means for conveying information. Each of these concerns has technical and financial implications.

There are also logistical considerations (such as transportation, communications networks, and market mechanisms) and intangible factors (such as the policy environment or cultural norms and constraints) that affect an initiative's prospects for sustainability and scalability. All of these factors may vary in different regions of a host country, making it difficult to move a project from one area to another.

As a result of these challenges, the aim of capturing project innovations in a guide should not be to codify them strictly for future imitation, an all-too-common approach. Rather, the challenge is to embody within the documentation notions of the process as well as the product. Take, for example, a project that created a guide for raising corn yields by applying conservation techniques. A recipe approach to the manual would lay out each step taken in the region where a project operated. By contrast, an approach that aspires to sustainability would integrate into the guide measures needed to account for different environments, material assets of users, access to resources, and crop variety. It would present the range of decisions a farmer must make, indicate the information needed to make the decision, and propose strategies for acquiring this information. It might also share the underlying science. All of these elements permit users to dismantle the original project scaffolding.

A Supportive Policy Environment

Sustainability also requires a policy environment that encourages the adoption and use of project innovations. This condition begins with an official endorsement of the project, but other support must ensue to ensure that the commitment is not mere rhetoric. Among these elements are:

- the official public adoption and routine promotion of strategies to train stakeholders in project components;
- the integration of project components into national plans and budgets;
- the inclusion of direct responsibility for project activities in official job descriptions and direct references to project elements in performance appraisals;
- reporting on the project in the media; and
- the revision of other policies to ensure they align with the requirements of a project.

The success of a project does not always depend on a conducive policy environment. In fact, a justification for many projects is that they provide an antidote to failed local policies and structures. To carve out a successful activity in an otherwise failing setting requires not just that a project introduce new techniques but that it create a new context in which to flourish. In Morocco, where I led a five-year USAID-funded education project (discussed below), my first request to regional and district education officers was to provide the project a "*marge de manœuvre*," or "wiggle room," in which teachers, school heads, and other frontline actors could operate without being shackled by official and conventional constraints. The teachers and participants needed the space to innovate *and even fail* in order to succeed, along with the confidence that they would not be penalized for eschewing official expectations.

Yet the problem remains: The obstacles to improved performance are often a matter not of knowledge but of conditions. A teacher may know quite well how to use learner-centered methods, but, if the education system tests rote knowledge, both the motivation and the opportunity to adopt new methods are largely absent. If the special conditions of a project disappear with the end of funding, its innovations will likely also wither. To persist with the project's strategic elements will either place the actors in conflict with official standards or condemn them to frustration and diminishing returns.

The long-term success of a project, then, hinges largely on the degree to which it clarifies the fundamental environmental conditions for success and works to cultivate needed institutional changes. It is incumbent on a project that is truly committed to long-term impact not to propose methods that will put its future practitioners at risk of failure.

The Deliberate and Strategic Pursuit of Sustainability

To state the case bluntly, if project designers and implementers are committed to sustainability and scalability, they must plan for it. There is little sense in cultivating a "hothouse flower" that will wilt in the host landscape without external funds. Unfortunately, early planning for sustainability rarely occurs. Too often, a project ends in a perfunctory hand-over ("turn-key"), and the donor and host-country authorities move on to other things. A project's original beneficiaries may continue to employ project models, and there may be some informal spill-over to new groups. But the systematic perpetuation of the project is unlikely.

In development practice, new projects frequently emerge around new priorities and disregard what preceded. If there are links to previous efforts, these are often attributable to key staff who move from one project to the next. This haphazardness produces little continuity. But when a project is truly embedded in local structures and plans, the prospects for both sustainability and scalability increase. The following case study illuminates both sides of this dynamic.

An Example of Education Project Success[2]

In 2005, USAID launched the $27 million Advancing Learning and Employability for a Better Future (ALEF) project in Morocco. Its core aim was to support Morocco's ambitious national education reform strategy. ALEF embraced many elements of that reform, beginning with two distinct and only loosely connected components: Basic Education (implemented by the U.S.-based NGO Academy for Educational Development [now FHI 360]) and Professional Training in Agriculture (implemented by the American firm Management Systems International [MSI]).

The Basic Education component operated at the junior secondary level and comprised many elements that are rarely included under a single mechanism: school development planning, social mobilization, information and communication technologies (ICT) for pedagogy, curriculum delivery, entrepreneurial education, teacher professional development, women's literacy, and a strengthened girls' dormitory model. The last of these was the only element drawn from USAID-Morocco's previous education investments. The Professional Training component emphasized training in entrepreneurial and core personal competencies delivered in agriculture schools and to business professionals.

ALEF officially operated in four regions of the country: Casablanca, Meknès-Tafilalet, Chaouia-Ouardigha, and Oriental. In agreement with USAID, the project also introduced the Basic Education component in five additional regions in its last year: Rabat-Sale-Zemmour-Zaër, Tadla-Azilal, Souss-Massa-Drâa, Tanger-Tétouan, and Fès-Boulemane. These regions received only technical assistance from the project; other expenses commonly covered by projects were instead handled by the respective Regional Academies of Education. Similarly, ALEF worked with the Ministry of Agriculture to introduce the Entrepreneurial Development Program to training institutions in two other regions in the project's final year.

The main purpose of this extension was to demonstrate the sustainability and scalability of the components' core models. Strategically, this effort required piloting activities under typical Moroccan conditions—outside the hothouse of the funded project. The experience allowed the project and relevant Moroccan institutions to identify challenging aspects of the strategy and propose "fixes" for them. It alerted the regional academies to institutional weaknesses they would have to address if they were to incorporate the ALEF model.

When the project closed, it was judged successful by virtually all who interacted with it. But how sustainable was it? Now, over six years since the project's end in September 2009, colleagues in Morocco report that elements of ALEF still endure. Six components have lasted more or less intact, while others have left clear traces in project regions, though not a systemic imprint. From the Basic Education component, the ICT for improved pedagogy model, including its distance learning platform, was embraced by the Ministry of Education and remains central to its operational strategies. The Ministry also continues to use the peer-driven teacher training and professional development model, which the project dubbed APAR—the Atelier de partage, d'approfondissement, et de regulation (the Sharing, Deepening, and Revision Workshop). The Entraide Nationale, a government department devoted to social welfare, has adopted and expanded the girls' dormitory model. And ALEF's pedagogy program has been included in the national pre-service education training curriculum, the Ministry's official curricular guidelines, and the Ministry's Programme d'Appui à la Réussite Scolaire, as well as a few independent schools.

From the Professional Development component, two aspects have endured. The Ministry of Agriculture has integrated the entrepreneurial development program and the associated employment support module into its technician and specialized technician training programs. And the career guidance and training website moustaqbali.ma continues to evolve since it was adopted by the ALEF partner MTDS, a private local firm that was responsible for the site's original development and management (see www.laformation.ma).

Other aspects of the project have also found continued life. The junior secondary entrepreneurial spirit training program was taken up by UNICEF, which transformed it for use in primary schools. The APAR mechanism featured prominently in two subsequent USAID projects that adapted it for use in the Ministry of Education's teacher training and professional development program.[3] And the school development project, or the *Projet d'établissement*, was adopted by the Ministry of Education in an official set of related guidelines, strategies, and policies.

In the final months of ALEF, the senior leadership of the Ministry of Education, many of whom were new appointees, realized how much the project had succeeded at addressing key priorities of Morocco's national education reform, something that partners at the regional level had long known. They also realized that a simple end-of-project handover would not equip the Ministry to sustain or expand ALEF's programs. Though it was too late to integrate the models fully into national policies, the Ministry and the project team seemed to have learned that the ultimate value of ALEF was the institutionalization of its models within formal government structures. Ultimately, much of ALEF's teacher training model was incorporated into the national education program. Sustainability and scalability seem to have occurred.

The aim of this case study is to highlight some of the factors that favor or disfavor sustainability. Although the subsequent string of donor-funded projects might be likened to a game of "whack-a-mole," with strategic objectives, implementers, locations, and host country partners popping up and then disappearing, ALEF stands out in Morocco for its apparent sustainability. If indeed this happened, it was the result of a deliberate effort to promote institutionalization as part of project operations from the start.

Planning for Sustainability and Scale: Core Principles and Strategies

A fundamental challenge to project sustainability is that implementers are not in control of many factors that determine success. Host-country institutions have a broader—though still incomplete—range of control, while donors must essentially surmise how best to align their projects with local and national priorities.

In this regard, a fundamental question about any externally supported project is whether it helps the host country accomplish its priorities or, conversely, the host country helps the donor implement a project. While one might reasonably expect the first, frequently the latter occurs. Certainly no donor would claim that its project trumps government's priorities. Yet one can argue that this often happens. If a donor country's parliament allocates funds for girls' schooling, HIV/AIDS, or food aid, those are the priorities its development aid agency will pursue, even if host countries are more concerned with malaria prevention and agricultural productivity. The host must accept donor rules if it wants to receive funding, even if its priorities lie elsewhere.

This misalignment also results from the competitive bidding process. Typically, a donor call for proposals launches a mad dash on the part of contractors to formulate a strategy, secure partnerships, and develop a "winning" bid. This frenzy is not conducive to reflection or negotiation on the suitability of the project to prevailing country priorities. Nor does it encourage challenges to the donor's assumptions and aims, at least not if a bidder wants to win.

Donors and host governments alike argue that deep reflection and negotiation are essential to project design. Indeed, the Paris Declaration on Aid Effectiveness (2005) designates the host-country government as the negotiation leader and requires that all donors align their efforts behind it. Nonetheless, donors retain their own agendas, and brief project design periods, which may involve proposal teams with little country experience, raise serious doubts about the degree to which local needs are accommodated.

Once a project becomes a country agreement and an official contract, its core elements are legally codified. For a contractor, any serious digression from the formal terms can result in accusations of non-compliance, reducing chances for future work and even jeopardizing the present contract. Latitude for experimentation depends largely on the flexibility of a donor's technical or contracting officer; and there are limits to what is possible even with a contract amendment. Another approach to project design and planning seems necessary if true sustainability is desired.

The Need for Reactivity and Flexibility within a Project

Unfortunately, the conventional conditions of project design and implementation often prevent managers from adjusting to changes that occur throughout the life of a project. Sometimes these changes represent important opportunities. The original ALEF plan, for example, called for piloting an ICT strategy for improved pedagogy in a mere dozen schools over the project's life. An opportunity to expand arose when the government decided after the project's design was formalized to establish computer laboratories in over 9,000 schools connected to the electricity grid. A subsequent agreement with USAID enabled ALEF to move beyond its initial mandate in order to assist the national Ministry in shaping its ICT instructional model.

When a project's plans are not engraved in stone, when project implementers can react to new needs and opportunities with its donors and host partners, the prospects for sustainability rise greatly. This flexibility allows project activities to respond to evolving circumstances, not just the hothouse conditions of a project laboratory. In addition, open collaboration between project staff and host-country stakeholders strengthens local institutions by improving both commitment and capacity. As noted earlier, this engagement produces not just a fishing rod but also the knowledge to repair, replace, or reject the rod as circumstances dictate.

Sustainability Begins on "Day 1"

Ideally, implementers should collaborate with host-country stakeholders during the design phase, negotiating to ensure that the project fully reflects local priorities and conditions. Unfortunately, proposal preparation deadlines rarely allow for such consultation, especially as there is only one government that must consult with many applicants. Since few applicants want to divulge their strategies for fear of revealing "secrets," consultations can be vague even when they do occur— hardly a foundation for cooperation and sustainability.

The second-best option is to undertake consultation once a project is awarded. Yet even here, the latitude for shared decisions is constrained since both the contract between donor and implementing firm and the bilateral agreement between donor and host-country government have been signed. Nonetheless, assuming sincere interest among the main parties to a project, critical decisions are still possible. Among those that might enhance sustainability are:

■ the selection of project locations (which should include diverse settings in order to ease planning and adjustment for later dissemination);

■ the identification of key political and strategic partner agencies within host institutions (early selection helps to establish a strong working relationship and allows the project to strengthen official capacity and commitment);

■ the establishment of concrete objectives, strategies, guidelines, and protocols for effective collaboration between the project and host-country institutional partners;

■ the shared articulation of clear outcomes, which the host country agrees to appropriate at the end of the project;

■ the anticipation of steps required for project success; and

■ the elaboration of a plan for the life of the project, including strategies, timing, resources, and benchmarks to ensure successful implementation and eventual scaling and sustainability.

All of these decisions depend greatly on the degree of latitude allowed in the original contract.[4]

Demonstrate That Sustainability Is a Desirable Outcome

Sustaining a project can place great demands on host-country institutions. It may require local officials to learn new methods, expend significant resources, and deal with negative reactions from the press or public. The most effective way to encourage this kind of effort is to demonstrate that the project generates valuable results. The successes most likely to convince stakeholders are fourfold. First, the project must yield outcomes that matter to all concerned and that outweigh the costs of operation. Second, it should introduce effective new techniques that local practitioners can learn with relative ease and adapt as circumstances require. The project may have to incorporate end-user training and capacity-strengthening to ensure that practitioners have the needed competencies for both results. Third, intended users must have access to core technology and other essential inputs. The classic experience of installing water pumps across the developing world offers a vivid example of these needs. While improved pumps are effective and simple, early versions failed for three main reasons: Replacement parts were difficult to obtain; many projects did not train maintenance technicians; and few projects anticipated the challenge of promoting careful use of the equipment. Finally, sustainability depends on the ability of practitioners and beneficiaries to derive continued benefits from a project, which may require action in separate domains. For example, training youth in a vocation can result in high levels of learning, but the real motivation for beneficiaries is usually future employment. Without improvement in a range of peripheral areas—such as access to credit, business training, market access, or equipment—there may be little interest in sustaining even a highly touted vocational training program.

While a project may not foresee all the ramifications of its interventions, it is disingenuous to speak of sustainability if project planners do not at least anticipate some of them. A project should ensure that its activities are compatible with the contexts in which they will operate. It should work with future implementers and beneficiaries to strengthen their capacities. And it may need to promote or consolidate new systems if those in use are ill-suited to sustainability and expansion.

Have Reasonable Expectations for the Scope and Rate of Successful Adoption

The history of international development is littered with projects that did not outlast their external funding. In many instances, they simply failed to satisfy the conditions mentioned above. Yet failure also results from an overly ambitious sense of what sustainability and scalability mean. Many stakeholders judge sustainability by whether the full population of beneficiaries—all farmers, women, teachers, or administrators—adopts a project innovation. Without full uptake, decision-makers may look for a different solution. This precipitous conclusion unduly pressures both a project and its intended beneficiaries.

People embrace risk and novelty in different ways, and there is no reason to expect that everyone will embrace a new technique. One way to characterize the path to project dissemination involves a typology of practitioner personalities and their willingness to accept risk. Those who are most likely to embrace an innovation can be called *Idealists*. They are convinced by an initial idea and are willing to use an innovation as first adopters. A second group might be called *Empiricists*. These are persons who wish to see evidence that an innovation works before espousing it. They are open to change, but need proof of its benefits. A third group may be called *Cynics*. They may simply be uninterested in change, or they may be jaundiced, having experienced too many failed projects in the past. They may also feel that the status quo is adequate. The last group are *Conformists*. These are practitioners who follow current trends. Their embrace of innovation marks a "tipping point," the moment when a "critical mass" is reached.

In the end, no project will affect all potential beneficiaries. Project managers must set realistic goals for both adoption and sustainability, disregarding rejection by some groups when deciding whether or not to persist with an activity. While Cynics may offer valuable observations, they must not be allowed to govern decisions about the relevance of a project.

Plan and Implement for Sustainability as a Participatory Process

Front-line actors and officials in local agencies will ultimately be responsible for a project's sustainability. It is crucial, therefore, to engage experts from key national and local institutions at all phases of a project's life. External experts may bring advanced methods and technologies, but they are often ignorant of the wide range of local conditions that will determine a project's ultimate durability. An international agriculture expert can bring cutting-edge strategies in conservation agriculture; but he or she requires local extension agents to identify relevant social, economic, and cultural factors.

Local participation helps to ensure the technical and socio-cultural appropriateness of a project and provides an avenue for concrete revisions that would be missed by an outsider. Perhaps most importantly, local participants maximize the prospects of "buy-in" by implementers and beneficiaries. Not only will project innovations conform more closely to local needs if they participate, but they will also be motivated by a sense of ownership and pride. The project will be theirs. A similar logic pertains to the participation of local authorities, since their influence will shape prevailing policies, plans, and budgets.

Sustainability as a Strategic Component: A Five-Phase Model

At base, a project is a hypothesis about a particular solution to a specific problem. As Rodrik noted, even if a solution is successful once, its reiteration in a new

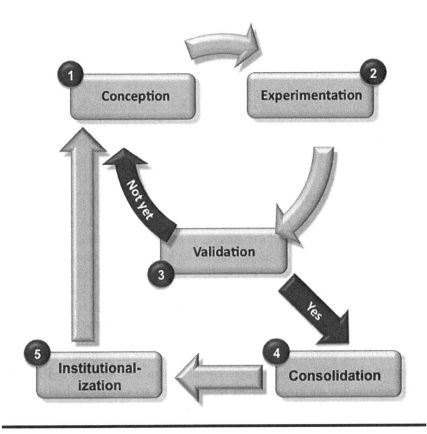

Image 5.2 Five-step framework for project sustainability

place and time demands new proof. The diagram on this page presents a five-step framework for accomplishing this revalidation. While the model is presented here in sequence, the first three steps typically occur as an iterative process, cycling repeatedly until the result turns out positively.[5]

Step 1: Conception/Design

Any project is essentially concerned with fitting a proposed innovation (or innovations) to a novel context in order to address a particular set of challenges. In some instances, this process involves creating a new technique or method, while in others it entails a version of something done elsewhere. In both cases, it is necessary to treat the project as new. Even with a "proven" approach, a new context demands that participants conduct design steps as if they were creating the model afresh.

This advice might seem to contradict the common wisdom that projects should not reinvent the wheel. But that is precisely the point. The design of even a conventional wheel must consider the surface on which it will roll, the weight it must bear, the materials available for its manufacture, and the speeds at which it will travel. It is not a matter of coming up with an alternative to the core notion of a wheel; but it is crucial to adjust every wheel to the surface it will navigate.

This accommodation of past models to current circumstances enables both the implementing agency and the host country partners to identify conditions that will facilitate project success and sustainability. And it provides local actors with a base of operational expertise as part of the process.

Step 2: Experimentation

The experimentation phase functions as a continuation of the conception phase, testing various techniques and technologies in order to refine them. At this stage, the major goal is to cultivate project success by honing and revising core project approaches for the new project setting. It is important to stress that conception and re-conception are permanent features of any strong project, though the early phases are particularly intense. The early process includes a triage that eliminates some aspects of a proposed model and introduces others in order to address unmet needs or enrich the range of choices.

To optimize prospects for sustainability, front-line practitioners should be heavily involved in this process, experimenting with new methods and materials in settings that are propitious for future project success. By multiplying the number of experimentation sites, project implementers and host-country partners have the opportunity to capitalize on a diverse range of local expertise and find the most appropriate adaptations. A participatory, field-led approach to experimentation can also safeguard against the incorporation of elements that are ill-suited to the local context.

Step 3: Validation

The validation stage takes experimentation to a new level. Its main goal is to confirm the legitimacy of the project model while revealing any lingering weaknesses, paying particular attention to the interworking of the model's components. If project sustainability is desired, it is vital to identify vulnerabilities early.

Achieving success at this stage is often relatively easy given the resources associated with a typical project. However, the risk of creating a sort of Potemkin village—an impressive façade that conceals an impoverished reality—is great. Many interventions crumble when they confront the hardscrabble terrain of a non-project setting. Preventing such "hothouse flowers" requires attention not just to the model but also to dissemination and support strategies as well as the overall policy and institutional environment.

In practice, creating a proper "stress" test of project models means expanding the number of implementation sites and adding locations that are representative of the target sector's diversity. The ALEF Project in Morocco, for example, grew from 39 schools at the experimentation stage to around 350 schools for validation. This knowledge should enable partners to revise the project as appropriate. Validation should also reveal environmental factors and capacity needs that are essential to a project's success.

When testing project interventions in true field conditions, one should expect that quality will be sacrificed. While this may seem worrisome to donors or officials, it is in fact purposeful and, I argue, desirable. A state-of-the-art intervention that succeeds in ideal conditions is more prone to failure when moved elsewhere. Conversely, a "lesser" version that accommodates a resource-poor, time-constrained reality has a greater chance of sustainability and expansion. Yet adapting a project to host-country conditions does not mean that it will always remain second best. As front-line actors perceive its value, they may identify ways to strengthen it. Leaving a project to local actors allows it to evolve in a variety of ways based on local particularities and ingenuity. In the end, this approach holds greater prospects for durable success.

In many projects, the validation phase occurs, if at all, toward the end of a project. The model proposed here situates it in the middle, perhaps followed by a mid-term evaluation. This placement gives partners time to identify two key project elements: (i) those aspects of a project's technical model that require revision to suit the prevailing context; and (ii) any political, technical, or strategic shortcomings of the responsible host-country institutions that require strengthening. With this information, the project can move confidently to the penultimate phase of consolidation.

Step 4: Consolidation

Having validated a project's models, methods, and materials, the next step is to finalize them for institutional appropriation and use by front-line practitioners. This process may run parallel to continued project operation, but with ever-decreasing engagement by the implementing partner. Indeed, one aim of the consolidation process is to secure the different aspects of a project in the natural conditions of the host country. In this regard, front-line practitioners may discover solutions to project weaknesses that the implementer could not solve. The ultimate proof of concept and consolidation of a project's model is its successful adoption by host-country institutions without project funds. This is what ALEF attempted to do by adding the four additional regions in the final year. The result of this effort was not just the consolidation of project approaches but also vital insight into how Moroccan institutions might strengthen their own policies to ensure their continued project operation.

Step 5: Institutionalization

Supporting host-country institutions as they incorporate lessons from the consolidation phase is the final step toward sustainability. Cutting the project umbilicus means adopting a purely advisory role as the project is transferred to host-country management. Prominent among the operational dimensions to address in this final phase are:

- the final transfer of project responsibility to host-country institutions and individuals who will manage it after funding;
- the formal appraisal of implementation and outcomes, as well as any decisions that follow from it;
- the incorporation of project models into the professional training curricula of relevant institutions;
- the integration of project models into the official plans and programs of relevant institutions;
- the inclusion in official budgets of costs associated with these activities; and
- the identification of project models as official host-country priorities.

If a project has planned for sustainability from the start, the final institutionalization should proceed smoothly and with little stress.

Risks to Sustainability

Imagine an education project that seeks to revise a country's national curriculum for the twenty-first century. What must happen to ensure its sustainability? While the project may successfully establish a new curriculum that guides students and teachers to high levels of achievement, this alone will not guarantee its survival. To ensure sustainable adoption, the curriculum must translate into new textbooks and support materials, updated school schedules, revised pedagogical methods, new teacher training programs, and new learning assessment measures. In addition, education systems must re-think their plans and budgets, supervision methods, and school governance mechanisms. Without such support, the new curriculum will wither on the vine, perhaps bearing fruit for a short while, but ultimately failing to alter the overall education system.

Unsurprisingly, project sustainability is unlikely to occur as seamlessly as described in this essay. For one thing, a project's duration may simply be too short to accommodate the steps needed to entrench it. Indeed, more than one project cycle may be necessary. Other factors may jeopardize sustainability as well, including the existence of competing innovations; reliance on unsustainable incentive structures; a "revolving door" of personnel; and overlooking a critical stakeholder.

Competing Innovations

It is not unusual for a country to host simultaneous projects in the same sector. While these initiatives should ideally complement each other, such coordination is rare. Funded activities may be distributed across a ministry's units, a strategy ostensibly undertaken to ease the burden and spread the benefits equitably. What sometimes occurs, however, is that agency directors use projects to assert their authority. At the same time, donors may disperse projects to influence a ministry's policies and plans. This multiplicity can leave front-line practitioners over-burdened by duties and wondering which interventions to prioritize. In such instances, sustainability may be arbitrary—a result of patronage, influence, or simple luck—rather than a decision based on robust evidence.

The allure of multiple projects for a country is understandable, as is the competition among agencies for leadership. Yet the risks of conflict can be severe. Both host-country institutions and their donor partners must endeavor to respect the Paris Declaration, which requires them to analyze the full roster of projects as a coherent whole and arrange them to maximize coordination and sustainability within a framework defined by host-country priorities.

An Unsustainable Incentive Structure

Sustainability may also fall victim to a lack of incentives among those responsible for a model's continued operation. Some incentives are extrinsic, such as payments, per diems, study tours, material resources, or orders from a superior. These may be hard to continue once external funding stops. Others are intrinsic, such as pride and prestige that come with enhanced capacity and improved performance, a sense of autonomy and fulfillment from participating in a high-profile intervention, an increased level of commitment to the system, or a belief in the goals and methods of a project. These intrinsic motivations are vulnerable on two fronts. First, practitioners who participated during the project phase may find that post-project conditions diminish their pride and effectiveness. Second, new practitioners may not have the same enthusiasm as early project adherents. Building incentives—both extrinsic and intrinsic—that can be sustained beyond the life of a project is therefore crucial, as is working with the host system to perpetuate them.

The Frequent Reassignment of Key Personnel

Development projects and developing-country institutions face frequent personnel turnover, which can stall a project during implementation or lead to new conditions that a project must accommodate. The loss of personnel means the loss of experience and expertise; at minimum, new practitioners require fresh training and investment. Given the inevitability of personnel changes, projects must take measures to anticipate and mitigate their effects. The choice of many front-line sites and many actors at each is one strategy for doing so. Even if a local manager leaves, other staff can then perpetuate what the project helped to introduce. Similarly, the more a project cultivates relations with many officials, the less vulnerable it will be to changing host-country personnel. Ultimately, a project's best defense against personnel changes is to be clearly advantageous to the careers of those responsible for its success. Veterans as well as new personnel should understand that association with the project will enhance their professional prospects.

This shift in perception was palpable within the ALEF project. In some of the original four regions, Academy directors and other officials saw the project as a USAID initiative. They were pleased that ALEF operated in their regions and were satisfied with the results, but it was almost always ALEF that organized activities and enjoined officials to participate. In other regions, however, including two of those added at the end, leaders recognized that ALEF provided solutions to challenges for which they were responsible. In these instances, ALEF supported their initiatives, and the activities usually came from them. With this shift in perspective, the routine turnover in personnel had fewer deleterious effects. Those who remained had sufficient motivation to persevere with the project's models and aims. And newcomers realized that association with the project could boost their professional success. This was evident in the large number of teachers and authorities working with ALEF who achieved prominence or gained promotions due to their ties to the project.

Neglecting a Critical Stakeholder

It is common for a project's supervisory responsibility to fall to only a few individuals within a host-country institution. As a result, a project may be little known outside the key stakeholders who interact with it directly. Implementers can endeavor to engage stakeholders beyond the project's orbit, but they have little authority to demand their attention. Furthermore, a project's institutional overseer may be stingy in his gatekeeper role, because he is trying either to protect others from being over-burdened or to control his own authority.

Nonetheless, without the involvement—even if minimal—of authorities from many technical and political domains, a project may prove unsustainable because it does not match the priorities of the overall system or because it lacks sufficient advocates. For example, promoting gender equality in education can require interventions related to health, poverty, culture, and infrastructure. Within the latitude provided, it is crucial for projects to involve as many host-country officials and stakeholders as possible.

It is certainly possible to manage many of these risks. Indeed, much of this essay is devoted to strategies for doing so. Sometimes, however, factors influencing a project may simply be a matter of chance. A new minister who opposes a project's extension, for example, will be difficult to anticipate and subvert. Conversely, a surprising new policy may provide precisely the impetus to progress that a project needs. In the end, if a project can generate solidly convincing outcomes, demonstrate its suitability in the prevailing context, entrench itself within a host country's institutions and priorities, and mobilize a critical mass of competent front-line practitioners, it should be able to overcome most risks.

Conclusion

The main message of this essay is that sustainability must be much more than an ambition. For an intervention to have real prospects for sustainability and scalability, these goals must be woven fully into its warp and weft. This process begins at the conception or design phase and includes a fully formed image of what sustainability will look like at a project's end. (This vision, of course, must also evolve.) The implementer must then coordinate with donors and host partners alike on a range of strategic decisions that form the foundation for sustainability: Who should be involved? What should be measured? Which methods should prevail? What inputs are required?

Ultimately, successful sustainability does not mean achieving a fixed project mold by the end of funding. Instead, it entails equipping beneficiaries and host institutions to maintain and even surpass project improvements as the activities evolve into the future. This can happen only if those responsible for sustaining a project's core elements 'own' them fully. Responsible implementers and beneficiaries must embrace the project model and master its working parts, accepting the process even more than the product as their own. In this regard, promoting sustainability is much less a matter of handing over reins at the end of project funding than it is of fading slowly into the background and, eventually, completely out of the picture.

Notes

1. Two considerations justify this claim. First, the information that is available over the short time horizons of many projects—often two to five years—can be relatively slim, favoring data on inputs (e.g., the number of agents trained and materials delivered) and outputs (e.g., the number of beneficiaries reached or materials developed), but not outcomes or impact. When outcomes are treated, they are necessarily short-term, such as higher test scores on a project-related test, improved nutrition measures, or businesses launched. What projects cannot measure over their short lifespans are the long-term effects of an intervention. How do improved scores on a test of letter recognition, spelling, and even simple comprehension translate into school retention or other measures of future academic, professional,

and personal well-being? How successful and long-lasting are new businesses, and how do they contribute to overall employment and economic gains? The second consideration relates to the first. Typically, project implementers are motivated to measure what they can control during the life of their activities. The problem with this tendency is that short-term indicators of project achievement may or may not be adequate proxies for long-term impact. For example, the global commitment to early grade reading seems fully justified by the finding that children are failing in this area. The nearly universal response is to increase the focus on reading in the classroom while robbing time from other aspects of learning. In measuring student acquisition of the mechanical aspects of reading, a project can capture an impact that is attainable in a few years' time. What it cannot measure are outcomes beyond the project's narrow frame. While there is no doubt that reading fundamentals are important, it is not certain that the methods used to achieve them, as opposed to others that might perform less well in generating short-term success, will translate into improved future performance in and outside of school. In other words, positive outcomes achieved within the context of a project are not necessarily proof that the project methods warrant sustaining or expanding.

2. Full disclosure: The author was the Chief of Party of the project in this case study.
3. These projects, however, operated in different regions and with a different lead implementer (the U.S. firm Creative Associates).
4. It is worth noting that all of these agreements will require re-visiting and adjustment over the course of implementation.
5. For a similar but alternative planning and implementation framework for sustainability, see the World Health Organization's (2010) *Nine Steps for Developing a Scalability Strategy*.

Bibliography

Agence Française de Développement. (2015). Dictionnaire du développement. Accessed November 20, 2015 at www.afd.fr/home/AFD/dictionnaire-developpement.

Asian Development Bank. (2010). Post-Completion Sustainability of Asian Development Bank-Assisted Projects. Special Evaluation Study, Reference Number: SES:OTH 2010–46, October 2010. Accessed January 7, 2017 at www.adb.org/documents/post-completion-sustainability-asian-development-bank-assisted-projects.

AUSAID. (2000). "Promoting Practical Sustainability," a paper submitted for the DAC Working Group on Aid Evaluation, 33rd Meeting, 22–23 November 2000. Accessed November 20, 2015 at www.oecd.org/development/evaluation/dcdndep/31950216.pdf.

Cooley, L., and J. F. Linn. (2014). *Taking Innovations to Scale: Methods, Applications and Lessons*. Washington, DC: Results for Development Institute.

Cooley, L., and R. R. Ved. (2012). *Scaling Up—From Vision to Large-Scale Change A Management Framework for Practitioners* (2nd ed.). Washington, DC: Management Systems International.

Fixsen, D. L., S. F. Naoom, K. A. Blase, R. M. Friedman, and F. Wallace. (2005). *Implementation Research: A Synthesis of the Literature*. FMHI Publication #231. Louis de la Parte Florida Mental Health Institute, The National Implementation Research Network, University of South Florida, Tampa, Florida.

Gugelev, A., and A Stern. (Winter, 2015). Nonprofits, What's Your End Game? *Stanford Social Innovation Review* 13:1.

Incluso. The Incluso Manual, Chapter 4: Project Sustainability (n.d.). Accessed January 7, 2017 at www.incluso.org/manual/project-sustainability.

Ingle, M. D. (2005). *Project Sustainability Manual: How to Incorporate Sustainability into the Project Cycle*. Executive Leadership Institute, Mark O. Hatfield School of Government: Portland State University. Portland, Oregon. (Revised).

Khan, M. A. (2000). Planning for and Monitoring of Project Sustainability: A Guideline on Concepts, Issues, and Tools. *From MandE News*. Accessed January 7, 2017 at www.mande.co.uk/docs/khan.htm.

Miseda, B. A. (2014). Influence of Community Participation on Sustainability of Selected Njaa Marufuku Kenya Food Security Projects in Kisumu West, Kisumu County, Kenya. Accessed January 7, 2017 at http://erepository.uonbi.ac.ke/bitstream/handle/11295/73986/Miseda_Influence%20of%20community%20participation%20on%20sustainability%20of%20selected%20Njaa%20Marufuku%20Kenya%20food%20security%20projects%20in%20Kisumu%20West,%20Kisumu%20County,%20Kenya.pdf;sequence=3.

Pink, D. H. (2009). *Drive: The Surprising Truth About What Motivates Us*. New York: Riverhead Books.

Rodrik, D. (2008). *The New Development Economics: We Shall Experiment, but How Shall We Learn?* Faculty Research Working Papers Series. Harvard Kennedy School, January 7, 2017. https://papers.ssrn.com/sol3/papers.cfm?abstract_id=1296115.

Shepherd, J. W., Jr. (2016). Four Strategies for Staying on the Path to Scale, Stanford Social Innovation Review. Accessed January 7, 2017 at https://ssir.org/articles/entry/four_strategies_for_staying_on_the_path_to_scale.

Solomon, S. (2015). *Making a Lasting Impact: The Quality Learning Project Sustainability Framework (A Case Study)*. Washington, DC: Creative Associates International. Accessed January 7, 2017 at www.creativeassociatesinternational.com/wp-content/uploads/2015/07/QLP_UPDATE.pdf.

Tango International. (2009). *Sustainability of Rural Development Projects: Best Practices and Lessons Learned by IFAD in Asia*. Occasional Papers. International Fund for Agricultural Development. Accessed January 7, 2017 at www.ifad.org/documents/10180/538441f4-bb55-4e99-9e23-854efd744e4c.

USAID. (2015). Sustainability and Country Ownership. Accessed November 20, 2015 at www.usaid.gov/what-we-do/global-health/hiv-and-aids/technical-areas/aid-investment.

World Health Organization and ExpandNet. (2010). Nine Steps for Developing a Scaling-Up Strategy. Accessed January 7, 2017 at http://expandnet.net/PDFs/ExpandNet-WHO%20Nine%20Step%20Guide%20published.pdf.

World Health Organization and ExpandNet. (2011). Beginning with the End in Mind: Planning Pilot Projects and Other Programmatic Research for Successful Scaling Up. Accessed January 7, 2017 at http://expandnet.net/PDFs/ExpandNet-WHO%20—%20Beginning%20with%20the%20end%20in%20mind%20—%20January%202011.pdf.

Chapter 6

The Walls of Kano

USAID Education Programming in North Nigeria and the Problem of Sustainability

Michael Gubser

"Education in Kano is under system failure," declared a local donor agent in north Nigeria's largest metropolis in 2011. "The government makes efforts but there are no results. They lack funds, lack an overall plan." Despite a decade of donor aid, a state official concurred, the education system has so many problems that it resembles a "compound fracture"; if you can name a problem—insufficient instructors, unqualified teachers, mass illiteracy, crumbling infrastructure, inadequate furniture—it exists.[1] Even in good schools, students sit on concrete floors and lack reading or writing materials. A population explosion fed by high fertility and steady in-migration has trebled school intake (according to common estimates) since the mid-1990s and more than doubled pupil-teacher ratios.[2] And urbanization increased the problem of itinerant Quranic school students (*al-majiri*), who beg in city streets rather than attend formal institutions. To be sure, some things have improved for Kano schoolchildren since the end of military rule in 1999. Demand for education has increased, teachers have encountered new pedagogical methods, and parents can engage more freely in their children's education.[3] But all of these changes place further strain on Kano's traditional and modern school systems.

This essay examines two primary education projects—the Literacy Enhancement Assistance Project (LEAP) (2001–2004) and the Community Participation for Action in the Social Sectors (COMPASS) Project (2004–2009)—run by the United States Agency for International Development (USAID) in Kano State during the decade after Nigeria's return to democracy.[4] Its aim is twofold. First, it chronicles the experience and legacy of two bellwether projects. Originally intended as a sequence, with LEAP introducing reforms in three districts (known in Nigeria as Local Government Areas or LGAs) and COMPASS expanding the most successful, the projects marked USAID's entry into Kano's education sector after an absence of over two decades. As the first bilateral donor to work in the sector under the new democratic dispensation, USAID is seen as a trendsetter whose experience influenced donor engagement across north Nigeria.[5] Second, the essay uses this recent history as a case study on how aid practitioners define and evaluate project success. LEAP and COMPASS, I argue, reveal the wider paradoxes of a ubiquitous aid focus on sustainability.[6] While both were service-delivery projects, designed to provide assistance to flagging schools, teachers, and students, they are often judged for their failure to entrench reforms that could last beyond project operation. This criticism may be misapplied: International donors, including USAID, have long touted sustainability as one of their core mandates. Yet while project planners talk of introducing long-term developmental changes, they often design activities that look more like temporary relief, using scant resources to deliver services for derelict institutions. LEAP and COMPASS exhibited this paradox: Both projects courted the hope of sustainable reform while dedicating much of their effort to filling the significant educational needs of the moment.

This discrepancy reflects the contradictory demands placed on projects. Most contracts combine numerical targets for goods and service delivery with vague demands for indicators of sustainability and long-term impact. Naturally, project managers worry more about specific and immediate injunctions that can be measured in assessments (such as reaching numerical targets by deadline) than about ensuring the sustainability of reforms years after project closure (when evaluators will have forgotten the project and managers are no longer responsible). The presentist focus of projects can also be defended ethically: With limited funds, a manager may well choose to offer discrete benefits to individuals now rather than gamble on the vagaries of long-term institutional capacity-building and future political will. Yet dispensing with sustainability as a criterion of project success also raises concerns. For what good, we might legitimately ask, is even a successful intervention if its achievements vanish within a year, leaving populations dependent on further outside aid? Temporary service delivery that sidesteps local systems can become a form of relief rather than a spur to development.[7] As LEAP and COMPASS suggest, there is no formula for balancing the alleviation of today's need with the promotion of long-run sustainability, only a dilemma of tradeoffs.

In trying to achieve this balance on any given project, however, aid practitioners tend to limit their knowledge of local resources by neglecting wider contextual and historical factors that affect their work.[8] The contractual now that governs project implementation and evaluation induces planners to evade questions of local context and long-term impact. And sustainability, while honored in rhetoric, is largely ignored in practice. The result is the oddly ephemeral quality of most project activities, here and gone despite enormous investments of energy and hope, vanishing after project closure into a largely forgotten past. This essay concludes by arguing that greater historical awareness among aid planners could help to deepen project impact.

The Nigerian Factor

Education has long been a fraught issue in the north, supporting both entrenched Muslim identities and the needs of a modern polity. This dual role is expressed in the most evident feature of Kano's educational landscape: its parallel Islamic and secular school systems. With a Muslim heritage dating back to the fourteenth century, Kano has a centuries-old Quranic school tradition. Led by a mallam, Quranic-school pupils memorize the holy book, with the most advanced passing upward through a religious school system that made Kano a nineteenth-century center of learning as well as the key emporium of Sahelian West Africa.[9] It is important to recall that what appears underdeveloped according to modern educational standards was a pioneering and advanced literacy program for centuries. Educated Kanawa (residents of Kano) take pride in this heritage, and locals not educated in the Western tradition trust it implicitly; the common view of the north as backward, a view bolstered by statistics and donor documents, contrasts sharply in this regard with local self-awareness and cultural memory.[10] The slow spread of modern secular schools and integrated Islamic-Western curricula, starting under colonialism and increasing since independence, fuels the tendency to invidious comparison. While it is tempting for Westerners to see the inevitable forces of 'progress' in the move away from traditional religious learning, few Kanawa share this attitude, nor would even the most cosmopolitan wish for the disappearance of a Quranic system that buttresses the religious and social order. In fact, the expansion of Western schools since the 1970s has stimulated something of a Quranic school renaissance, as parents seek to provide their modern children with moral and religious foundations. Even families committed to secular learning often send their kids to Quranic schools in the evening.[11]

North Nigeria's earliest encounters with Western education came in the form of nineteenth-century missionaries who sought to convert their pupils to Christianity. Incorporated from 1809 to 1903 in Usman dan Fodio's jihadist Sokoto Caliphate, northerners rejected the missionaries as a cultural threat, setting up an enduring association between *Boko* (Western education) and Christian conversion.[12] When the caliphate fell in 1903 and British forces entered Kano, High Commissioner Frederick Lugard, aware of the dangers of jihad from Britain's experience with Sudanese Mahdism, banned Christian missionary schools from the northern protectorate and allowed his new subjects to retain their religious institutions. Thus, while Western schools enrolled thousands of students in the southern part of the Nigeria colony, a flourishing Quranic school system remained the near-exclusive option for northerners under British rule. To meet local manpower, the colonizers established several exclusive Western institutions that trained the children of elites—or, as was often the case, of their slaves.[13] Nonetheless, by the eve of independence, Muslim northerners, once the vanguard of nineteenth-century learning, found themselves trailing their southern confederates in all measures of educational attainment.[14] Numbers tell much of the story: M. G. Smith reported that Kano Province had only 63 elementary schools in 1951.[15] Albert Ozigi and Lawrence Ocho found that northern primary schools graduated 70,962 students in 1947 compared to 218,610 in the south; the secondary school discrepancy—251 to 9,657—was even sharper.[16] And if the northern rate of graduation slightly outpaced the south during the 1950s,[17] the gulf at precisely the moment when a new Nigeria was staffing its political and economic institutions was chasmal. A shortage of skilled northerners meant that southerners and foreigners filled professional posts. Not until the 1980s did native Hausa come to dominate the teaching profession as well as other skilled positions in the north, an experience that helped to sediment northern resentment within the federal union.[18]

The 1970s came as a watershed for Nigeria as a whole—a chance at rebirth after the fratricidal Biafran war. Because Nigerian oil is now so closely associated with corruption, it is hard to recall the promise that accompanied the initial petroleum boom. A benison from below, Nigeria's black gold launched a hopeful epoch when it seemed the government might finally be able to finance the country's development, including a dramatic educational expansion. Investments swelled the urban agglomeration of Kano, boosting the modern sector until it replaced farming as the main source of state income.[19] Fueled by new revenues, the city witnessed an industrial burst that helped to revise attitudes toward modern education, as Western schools suddenly seemed to offer valuable employment skills.[20] The national government bolstered these prospects with a new education policy that replaced the British school system by a uniform 6-3-3-4 setup (designating the number of years assigned to primary, junior secondary, senior secondary, and tertiary education, respectively). As part of the push toward "education for self-reliance," a junior-secondary vocational block helped students who would not continue in school.[21] Perhaps the most noteworthy aspect of this policy was the 1976 commitment to free and universal primary education (UPE), an initiative supported by awareness campaigns that drew millions of first-time students into public schools and contributed to a temporary enrollment hike.[22] But education fever was not ubiquitous. It prevailed more in urban than rural areas, where the mistrust of government schools endured. President Gowon's demand that northern elites enroll their children may, in fact, have hardened resentment, associating public education not only with Western Christianity but with government coercion as well.[23] Yet as educated students became powerful civil servants, another link was forged: By the 1980s, many Kanawa recognized that modern schooling was a necessary qualification if they hoped to hold power in their own state.

Nigeria's brief window of democracy between 1979 and 1983 reinforced this link, as elected governors expanded jobs for educated candidates. Governor Abubakar Rimi (1979–1983) required signatures, rather than the typical thumbprint, to secure a government job, demanding at least a basic level of literacy to work for the state's largest employer. In education, moreover, the state government started guaranteeing jobs for locals with teaching degrees.[24] The economic rewards of modern skills, combined with the revelation that a shortage of qualified Hausa could undermine local self-governance, slowly eroded the longstanding fear that Western schools might sabotage northern culture. Instead, modern education came to be seen in some circles as a tool for political and personal advancement—and even for cultural assertion.

New economic and political opportunities drove not only a rising interest in Western education but also the growth of Islamiyya schools that combined religious instruction with modern secular subjects.[25] Religious innovations contributed to this effulgence. Most prominent among the many Islamic reform efforts of the 1970s, the Salafist Izala movement, popular among Kano's nascent entrepreneurial and civil servant class, promoted a modernist outlook that integrated Islamic and Western schooling and encouraged the education of women.[26] By claiming to purify Islam of syncretic practices, including the esotericism and master-disciple structures of the dominant Qadiriyya and Tijaniyya Sufi orders, and return to the Prophet's undefiled Islam, Izala attracted adherents and challenged Kano's traditional religious elite.[27] The shift to anti-Sufism, writes religious scholar Muhammed S. Umar, "entailed a reorientation from a communal to an individualistic mode of religiosity [that] seems to be more in tune with the rugged individualism of capitalist social relations."[28] This intra-Islamic pluralism complicated Kano's educational dualism as well; today's education landscape reveals a diverse spectrum of primary schools, representing various sects, ranging from Quranic through Islamiyya to strictly secular institutions—none of which reject Western education per se!

The year 1980 struck in devastating fashion when the Maitatsine riots, sparked by religious militants, killed over 5,000 people in Kano and drove residents from the city.[29] Religious unrest reverberated across the north for the next few years, the bloody harbinger of a lost decade when oil revenues plunged and a debt crisis dashed the developmental hopes of yesteryear. By the mid-1980s, Nigeria had become a byword for corruption: The economy tanked, poverty soared, and oil money plumped private fortunes. In 1983, Major-General Muhammadu Buhari overthrew the elected president, ending the country's brief democratic chapter and inaugurating 16 years of praetorian rule. Two dictators later, Sani Abacha (r. 1993–1998) turned Africa's most populous state into an international pariah. Education suffered with everything else: Enrollments, on the rise for nearly a decade, plummeted, as dismal school performance led parents to withhold their children.[30] The federal education budget, pegged at ₦3.1 billion between 1975 and 1980, fell to a meager ₦7.7 million over the next five years.[31] Teachers went unpaid; school infrastructure eroded. The opportunity of the 1970s turned to betrayal at the millennium's end, and Quranic schools, with their moral education, remained a prized alternative to "total decay."[32]

Even this 16-year neglect, however, did not entirely cancel the recent favor for modern schools. The legacy of 1970s industrialization, the push for universal basic education, the prevalence of religious reform movements, the establishment of Islamiyya schools—these trends had altered the educational landscape, especially in Kano City. Generational passage cemented the shift: As educated Hausa entered the civil service, the skilled professions, the teaching ranks—claiming posts previously held by outsiders—they came to embody the fusion of local tradition and modern sensibility. Particularly significant were educated women who combined professional commitments with traditional family roles.[33] Nor should we overestimate Kano's economic decline. Throughout the 1980s and 1990s, the city's light industrial sector demanded skilled workers, attracting a continuous flow of migrants. Urbanization itself encouraged educational modernization, as migrants witnessed model schools available only in the city. Although the Quranic system retained the majority of students, countervailing trends persisted.

It should also be stressed that the military era did not entirely lack for educational innovations.[34] Kano in particular was a pioneer within the federation, despite its reputation for conservatism. The city was "the first to introduce Science Secondary Schools in Nigeria in 1977—a highly-focused scientific and technological manpower development initiative," writes education professor Abdalla Adamu.

[I]ts Girl-Child initiative at Wudil was the most comprehensive reform package of its kind anywhere in the Federation, and was used as a model by UNICEF which [it] urged other states to copy. Its network of further education colleges is the most diverse of its kind in the federation—giving opportunities to thousands of students from Kano to acquire middle-level and higher-level educational qualifications. It is also the first to produce a fully Integrated Islamiyya Curriculum which seeks a synergy between Islamic educational tradition and western schooling systems.[35]

In 1987, Kano introduced the state-level Primary School Management Board to oversee school and teacher welfare, removing instructor oversight from local government purview after repeated failures to pay salaries. Within a year, Nigeria had adopted the state management board as an education governance model for all federal states.[36] After a brief reversion to LGA control following the election annulment of 1993, the renamed State Primary Education Board (SPEB)—which became the State Universal Basic Education Board (SUBEB) in the middle of the next decade—has remained the national model.[37] It is worth highlighting the national and local character of these innovations. Very few international donors operated in Kano during the years of military rule: the World Bank, UNESCO, UNICEF, and, after 1989, USAID.

"Let's Go Learning!"

USAID had operated in Nigeria's education sector from independence through the early 1970s.[38] By the middle of that decade, straitened by the same OPEC embargo that flushed Nigeria with revenue, the U.S. government decided to turn its resources to needier countries.[39] USAID left the education sector and reduced its country program to a minimal portfolio over the next 25 years. Thinned to a skeleton staff of 11, the Mission became so marginal in USAID's global portfolio that there was talk of closing it altogether in the mid-1990s. With little support and few resources, the Mission oversaw one program: a health initiative, launched in 1989, that evolved into the BASICS (Basic Support for Institutionalizing Child Survival) project by the middle of the next decade.[40] Kano was one of its target states.

To run the program, the USAID-Nigeria Mission engaged several grantees who would later reappear under the democratic dispensation: Family Health International (FHI), Pathfinder International, Johns Hopkins Bloomberg School of Public Health Center for Communication Programs (JHU-CCP), and the Center for Development and Population Activities (CEDPA).[41] Sharing USAID offices in Abuja and Kano,[42] these partners faced stringent restrictions. Not only did Abacha's regime frown on international organizations, but the U.S. government banned collaboration with military rulers or their appointees. As the regime picked state and local leaders, USAID had no viable official partners. Moreover, implementers faced frequent anti-American rallies in Kano, and mosque protocols condemned U.S. policies in the Middle East.[43] Nor were state and local officials pleased at being bypassed by U.S. funds. "We had to constantly rely on good will in order to keep the projects operating," said a local staff member who tapped personal friendships and connections.[44] These were, in the words of another staffer, "the toughest but the most innovative" years.[45] Without official access and faced with few capable civil society organizations, implementers began funding individuals to provide health services in their communities.[46] Unbidden, these "suitcase NGOs" or "NGIs (non-governmental individuals)," as they were dubbed, hired staff to sustain their work, creating what evaluators called impromptu community partnerships for health.[47] When the U.S. embassy, joining the post–Cold War push for democratization, asked the Mission for democracy programming in the mid-1990s, implementing partners replied that they already promoted civic engagement through health activities. The projects formed community coalitions and convened mock parliaments to discuss needs. "Men even brought their wives, women in purdah," recalled a donor staff member. "USAID would never have imagined this possible, especially in conservative Kano under a dictatorship."[48]

Thus, when in 1999 Nigeria's 16-year-old military regime handed power to the elected government of Olesegun Obasanjo, USAID was better positioned than many donors. The return to democracy was a dramatic shift in Nigeria's recent history, but it was not uniformly beneficial. Contrary to hopes, democratization coincided with a northern industrial decline that lowered living standards even as the population exploded. The stark and growing gulf between southern and northern development indicators seemed to bear out northern fears of neglect by a southern-dominated government. Indeed, the 12 northern states took their new freedom as an occasion to assert cultural and political autonomy by declaring sharia law.[49] While southern Nigerians viewed the promulgations as a threat to constitutional unity, most northerners saw them as an assertion of Muslim distinction. Islamic law, they averred, provides a touchstone for social and moral order in a society facing rampant corruption. Westerners, of course, saw the declarations as Muslim extremism, and viewed them primarily through the post-9/11 prism of the one sharia story to make international news: the 2002 stoning sentence of a woman accused of adultery.

USAID's new chapter, then, began at a time of heightened suspicion, not democratic euphoria. And while USAID had a head start among bilateral donors, 20 years of skeleton programming limited its knowledge of sectors beyond health.[50] To its credit, the donor acknowledged its ignorance of education trends by displaying unusual curiosity and even deference toward local viewpoints, actively courting political and religious leaders and undertaking study tours of the sector, exhibiting far more receptivity than is common in more established USAID countries.[51] Although the Mission preferred to concentrate its investments on literacy in the north, political pressures forced an expansion: Obasanjo insisted on project representation in the country's three geopolitical zones (the north, south, and Middle Belt). And Nigeria's strategic importance meant that USAID was not allowed to act alone. In the aftermath of democratization, recalled a Mission staff member, "twenty-seven different US government agencies" descended on the country to define portfolios in health, education, and democratization.[52] With standing commitments to a variety of programs in Africa,[53] U.S. government officials expanded initial education goals to include numeracy, teacher training, community participation, and data management.

Led by prime grantee Educational Development Center and partners RTI International and World Education, the ensuing $12 million LEAP project embraced this wide-eyed curiosity, undertaking many more research studies than is typical of activity-heavy USAID packages.[54] Whereas most projects generate reports simply to establish baseline indicators or evaluate their own activities, LEAP produced a range of surveys and analyses on topics such as teacher identity, education finance, girls' education, teacher recruitment, teacher supervision, career incentives, and student-centered methods. In its opening term, it undertook the detailed political mapping of institutional partners and their historical relations, an activity born of the frank admission of ignorance.[55] "LEAP was like a research project," admitted one Kano staffer. "We didn't know the system in which we were trying to work."[56] And so the project heeded the opening refrain of one of its popular instructional radio programs: "Let's Go Learning!"[57]

This receptivity paid local dividends at a time when anti-American sentiment ran high, when selling an American project designed to educate Muslim children—with English-language radio programs that few northerners understood—required particular discretion. "It was not easy to introduce the project as American," reported a former manager, and staff members used a gamut of techniques to appeal for support, explaining project activities in Islamic terms, even hiding the fact that LEAP was U.S.-funded.[58] In its first year, the project launched "sensitization campaigns" designed to introduce its efforts, raise awareness of the educational needs, and recruit local support.[59] It sought endorsements from religious leaders ranging from local mallams to the Kano emir, the traditional Hausa-Fulani leader who alone could overcome conservative resistance by vouching for project compatibility with Islam.[60] Personal connections mattered immensely. LEAP cultivated the support of Kano's governor Rabiu Kwankwaso, whose numerous primary education initiatives made him an obvious ally.[61] These efforts paid off in 2003, the year of Nigeria's second national and local elections when the All Nigeria People's Party (ANPP) of former teacher Ibrahim Shekarau swept Kwankwaso from state office. LEAP had planned for a possible transition by cultivating relations with opposition parties, and, despite the challenge of a new administration that replaced Kwankwaso's demand-oriented policies with the supply strategy of hiring new teachers, LEAP enjoyed, in the words of one local partner, a "smooth ride."[62] Rockier was navigating the surge of anti-Americanism stoked by the Iraq War and the polio vaccine crisis; it took the emir's intervention, as well as lobbying from LEAP staff who knew the new governor, to sustain the project uninterrupted.

Another mark of LEAP's reserve was the decision to avoid Quranic schools altogether and engage only their secular and Islamiyya counterparts—and the latter only when they expressed interest. Quranic schools substantially outnumber government-supported institutions,[63] and Western concern for similar schools in other regions heightened after the 9/11 attacks. Nonetheless, for fear of imperiling other investments, LEAP avoided Kano's most conservative educational establishments. The only substantial intervention came at the behest of local staff members: Under a 2003–2004 grant designed to promote new initiatives, several pedagogues introduced LEAP instructional radio programming in selected Quranic schools. Student enthusiasm, they reported, overcame initial mallam resistance to the "radio teacher."[64]

LEAP was designed to introduce activities in three main areas—teacher training, community participation, and education management and information systems—the best of which would be expanded by a subsequent project. From the start, then, LEAP was viewed as a pilot activity, conducting studies and launching activities that would continue beyond its three-year run. Operating in three LGAs and 110 schools,[65] the project organized meetings among key state and local stakeholders to discuss literacy and numeracy instruction (a process known as the Literacy and Numeracy Agenda [LNA]); trained teachers in literacy and numeracy pedagogy, student-centered methods, and the production of low-cost instructional materials;[66] introduced an Interactive Radio Instruction (IRI) program designed to promote interactive learning methods in grades 3 through 6;[67] trained widespread but dormant PTAs on school improvement and parental involvement; offered grants to PTAs and community coalitions for school renovations; and worked with SUBEB offices to improve government management and data gathering. Much of this work is standard fare on donor education projects, but, in post-1999 Kano, it was brand new. "There was no program like LEAP before it arrived," said a former SUBEB official.[68] It "made a tremendous impact in changing people's minds and getting people engaged."[69]

But novelty does not ensure successful change. LEAP instituted several policies designed to entrench its reforms in the education system. In order to win government allegiance, it set up headquarters at the SUBEB compound on BUK Road, a strategic choice that mitigated past resentments about U.S. insistence on retaining control of funds rather than operating through government systems.[70] The decision was especially shrewd as most LEAP activities were community-based rather than government-focused, further inviting the charge of bypassing proper authorities.

LEAP also maintained USAID's earlier approach of localizing implementation by hiring indigenous staff and NGOs to manage the activities. LEAP's Kano State managers—often seconded from government ministries—were granted unusual latitude within the program's strategic rubric. Staff members describe how they were encouraged to use their knowledge of Islamic culture and history, their personal connections, and their local familiarity to introduce activities to suspicious parents and leaders, adapting materials to avoid offense and realigning events to fit local schedules and expectations.[71] For a donor driven by mandates from Washington, this flexibility marked a significant concession to local pace and sensitivities. In addition, LEAP cultivated local trainers, frequently recruited from teacher training colleges, to conduct workshop sessions. Similarly, building on approaches pioneered under BASICS in the 1990s, two local NGOs—Neighborhood Education Committee and Basic Education Association—conducted PTA trainings in the three districts. To this day, they remain among LEAP's greatest champions, praising the partnership for cultivating organizational growth and improving parental commitment to schools.[72] The faces of the project, in other words, were indigenous— hardly an innovation in aid programming, but important nonetheless.

Of course, as a pilot project, LEAP's primary sustainability strategy was to continue and expand under a sequel; implementers were called from the start to think beyond the project terminus. Although administrative turnover in the Abuja head office—the project passed through three Chiefs of Party during its last months—complicated the transition, and although at least one consultant feared that project findings were not adequately synthesized for policymakers, several staff and partner organizations recall a concerted effort to gather and catalog materials, plan for the local continuation of efforts, and convene a meeting to discuss project continuity.[73] In some ways, this effort paid off: "LEAP was the basis of everything," affirmed a manager of the subsequent COMPASS project, and the approach pioneered by LEAP "was key, making sure locals bought in and felt comfortable."[74] The transition, however, was anything but seamless.

A New Project

"LEAP was too short," lamented a staff member. "If it had stayed seven years, it could really do something."[75] Ironically, staying seven years was precisely USAID's plan, even as a new solicitation placed activities under fresh management. According to numerous respondents, the switch came as a surprise in Kano, where many felt that LEAP had pioneered a successful model and deserved to continue. USAID's 2003 solicitation, with a scope of work that was different from and larger than its predecessor, might have warned them that change was afoot. A $95 million bid, the new tender combined education and health activities into one social sector project, an omnibus pushed by a Mission director fresh from Uganda, where similar integration was underway.[76] Education was allotted approximately $20 million—just over one-fifth of the budget. With the increased funds came a dramatic expansion in scope. The solicitation demanded that implementers reach hundreds of new schools and many more LGAs in each state; introduce new education activities (a school health and nutrition program, pre-service teacher training support); and expand previous ones in dramatic fashion (local language radio instruction for grades 1 and 2).

Perhaps the surprise should have been less, therefore, when a new team won the bid. The new education implementer, DC-based Creative Associates International, lacked Nigeria experience when it took over in 2004, but it could rely on guidance from seasoned partners in the five-member COMPASS consortium— Boston-based prime grantee Pathfinder International, JHU-CCP, and the Futures Group—all of whom had worked for USAID-Nigeria in the 1990s. Any administrative turnover produces disarray. To hear LEAP staff tell it, a successful initiative was replaced by a much more rigid and diffuse one, a view that partner NGOs shared. COMPASS, local collaborators allege, was so determined to dissociate itself from LEAP that it rejected experienced staff and ignored materials prepared to ease the handoff. It seemed to fear that it might be "dominated" by former staff, remarked one respondent. COMPASS managers refute this claim. The LEAP team, they rebut, tried to "play politics" by urging the SUBEB to demand that COMPASS hire all former staff on the new project. Instead, initial interviews yielded three new state managers and only one carryover.[77] The choice of Rabia Eshak, a former senatorial candidate, as Kano Team Leader caused particular concern, primarily because she was from neighboring Jigawa State.[78] Furthermore, the project seemed to lose some of the goodwill extended to LEAP by Governor Shekarau, despite Eshak's public relations efforts.[79]

Far more problematic, the education component was now tethered to the needs and controversies of a very different sector: health. Between 2001 and 2004, LEAP had operated concurrently with a separate USAID health program, BASICS II, a successor to the initiative of the 1990s. With COMPASS, however, the two were joined, and education, at one-fifth of the project budget, appeared subordinate. The new team, remarked a SUBEB representative, segregated itself from local education officials, moving out of the SUBEB where LEAP had been headquartered and joining its health colleagues in an office behind Farm Centre. Moreover, reported the administrator, "sometimes the project clashed with activities in the SUBEB. COMPASS only informed the SUBEB"; it did not collaborate as LEAP had.[80]

Significant additions to COMPASS's education mandate also changed the character of the program and the intensity of its activities. The bimonthly three-day teacher training sessions implemented under LEAP were reduced to one day as COMPASS expanded from 110 to 605 schools and from three to 16 LGAs.[81] The project introduced a cluster structure that grouped teachers from proximate schools for training purposes and linked them with local clinics for pupil health care. Most respondents agreed that these changes reduced the depth of pedagogical training. NGOs who implemented PTA trainings reported a similar attenuation.

COMPASS also expanded radio instruction by adding Hausa programs for grades 1 and 2 to the upper-grade English broadcasts inherited from LEAP. Transmitted on Radio Kano's AM station with a 50% government subvention, the half-hour shows incorporated rhymes and songs that became popular with teachers and students statewide.[82] The project also added a pre-service training component, based in the Primary Education Studies (PES) Department of Kano's Sa'adatu Rimi Teaching College. The initiative trained staff members, provided scholarships to female students, and funded the development of a new reading curriculum. And finally, COMPASS introduced a school health and nutrition (SHN) activity in which teachers learned to diagnose common illnesses, administer basic medicines, and make clinic referrals. Under SHN, PTAs applied for small grants to establish school gardens, build toilets for girls, and construct clean-water sources. These additions made COMPASS more wide-ranging than LEAP, but they also taxed its capacity.

Yet while COMPASS was a more typical activity-laden project than LEAP, it also had pilot ventures that marked USAID's continued experimentation. The pre-service teacher training program at Sa'adatu Rimi College was particularly successful.[83] As in much of Africa, primary-school teaching is widely unpopular and under-remunerated. "No one wanted to come to Sa'adatu Rimi to study PES," recalled a lecturer in 2011. "It was associated with 'old people,'" mid-career teachers who returned to upgrade their certification.[84] COMPASS scholarships to women—40 and 60 in the first two years, respectively—improved the program's status.[85] And the introduction of an English-language curriculum placed the PES program at the cutting edge of pedagogical innovation.[86] The effect on matriculation was dramatic. From a low of 20–30 enrollees in the lean years, said one lecturer, the program increased to around 700 students in 2011.[87] There was "an explosion of females who wanted to read PES."[88] Unlike most COMPASS activities that delivered school and community services, the pre-service initiative addressed a system-wide need for qualified teachers with "a relatively low-cost, high-impact investment."[89] It was also an investment with potentially lasting gains, as lecturers trained by the project have continued to instruct teachers, either in Kano's higher learning institutes or on state contracts to provide in-service support for classroom instructors.[90]

The effectiveness and sustainability of other activities were less obvious. The school health initiative in particular suffered from the vaccination controversies of the mid-decade: De-worming did not begin in Kano until 2008, later than in the other COMPASS states (Nassarawa and Lagos). And while there were cases of teachers making diagnoses, schools building toilets, and communities purchasing medicines, many respondents felt that the integration of education and health did not achieve its promise.[91] "We all pretended that integration worked because we wanted it to work," said a former COMPASS manager. "People talked about the links at the community level, but the services simply aren't there because officials refused to collaborate across sectors."[92] Without the cooperation of line ministries, local sensitization on health and education links produced little systemic reform. There is even some sense that integration hampered the education team by creating the impression that its activities were secondary. Several local implementers and NGOs feared that health had "hijacked" or "drowned out" education; one even recalled being told by a project manager that COMPASS is "mostly health. Education is just a bonus."[93] Ultimately, health and education were distinct sectors with different target groups coexisting under the same umbrella, side-by-side but not integrated, and references to health activities are surprisingly infrequent among those who knew the education program. But while this segregation may have granted the education team more latitude, it could not stem the belief that education had been demoted in USAID's portfolio.

The size of the cross-sectoral COMPASS consortium—five international and four local organizations—may also have taken a toll on management and partner relations, with Nigerian partners feeling particularly excluded. Like LEAP, COMPASS relied on local NGOs to implement mobilization and training activities. The project engaged four Nigerian NGOs as formal partners, two—the Federation of Muslim Women Association of Nigeria (FOMWAN) and the Civil Society Action Coalition on Education for All (CSACEFA)—in the education component.[94] And it maintained smaller resource organizations, including those used by LEAP, to run community mobilization efforts and PTA trainings.[95] Yet partner relations were not as smooth. CSACEFA and FOMWAN complained that their roles were vague during early implementation phases and that they did not enjoy equal status with international partners as the project progressed.[96] The resource organizations also felt marginalized: COMPASS was not consistent in signing formal agreements, they complained, so their roles remained piecemeal and ill-defined.[97] Project staff acknowledged these problems but blame inadequate organizational assessment during the proposal phase: The Nigerian organizations simply lacked the capacity to manage such a large program, a limitation that should have been known before they were signed as full partners. The ensuing compromise—representatives of local offices were invited to sit in the Abuja head office where they could be trained—pleased no one entirely.

In the end, it is hard not to concur with the Abuja-based Mitchell Group's 2008 assessment that the COMPASS project was spread too thinly, that its ability to make systemic changes was compromised by its reach and ambition:

> COMPASS . . . has experienced some serious challenges, mainly because the targets are too ambitious for the limited resources (1,400 schools and 712 health facilities). In both education and health, the COMPASS program inputs are stretched too thinly to make any impact. The project is labeled as a service delivery program, but given the small population it serves (about 9 percent of the total population) in reality it is more of a pilot program for Nigeria. The project approach has been correct and in that it has developed emerging models that can be brought to scale by the larger community to have greater impact. Although there have been some good attempts

at capacity-building at the clinic, school and community levels, the project has had insufficient resources to develop a critical mass of local capabilities to ensure long-term sustainability.[98]

While COMPASS introduced valuable models of service delivery and achieved some success in pre-service training reform, its efforts, feared evaluators, were too diffuse to produce lasting, "sustainable" change.

Success and Sustainability

In 2009, USAID moved the bulk of its education programming out of Kano, closing an eight-year chapter of state involvement. Were its efforts successful at reforming Kano's primary schools? The answer depends on what is meant by success. Development donors typically measure project achievement against the litmus of sustainability, a term that designates reforms or practices lasting beyond a project's life. Lacking the sustainability achieved through successful behavior change or institutionalization, the argument runs, project achievements vanish and communities fall back on old habits—or, worse, become dependent on assistance to fund and manage their affairs. "If donors move out of Kano," insisted a former staff member, expressing the ideal of sustainability, "government should be able to replicate their programs because there are resources in Nigeria."[99] Yet aid programs can also supply discrete goods whose provision is clearly not 'sustainable': They may better the education of a cohort of students or offer relief support for failing schools; they can introduce new pedagogical ideas that may or may not win immediate converts. Indeed, outside the cohort of direct beneficiaries, novel pedagogies may lie dormant for years until a former student becomes an adult administrator charged with a mandate of reform, a future that is impossible to predict on the short yardstick of development sustainability. There is, then, no necessary correlation between the immediate gains a project offers to some people and the long-term, systemic reforms it is usually called to enact. At times, directing resources to the one may even compromise the other. To put the matter another way: Though development projects tend to cast their mission in systemic terms (institutional reform, overall performance improvement), the benefits of projects such as LEAP and COMPASS generally accrue to individuals (teachers and students, parents and individual schools) rather than social collectives. This is not in itself a demerit, though it is not what is advertised on most project briefs. But it does demonstrate the tendency of aid projects to gloss the difference between individual gain and system reform, to promise the latter while effecting primarily the former.

Both COMPASS and LEAP achieved many individual successes: Teachers hailed the interventions, some saying they encountered interactive pedagogies and school health initiatives for the first time. Rural communities and Islamiyya schools reported greater parental engagement and improved teacher performance.[100] But these benefits rarely lasted. One model school, for example, praised COMPASS for its impact on teachers and students but acknowledged little sustained reform since the government transferred trained instructors to other schools where enormous classes prevented them from applying their new skills.[101] One project advisor even worried that school reforms might have troubled Kano's educational equilibrium by disrupting traditional practices and generating demand that could not be met by officials, intensifying the gulf between government and citizens.[102]

Yet while successful training does not guarantee sustainability, it may offer discrete benefits. In Kano today, one still hears praise of the services LEAP and COMPASS delivered. The case of Gwarzo district, at the western edge of the state, is exemplary. Championed by an effervescent Education Secretary, COMPASS worked in 37 of its 121 public primary schools, providing teacher training, health interventions, school renovations, and PTA support.[103] Recognized as a top project jurisdiction, Gwarzo received additional funding for a three-month expansion in 2009 that introduced activities to all public schools in the district. With the project's closure, according to a 2009 report, the local government council tried to continue some of the activities and encourage a school "maintenance culture."[104] Primary school enrollment, according to local statistics, rose steadily from 30,000 pupils in 2004 to 39,000 in 2011.[105] Though hardly representative, Gwarzo suggests the change a service-delivery project can make when it enlists well-positioned advocates. Yet even here, sustainability is not assured, for the district faces the same enrollment and population boom experienced statewide.[106] And the project's most zealous champion, who served under the eight-year Shekarau governorship, no longer helms the local education authority since Kwankwaso retook office in 2011. The lack of systemic incentives for continued reform threatens even the most committed jurisdictions and well-entrenched innovations.

LEAP seems particularly unsuited to the measure of system sustainability, for it was a maiden voyage. What staff members and participants remember instead was its spirit of novelty and experimentation. "Our purpose," opined a former manager, summarizing a widely held sentiment, "was to lay the foundation of education reform, not to do the reform itself."[107] This preparation required that the education system, intuitively understood by locals, be translated into terms that enabled donor intervention.[108] The lines of authority had to be clarified, data on enrollment and teachers collected, points of entry for project activities identified. None of this was available in Kano at the start of the millennium, and thus, as one LEAP staffer maintained, the project's task was not system strengthening but system creation.

This initiative was expressed in the localized approach of both LEAP and COMPASS, a source of particular pride among project managers. Teams composed of Kano experts were granted significant latitude in programming and pacing within the project framework, a concession to the relatively unusual circumstance of a mission with longtime core staff who trusted local input at a crucial historical juncture.[109] But local direction was not complete. Kano team managers bemoaned the haste of USAID's results-driven approach and felt that project goals, if not method or approach, were ultimately driven from the outside. USAID uses a "clipboard approach," complained two local consultants, "this activity 'tic,' that activity 'tic.' Sometimes we feel like rats in a lab."[110] While this censure was particularly strong, other commentators also deplored rigid donor rules that prevented the elaboration of "a Nigerian solution" for "a Nigerian problem": "They package something in Boston," said an exasperated NGO representative, referring to the home city of COMPASS prime grantee Pathfinder, "and bring it here and say it will work but it won't."[111] USAID tended to assume it knew what was wrong and how to fix it, admitted a former COMPASS manager. "We led the process, saying we'll do this and this based on the initial proposal. It made the project rigid."[112]

Staff expressed particular regret about a tendency to shortchange crucial social processes in the rush for "quick wins" to meet reporting deadlines. Insufficient attention was placed on explaining the project to its beneficiaries, lamented one COMPASS manager. New activities require extensive public outreach to gain local confidence; instead, project "sensitization" tended to be brief and perfunctory, designed to win the support of leaders but not of the teachers, parents, and children who were its primary targets.[113] COMPASS also skimped, said another, on the organizational development of Nigerian partner NGOs, engaging FOMWAN and CSACEFA without either predetermining their ability to do the required work or launching an adequate organizational training process.[114] Furthermore, said a representative of both projects, USAID tended to privilege quick completion of activities over the slower process of cultivating local ownership, putting up most or all of the money for training or renovations and asking communities only to monitor and provide labor. "People must tax themselves so they have ownership," she insisted. "People don't believe it is their project. It is COMPASS."[115] And finally, lamented a local program reviewer, the projects did not publicize their achievements sufficiently to ensure a legacy.[116] Outside of the IRI program, there is little indication that LEAP or COMPASS interventions were known beyond the circles of their overseers and beneficiaries. Although it was the early achievement of public schools under LEAP that drew skeptical Islamiyya schools to seek assistance from an American donor, project schools rarely attracted their neighboring institutions to available facilities such as computer labs. All of these shortcomings bear the stamp of deadline-driven haste, a hallmark of aid projects beholden to yearly funding cycles. The result is often measurable but superficial accomplishment.

What of IRI, the centerpiece, according to some staff, of both LEAP and COMPASS and one of their clearest public relations boons?[117] The popularity of the radio programs, within and outside the state,[118] is a certified achievement:

Pupils were excited for the half-hour broadcasts, "telling teachers, 'It's time, it's time!'"[119] One teacher reported that students' "way of listening changed. Now they listen to radio and understand news."[120] Pedagogy was also affected; some instructors incorporated rhymes, games, and interactive methods in their lessons where before they had taught by rote. The result? According to several teachers, new methods led to better student scores in English and math.[121]

This anecdotal evidence of learning gains, however, was not corroborated by student assessments. Under LEAP, student math and English scores from 2002–2004 indicated little or no improvement. "There was no consistent evidence," according to the final evaluation by the University of Massachusetts, of the "positive impact of the LEAP treatments."[122] This finding is partly due to a troubled evaluation design, which had to devise assessment tests from scratch and failed to establish a comparable control sample.[123] The evaluation used student tests administered before and after project interventions—what are known as pre- and post-tests—to chart learning gains and compare them with changes in control schools during the same period. Schools in Kano were partnered with a control group in faraway Sokoto State, where evaluators were confident that teachers had not picked up the Kano-based radio transmissions whose effectiveness was under scrutiny. Yet while Kano schools were drawn from among the poorest in project locations, Sokoto solicited volunteers for its control sample, with proficient schools jumping at the chance to tout their success. The result was an incompatible pairing of the strong and the weak. "Once you get in that situation you are screwed from an evaluation perspective because there are two different populations," rued an auditor. "It was hard to make the project look good."[124] Disappointing data in turn prompted skepticism about many project activities.[125] Indeed, one advisor worried that "everyone had a jolly good time with IRI and liked the opening song," but "students didn't learn a thing."[126]

COMPASS findings were more positive though still varied: According to a representative of the Canadian firm EDUCAN (which conducted student assessments), "If COMPASS had continued you would have a seen a major difference. We thought it was very effective."[127] COMPASS activities "had a strong, positive impact on student achievement over the life of the project," they told participants at a 2010 education conference in Istanbul.

> Not in every school, every class or every student, nor always in both English and Mathematics but certainly on the broad spectrum of pupils involved. Furthermore, where principals and/or teachers and/ or pupils acknowledged a committed engagement of the COMPASS activities, there is clear evidence of substantial improvement in learning in those particular schools, classrooms and pupils.[128]

Their data somewhat mitigates this enthusiasm: While a four-year survey of the 2006 cohort and a two-year survey of the 2008 group showed gains in math and

English, a three-year tracking of the 2007 group revealed little program effect.[129] And a second set of evaluators from the Abuja-based Mitchell Group disputed the learning benefits of IRI: "Given the very small number of weekly contact hours devoted to literacy and numeracy—about 30 minutes each for math and language—the evaluation team was very skeptical that much impact could be attributed to the IRI program," especially in rowdy, overcrowded classrooms with poor radio transmission.[130] EDUCAN officials, it is important to note, insist that Mitchell Group assessors barely perused their data when conducting the analysis.[131]

What shocked EDUCAN was the apparent indifference of COMPASS managers to their detailed positive findings. The small firm gathered data not only from the student tests required by contract but also from questionnaires designed to make sense of school context and student life experience. Their final report drew correlations between test scores and questionnaire responses. But the project, lamented a representative, wanted only a performance improvement average and ignored much of the data—disaggregated not only by state and grade but by subject matter, previous donor experience, region, and other categories—that EDUCAN offered:[132] "Still today there is no interest in this data. We were very disappointed."[133]

If achievement measures give the edge to COMPASS, LEAP is the more fondly remembered project. Several factors contribute to this nostalgia: LEAP's community and school interventions were novel in post-millennium Kano, "the first of its kind." Staff and partners remember the project as "more intense" than its successor, with trainings that lasted three days per session rather than COMPASS's one.[134] Here the later project clearly suffered from USAID's ambition. As a COMPASS manager put it, "1400 schools was too much. Are you looking for coverage or quality?"[135] LEAP also had better partner relations, again perhaps a function of size, as COMPASS had to merge five international and four Nigerian partners working in two distinct sectors whose integration left participants with the sense that education was secondary. LEAP, by contrast, seemed dedicated and focused.

In the end, if it is relatively difficult to point to 'sustainable' gains of LEAP and COMPASS, it is quite easy to find individual champions. If we judge projects according to whether they introduce activities that assist or inspire people, then USAID enjoyed significant success. LEAP and COMPASS won support in Kano and left models that may be tapped in the future. But if we seek lasting systemic change, then the projects must be judged more stringently. Perhaps the best we can say is that little evidence of permanent transformation survives. Both projects left trained individuals and NGOs who still tout new ideas before recalcitrant officials; neither really dented the enormous problems of a surging student population, an inadequate teaching corps swollen with unqualified recruits, and a Quranic system that attracts the majority of youth. Even IRI did not last, ending eight months after COMPASS's closure when the government ceased to pay Radio Kano.

Sustainability surely requires greater attention to systemic reform than either LEAP or COMPASS could devote. This focus could take many forms: managing a concerted behavioral change module in order to establish new attitudes; ensuring permanent school or government mentors to train new recruits in improved pedagogical techniques; cultivating local NGOs and training cadres that continue to work in schools—all strategies that LEAP and COMPASS employed to some degree but which they limited in favor of more direct school interventions with immediate individual results. Ultimately, however, there is no substitute for policy reform and official embrace of new activities. And here aid projects face a Nigerian catch-22. Civil society initiatives, led by individuals or NGOs, do not currently have the reach or funding to supplant government commitment in the modern education sector, especially with a bulging youth population.[136] Yet even as officials command respect in Kano's "big-man hierarchy,"[137] government corruption stokes widespread disdain. Donors should never give money to government ministries, insist respondents, or it will disappear. "The Nigerian factor"—*chuwa chuwa* in Hausa—is a byword for corruption, the disease of the country's body-politic. As a result, project funds tend to bypass government offices, even though this re-routing often alienates the very officials needed to sustain program efforts.[138]

This dilemma has led to a recent shift in donor programming away from community-based service delivery to 'system strengthening' that concentrates on policy and governance reform. LEAP and COMPASS represented the former. As one manager put it, COMPASS "was a service delivery, not a systems strengthening project. Sustainability was not really addressed in the design."[139] Later projects such as the World Bank's State Education Sector Project (SESP) (2008–2011), the British Department for International Development's (DfID) Education Support Sector Programme in Nigeria (ESSPIN) (2008–2015), and USAID's Northern Education Initiative (NEI) (2009–2013), despite some school and community-level initiatives, aim primarily to strengthen education policy and governance.[140] It is too early to judge their impact, but one thing might be said already: For system-strengthening projects to succeed, they *must* be sustainable; indeed, sustainability is the primary, perhaps the only, measure of their success. They cannot claim, as do community and school interventions, to offer discrete benefits by temporarily filling a dire need or directly serving a cohort of pupils. The system-strengthening approach courts the reverse problem: By collaborating closely with officials, projects risk remaining aloof from their ultimate beneficiaries, improving the administrative capacity to deliver education without necessarily securing the political will to enact reforms, increasing public willingness to accept change, or making immediate improvements in people's lives.

As a marker of project success, sustainability may ultimately be something of a canard. Not only does it distract from the immediate value of discrete goods, but measures of sustainability tend to emphasize the relatively short-run, post-project perpetuation of reforms, not their long-term social impact. Indeed, once final evaluations are concluded, a project's legacy enters the realm of history where it is largely forgotten by the aid community. Its longer impact remains generally unknown, despite constant talk of sustainable reform. This neglect is not simply the result of oversight but the byproduct of a managerial approach to aid programming that aspires to technical control of the reform process, divides the process into concise steps, and evaluates only those factors that contracts stipulate. Yet a project's ultimate impact is shaped by forces far beyond its managerial bounds, and the very best of projects may be overwhelmed by social and political events. How should we evaluate the legacy of even well-regarded school projects if the education system remains barely improved—or even worsens—after ten years? This is the dilemma confronting aid workers in Kano schools, for, despite a decade of effort, many commentators say that today's system faces graver challenges—in terms of classroom size and teacher quality—than it did on the eve of the millennium.[141] What difference, then, did a decade of donor intervention make? Answering this question requires greater contextual knowledge than most aid professionals marshal.

Conclusion: The Walls of Kano

In October 1999, on a diplomatic stopover in Nigeria, Secretary of State Madeleine Albright requested to visit Kano and its ancient city walls. Embassy officials in Abuja scurried to accommodate her wish amidst reports of "palpable joy" in the northern metropolis.[142] Her interest is striking, as few Westerners have even heard of the Sahelian entrepôt, let alone its notable monument. Kano's walls, which date back 900 years, are now quite dilapidated, little more than earthen berms or dirt glacis for much of their 14-kilometer girth.[143] German and American funding has restored some of the 15 original gates, but most of the ancient fortification has succumbed to harmattan winds and urban traffic. In one regard, of course, this decay reflects a culture of neglect: Few Kanawa worry about their fabled rampart. But in another sense, north Nigerians are more attuned to the past than Americans. If Westerners compartmentalize history in museums and monuments, Kanawa see it as a living tradition.[144]

Why should northern history matter to aid donors and project implementers? Recent calls for greater historical awareness in development practice seem particularly apt in Kano, where people live in and around the relics of the past, moving daily through the ancient gates. The Emir's palace, a hub of downtown activity, embodies an Islamic tradition that defines life for most residents. Like many Africans, Kanawa do not expect Westerners to appreciate their tradition, and efforts to learn the language or understand cultural nuances are met with pleasant surprise. But more than most places, north Nigerians resent the slight suggested by indifference and take umbrage at descriptions of backwardness that ignore the region's proud past. Aid programs in general tend to favor culture-neutral techniques over processes invested with local value. But this insistence not only limits cross-cultural understanding, it also prompts a local reticence that may stall program activities—or even thwart them. During the notorious polio vaccine crisis of 2003–2004, when Kanawa rejected inoculation as a Western plot, it was tempting for Westerners to blame a benighted culture. The truth is more complex, involving political snubs by southern and international leaders alike. Aid programs and their technical interventions are not devoid of historical implication, for they hark back to patterns of earlier Western encroachment when scientific reforms justified colonial hubris.[145] North Nigerians will collaborate with Western programs as long as implementers respect local concerns and encourage local leadership. But historically based suspicions run high, and an impatient or cavalier attitude that ignores or dismisses local values can alienate potential allies. "There is a need for a new development assistance paradigm," admonished one respondent, "that is realistic, transparent, and rooted in the needs of the recipients as identified by them."[146]

Aid projects erect their own walls, packaging social change in three-to-five-year compartments bounded by the managerial brick-and-mortar of contract requirements, target outputs, and interim deadlines that try to map the uneven terrain of development. In theory, the walled compounds of multiple donor projects should join together to form a sturdy architecture of social change. Rarely, however, does a long-term process carved into so many bits, each separately managed, cohere into the seamless evolution imagined by aid visionaries. Instead, projects often compete and reverse course, launch activities that are dropped when funding ends, and lurch between managerial approaches and strategic objectives. As one advisor put it, "We try to do 25-year programs in 3–5 year projects with one-year budgets."[147] Education in particular seems unsuited to a project modality because of the lengthy duration of human growth and the artificiality of short-term objectives. As institutions of cultural perpetuation and the transmission of values, schools are particularly sensitive in Kano, and projects that enter them require local trust. Under these circumstances, the demand for quick wins coupled with long-term sustainability may simply prove untenable.

Of course, in the build-it-and-they-will-come world of foreign aid, donor money does win compliance, and projects do change lives. LEAP and COMPASS were in many ways exemplary—spearheaded by local leaders, introducing practices that changed the way people viewed education. But as with many projects, the structures they built were soon eroded by the forces of population growth, economic decline, political indifference, and stubborn tradition. Their successes seem in many ways unreal when looked at from outside and afterward: positive memories of a hopeful investment and minor reforms of an education system that today faces challenges as dire as it did ten years ago. In the end, it is this wider context and trajectory, largely beyond managerial purview, that determines a project's worth.

Notes

This article would have been impossible without the assistance of many people. Ahmed Umar Jibrin served as my facilitator and co-researcher in Nigeria. His influence is felt throughout the essay. Nafisa Ado was equally important, providing contacts, advice, and encouragement at every step. In Washington, DC, Sandy Oleksy-Ojikutu and Semere Solomon readily offered their resources and expertise. Abdalla Abu Adamu, Terrence Jantzi, Lamont King, Mark Lynd, Dirk Moses, David Owusu-Ansah, and Alastair Rodd made valuable comments on earlier drafts. And the History Department and Office of International Programs at James Madison University funded the research. My interviewees, in Kano and in the United States, generously offered their time and memories. Some of them wanted their names to appear in print; others requested anonymity. Because this mixture would have stilted the presentation, I opted to remove direct attribution throughout. But in order to honor those who requested it, I list them here: I am deeply obliged to Dr. Garba Shehu of Sa'adatu Rimi College, Headmistress Rahinatu Yakubu Adamu and teacher Alima Usman Bari of Race Course Model Primary School, Sa'a Ibrahim of Radio Kano, and Ladidi Sani Fagge formerly of LEAP and COMPASS, as well as over 30 nameless others who provided information and opinions.

1. Respondents I and O.
2. Respondents A and K. Ratios vary widely from place to place. One state education official estimated that average state primary school class size had risen from one teacher to 40 pupils in 2000 to 1:60 in 2011, with numbers reaching an incredible 1:150 in urban areas. Others pushed it to 1:200 (Respondent E). This growth tracks overall state population growth. The 2008 DHS Nigeria Report (p. 65) places the maternal fertility rate at over 7.0, far higher than southern Nigeria and on par with impoverished neighbor Niger. A cultural and commercial hub for centuries, Kano continues to attract migrants despite a decade-long economic skid. Residents lament the shuttering of light industries that flourished under military rule, blaming unreliable electric power and favors from southern brokers. In a bitter irony, citizens of the world's sixth-largest crude oil producer pay exorbitant costs for diesel to run their ubiquitous generators, especially in the non-oil states of the north. In late 2011, a presidential proposal to remove fuel subsidies prompted country-wide riots.
3. Whether they are actually more active is disputed by education officials (Respondents J and P).
4. Both projects ran education activities in three states: Kano, Nassarawa, and Lagos. This essay focuses solely on Kano. In addition, though COMPASS involved health activities, this essay concerns education alone, addressing health only insofar as it affected the performance of the education team.
5. USAID left for other northern states with COMPASS's closure in 2009, and the subsequent Northern Education Initiative (NEI) operated in Bauchi and Sokoto States. USAID still works minimally in Kano under a grant to the International Federation for Education and Self-Help (IFESH), sending American educators to work in local schools, but many describe this effort as a placeholder for USAID's re-entry into the state under a future teacher training initiative.
6. For a critique of the aid concern for sustainability, see Kremer and Miguel (2008), 201–253.

7. This is precisely what Sachs (2005) accused Western donors of doing: providing enough money to alleviate some suffering temporarily but not enough to prompt development.

8. Recent pleas for greater historical awareness in aid practice include Lewis (2009); Gubser and Keilson (2010); and Bayly et al. (2011). For a case study of USAID programming in Uganda that ends in a similar call for *historiopraxis*, see Gubser (2011).

9. For classic accounts of Kano's history, see Hogben and Kirk-Greene (1966); Paden (1973); Hill (1970); and Smith (1997). See also Umar's intellectual history (2006).

10. One of the simplifications in donor literature is the equation of Quranic schools with mendicancy. Kanawa tend to distinguish between Quranic schools supported by local communities and Tsangaya schools with peripatetic mallams and pupils. The *al-majiri* (derived from the Arabic word *Al-mahajirun*, or "migrant") make up the latter. Both are venerable institutions of religious learning, and indeed the tradition of leaving home to seek knowledge dates back centuries. Typically, mallams were not paid, relying instead on support from host communities and farm labor undertaken by students. In recent decades, however, Tsangaya schools have suffered as a result of rising student population, increased urbanization, economic decline, and waning community support, with pupils spending much of their time begging. For a sample of the sizable literature, see Okoye and Yau (1999); Khalid (2001).

11. On recent education trends, see Umar (2001). For an older account of the remarkable adaptability of Kano's first school system, see Chamberlin (1975). For a defense of Islamic education against an exclusive, "one-eyed" focus on Western schooling, see Abdurrahman and Canham (1978).

12. The word *boko* literally means "false" or "false education." By semantic extension, it has come to indicate the supposedly false teachings of Western education, though it might also be applied to other types of misleading guidance.

13. On Hans Visscher's schools, see Fafunwa (1974), 106–109.

14. According to Peter Tibenderana (2003), Britain's dual policy had the effect of creating a dependent culture.

15. Smith (1997), 490. A survey ten years later, by contrast, reported 5,215 Quranic schools. Paden (1973), 59.

16. Ozigi and Ocho (1981), 57.

17. Fafunwa (1974), 174.

18. Respondent V. This dearth of local role models was especially acute for women: One interviewee noted that her secondary school was staffed by Westerners, Egyptians, and a few Hausa men.

19. On this era, see Kane (2001), 29–68. Loimeier (1997), 86, lists the industries as textiles, leather, chemical, machinery, food processing, and consumables. While many migrants were seasonal, moving back and forth between farms and factories, the trend toward urbanization kept farmland relatively cheap, drawing migrants to rural as well as urban Kano State.

20. Bayero University historian Bawuro Barkindo (1993), 94–95, noted that the temporary flight of Igbos from the Sabon Gari district of Kano during the war made it clear how dependent Kanawa were on southerners for essential city services.

21. Respondent D.

22. See Umar (2003), 151. This was neither the first nor the last push for UPE. The idea was floated in the 1950s by British colonialists preparing the country for

independence and then renewed as part of the Millennium Development Goals at the end of the century. On the former, see Fafunwa (1974), 167–175. Documents at the Hans Visscher Archive in Gidan dan Hausa contain numerous references to the colonial plan. See, for example, Folder EDU/29.

23. Respondent M. Indeed, children forced by either British colonialists or the post-independence government to attend public schools could be ostracized from their families and communities. Respondent V.

24. Respondent V.

25. As opposed to Quranic schools, Islamiyya schools also generally teach more than just the holy book.

26. This assertion will no doubt surprise Westerners who are used to equating Salafism with Saudi Arabia's rigid anti-modern fundamentalism. Respondents S and T confirmed the importance of the Izala movement in weakening traditional mistrust of *boko* and encouraging greater enrollment. Islamiyya schools and women's education first appeared in the 1950s on the agenda of the Northern Elements Progressive Union (NEPU), led by Aminu Kano, but the 1970s saw their real flowering. See Barkindo (1993), 102.

27. The Tijaniyya movement had itself expanded in the middle of the century as an intra-Sufi revolt against the caliphate's dominant Qadiriyya sect, which, its adherents claimed, was too closely tied to British colonialism. Works on the Izala movement tend treat it in Weberian style as the religious harbinger of social and economic modernity. The fullest analysis is Kane (2001). For a detailed history of Islamic reform movements in twentieth-century northern Nigeria, including Izala, see Loimeier (1997). For discussions of Izala and its impact on education, see especially the works of Muhammad S. Umar.

28. Umar (1993), 178. For a detailed implementer survey of intra-Islamic feuds, see also International Crisis Group (2010), 13–19.

29. It is important not to equate the fringe Maitatsine movement or its latter-day successor—the Yusufiyya movement of Boko Haram, which execrates Western education—with the traditional or modernist Islamic ideologies of northern Nigeria, which oppose the violent extremism and ideological hodgepodge of these cults. On recent religious violence in Nigeria, see Falola (1998).

30. Umar (2003), 151.

31. Umar (2003), 152.

32. Respondent AD.

33. Respondent V.

34. Though social services in general were severely underfunded, Abacha established the Education Trust Fund (PTF) to channel some oil income to schools. Democratically elected Obasanjo annulled this fund, replacing it with an Education Tax Fund (ETF).

35. Adamu (2003), 1.

36. These were overseen by the National Primary Education Commission (NPEC), which later became the Universal Basic Education Commission (UBEC).

37. Respondent P. The change from SPEB to SUBEB took place under the influence of universal basic education campaigns fueled by the Millennium Development Goals. The name change also involved a jurisdictional shift, as Junior Secondary School, formerly the purview of the State Ministry of Education (SMOE), now fell under basic education and shifted to the control of the SUBEB. Funding is

split in three parts: Federal and state offices share construction funds, with the state expected to match monies contributed by the Universal Basic Education Commission (UBEC); school materials come out of state budgets; and the LGA is responsible for teacher salaries, although states deduct salaries from LGA budgets prior to disbursement to avoid the recurrent problem of LGA failure to pay teachers.

38. Today's Hausa managers recall the presence of American instructors from land-grant colleges in the schools of their youth. Respondents X and V. For a report on one of these projects, see USAID (1981).

39. Respondent AA. This choice reflected a broader shift among donors away from the modernization of threshold countries and toward poverty-alleviation that targeted the world's poorest. Oil-rich Nigeria seemed capable of relieving its own poor.

40. There were three separate activities under this program: Family Health Services (FHS), AIDS Prevention and Control (AIDSCAP), and a Maternal and Child Health intervention entitled Combating Communicable Childhood Diseases (CCCD). See SBA Consultants (1992).

41. These partners were engaged by cooperative agreement, a flexible partnering mechanism that allows for improvisational programming, rather than by contract, a stricter, top-down form of partnership.

42. In 1996, USAID moved its northern regional office from Kaduna to Kano.

43. Frequent targets were U.S. relations with Israel, the embargo on Iraq, and the bombings of Sudan and Afghanistan. "We had to hide our vehicles every Friday as a precaution," recalled Respondent X.

44. Respondent X.

45. Respondent AA.

46. Respondents AA and V.

47. See for example Brieger and Ogunlade (1997).

48. Respondent AA.

49. The prospect of northern sharia law had also been debated during the previous democratic quadrennium. The best source for this topic is the five-volume Ostien (2007).

50. While there had been some talk of an education activity in the early 1990s, the annulment of Nigeria's 1993 election stanched the discussion.

51. Respondent H. One "discovery" during this period reveals how limited Mission understanding of northern school culture was at the time: Expatriate staff were surprised to learn that Quranic schools, traditionally male-only, enrolled "millions of girls." Respondent AA.

52. Respondent AA.

53. In 1998, for example, Bill Clinton launched the Education for Development and Democracy Initiative.

54. The project was initially budgeted for $9 million and later increased by $3 million. An interesting aside, LEAP began on a somber September 12, 2001, when RTI's policy advisor Alastair Rodd recalls flying from his California home to Washington to sign the project agreement on a plane with more crew than passengers.

55. Respondent H.

56. Respondent M.

57. Other programs were entitled "Aunty Bola's Workshop" and "Animal Garden." The latter has an interesting story: National staff developed LEAP radio programs for

all three project states. "Animal Garden" was scripted initially as "Magic Garden," which is how it played in Nassarawa and Lagos States. But staff in Kano warned against a northern broadcast because of Muslim prohibitions on thaumaturgy, so the program was re-written for Kano audiences.

58. Respondents M, O, Q, W, and X. Local staff members report being challenged in meetings by mistrustful community members who viewed the United States as warring with Islam, and they sometimes suffered the taint of American association.

59. Though advocacy and sensitization campaigns have become *de rigueur* in Kano, donors do not always use them adequately, at times with disastrous consequences: The most well-known failure occurred in 2003, when religious leaders condemned the international push for the polio vaccine after national and international authorities failed to consult them.

60. Respondent H.

61. To promote education demand, Kwankwaso introduced a school feeding program, free uniforms, and child-friendly schools. His Community Reorientation Committees (CRCs) mobilized communities to participate in local development in general, including education. For a discussion of these initiatives, see Adamu (2003), 16–54.

62. Respondent Z. Shekarau's hiring policy was partly initiated by an RTI-led Education Management Information System (EMIS) project that ran from 2003 to 2004, bridging LEAP and COMPASS. The activity found over 1,500 ghost teachers on state payrolls, which Shekarau tried to fill with real bodies. The EMIS activity also identified severe shortcomings in teacher qualifications, which Shekarau's hiring binge ultimately exacerbated.

63. A precise count is unknown, but all estimates demonstrate this gap. A 2003 census placed the number of Quranic schools at over 14,000 (Bano [2009], 10). A 2007 state census by the Special Advisor to the Governor on Islamiyya, Quranic, and Tsangaya Education (IQTE) estimated over 7,000 government-supported (public and integrated) schools and more than 20,000 non-integrated Quranic schools in the state (Respondent T; unpublished spreadsheets completed in 2008 with data generated by the office of the Special Adviser to the Governor of Kano State on IQTE). A 2009 Kano State ministry estimate placed the number of Tsangaya schools at 26,000 (www.citizensfornigeria.com/index.php?option=com_content& task=view&id=262; retrieved Feb. 15, 2012). Public schools, by contrast, number around 5,000, according to the Kano State Ministry of Education's 2009–2010 Annual School Census Results. Incredibly, a 2010 state census counted 5,024 government and 1,240 Quranic, far lower than any other estimate (Annual School Census Results, 2009–2010, Ministry of Education, Kano State). Since most public school students attend some kind of Islamic school in the evening or on school breaks, these institutions reach by far the most children in the state.

64. Respondents AF and V.

65. The three LGAs, representing that state's three senatorial districts, reflect a mix of urban (Kano Municipal) and rural (Tsanyawa, Ajingi). Schools were chosen at random "by pulling cards out of a hat," remarked one local staff member. Random selection, said an expatriate policy advisor, required some initial preparation and diplomacy since beneficiaries of government programs are typically chosen due to connections.

66. "Low cost or no cost" was the slogan, as the project encouraged teachers to make their own classroom aids rather than wait for government deliveries.
67. The program started in grades 3 and 4, the crucial transitional grades where pupil attrition mounts, and then expanded to upper primary levels. Respondent O.
68. Respondent P. "LEAP was the first of its kind among donors," agreed Respondent Q.
69. Respondent AD.
70. Respondent X. The World Bank and UNICEF, by contrast, passed money into state accounts, said Respondent O, and losses to corruption were high. Today, all donors maintain control of funds until they reach targeted beneficiaries.
71. Respondents O and W.
72. Respondents AG and AE.
73. Respondents R and AI.
74. Respondent AB. Furthermore, the Neighborhood Education Committee reports continuing LEAP PTA trainings and introducing vocational skills programs in former project schools. Respondent AG.
75. Respondent W.
76. "Thou shalt be integrated," griped a former employee when describing the top-down dictate. Though most Mission staff preferred to keep the sectors separate, integration was a prevalent USAID strategy in the early years of the millennium, touted as a way to reduce the managerial burden of multiple projects for an agency that had recently lost, according to Shawn Zeller (2004), 37% of its employees and $50 million in budget (p. 33.) Social sector integration is not without programmatic logic: Education increases the likelihood that a person will use health services, and healthy children demonstrate better learning achievements.
77. Respondents W and V. Two members of LEAP's Kano team returned to their government posts, where duties included overseeing aspects of COMPASS. One LEAP team member moved to USAID as an education officer; another contributed to COMPASS as a consultant with local NGOs.
78. Jigawa was part of Kano State until 1991, when the country was subdivided into today's 36-state federation, and Eshak was a lifelong Kano resident.
79. This deficit was noted by several commentators. One, for example, said that Shekarau seemed resistant to COMPASS (Respondent Q). Some speculate that Shekarau's tepidity had to do with typical political distancing from programs associated with a predecessor. Others note that Shekarau's policies may have affected COMPASS without targeting the project directly. SUBEB officials complained, for example, that after 2007 the governor ceased paying counterpart funds required to receive the UBEC school infrastructure revenues. And many respondents noted Shekarau's inconsistency in supplying Radio Kano with its promised 50% cost-share to broadcast IRI programs. The radio shows were interrupted once during COMPASS's tenure and ceased altogether eight months after closure.
80. Respondent E.
81. By the end of the project, training sessions were carried out quarterly, not bimonthly.
82. Respondents Z, N, Y, and AC.
83. This praise was given by numerous recipients, including those critical of other activities.
84. After 1998, the Nigerian Certificate of Education (NCE) replaced a grade II (or secondary school) degree as the minimum teaching qualification. The new policy, designed to improve teaching quality, exacerbated the dearth of qualified instructors,

partly because training colleges, which had ensured that teachers with secondary degrees got nine months of instruction before being posted, were closed in favor of a single statewide institute. Respondent AF. Moreover, reported Respondent M, the NCE program was geared toward secondary, not primary, school teachers.

85. The college added 40 more scholarships, targeting men as well as women, and has continued to provide scholarships, though fewer, since COMPASS ended.

86. The Proficiency in English Language Instruction (PELI) curriculum sponsored by COMPASS was never institutionalized at Sa'adatu Rimi, where it remained a supplemental weekend course taught without additional recompense. Ironically, though it is not taught at its place of origin, the curriculum is being considered for national adoption by the National Commission for Colleges of Education (NCCE).

87. Respondents L and AF.

88. Respondent Q.

89. USAID/The Mitchell Group (2008), 26. The Mitchell Group is an Abuja-based company contracted by the USAID Mission to evaluate its projects.

90. Respondents V and AB.

91. Even the school renovations are a mixed legacy. Toilets built under COMPASS still attract girls to school, but shoddy construction has not always lasted. Some school officials say they wish COMPASS had managed the renovations rather than leaving them to contractors hired by PTA grants.

92. Respondent X.

93. Respondents H, V, and N. Though project documents made this division clear, it was not always communicated to local partners.

94. CSACEFA and FOMWAN are umbrella organizations of smaller local NGOs.

95. In addition to Basic Education Association and Neighborhood Education Committee, it engaged a third organization: Child Growth, Youth and Women Empowerment Initiative.

96. Typically, full partners control their own budgets, but FOMWAN and CSACEFA operated mostly under the supervision of prime grantee Pathfinder.

97. Respondents G, B, AG, and N.

98. USAID/The Mitchell Group (2008), 2.

99. Respondent X.

100. "There was a drastic change of some schools, especially Islamiyya and Quranic schools that weren't integrated." Respondents AG and M.

101. Respondent Y. A model school serves as a center for educational experiments, receiving extra resources from the government and enjoying greater student selectivity.

102. Respondent H.

103. It worked in nine directly, with the rest engaged as extended program participants.

104. Respondent K; Unpublished Report, "5 Years COMPASS: Programmes in Gwarzo L.G.A of Kano State (The Journey So Far) 2004–2009," Compiled by Mushabu Sani Rimingado, Gwarzo Local Government Education Authority (LGEA) in 2009.

105. These figures, rounded to the nearest thousand, were provided in Gwarzo. Their most striking feature predates the COMPASS years: Enrollment for the five years from 1999–2003 is listed as 26,000; 25,000; 39,000; 50,000; and 55,000. I was informed that the pre-COMPASS figures were drastically inflated (a practice common in Nigeria since higher population numbers win greater funding) but that

numbers for the COMPASS years were correct. Worth noting here is the remark made by one Bayero University professor that "80% of the data in official reports is false, and lack of data prevents us from knowing the impact of local or donor projects." Today's data frenzy, he said, is more of a Western obsession, obliged but not shared by Nigerians who rely on donor aid. For a discussion of the technical and political challenges of estimating population in Nigeria, see Jerven (2013), 56–61.

106. One Gwarzo official estimated that the population had trebled since 1999, and enrollment rates had risen from 30–40% of the population to nearly 90%.
107. Respondent M.
108. Ferguson (1994) argues that social problems in developing countries must be rendered in ways amenable to donor intervention, with inequities depoliticized and cast as technical challenges.
109. Whereas expatriate staff members tend to cycle through USAID Missions and "piss on things to leave their mark," commented Respondent AA, the beleaguered and understaffed Nigeria Mission enjoyed a core group of relatively longtime employees, both local and expatriate, who survived the lean years under dictatorship.
110. Respondent D, but also AD, criticized COMPASS for this fault.
111. Respondent B. "These projects have an outside agenda," agreed Respondent D, "not the result of system analysis from within, but system analysis for without, where 'development needs' consistent with Agency agenda are identified and funding made available for execution. Agencies are often carried away with the 'messianic zeal' of bringing health, equity and democracy to Third World without finding out what the recipients think about these values and how they can mesh them with their own internal values."
112. Respondent X. Respondent I said, "USAID tended to view the staff as experts, not looking to the government. It told the staff to go and do the work"—an empowerment that could appear as imposition from the outside.
113. Respondent V.
114. Respondent X.
115. Respondent Q. Providing too much per diem, she worried, may spoil people so that they refuse to work with the government after the project closes. Respondent P, D, and B also worried that donors put up too much cash and that community cost-share was essential for local ownership.
116. Respondent U. COMPASS simply ended, remarked one NGO partner, without preparing its programs for local handoff. "We do not know what happened." Respondent AG.
117. Respondent AB described IRI as the "main initiative" of the program, complemented by all the other interventions.
118. The broadcasts were heard as far away as neighboring Niger. Radio Kano, reported Respondent Z, received delegations seeking help to implement the programs they heard. Respondent AH also noted outside interest.
119. Respondent AC.
120. Respondent Y.
121. Respondent Y and AC.
122. Royer (2004), x. A USAID respondent concurred: "Based on the data, we struggled to show positive gains from the project."
123. A 2002 document entitled "Summary of M&E Efforts for LEAP Pedagogy" reveals that the assumed availability of preexisting government assessment tests proved false, forcing evaluators to start anew well after the project had begun.

124. Respondent AI. A telling anecdote reveals the challenges entailed in devising assessment items. One assessor observed that rather than memorizing multiplication tables, students tended to count marks drawn on a board during class exercises, a practice encouraged by teachers. To determine the result of 8×5, for example, students came to the front board, drew eight bundles of five tics each, and then counted them. Thus, when evaluators assessed students outside the classroom by asking them to compare two equations and determine which was larger—8×5 or 7×6, for example—the children were baffled. "Classroom activities were totally divorced from the real world."

125. Respondent R. USAID representatives, according to several respondents, harbored longstanding doubts about both the ability of IRI to support classroom teaching and the emphasis on pedagogical methods to the near-exclusion of subject-matter knowledge. Both of these, it should be noted, were widespread trends in education programming at the start of the millennium.

126. Respondent H. Respondent AI offered a similar assessment: "By and large, LEAP didn't do anything."

127. Respondent AJ.

128. Mildon and Fournier (2010), 18. These findings appeared in earlier conference papers as well.

129. USAID, EDUCAN/COMPASS Nigeria Pupil Achievement Report (March 2009), 147–177. Student achievement was measured through annual pre- and post-tests administered in a random sample of schools.

130. USAID/The Mitchell Group (2008), 26. While COMPASS students outperformed those in the Abuja control schools, Mitchell Group evaluators felt this edge may have come from factors other than project training, including the greater concentration on math and English in target schools. USAID/The Mitchell Group (2008), 43.

131. Respondent AJ.

132. Surprisingly, the initial contract did not even request data by state, said Respondent AJ, though staff members quickly recognized its importance. Interestingly, EDUCAN also disaggregated by whether or not a school had received earlier LEAP inputs. At most levels, students in LEAP schools showed no advance over COMPASS-only kids (though COMPASS's improvement over LEAP may have stemmed from the project's longer exposure and later initiation).

133. Respondent AJ.

134. Respondents V, AD, and AG.

135. Respondent AB.

136. Private investments can, of course, supplement donor and government effort. Respondent A noted that after seeing LEAP interventions some private businessmen established their own schools.

137. Respondent H.

138. One official even averred that projects are designed to end at political transition points because of fear that change will subvert ongoing efforts anyway. Respondent P.

139. Respondent AB. Respondents V and X noted that USAID was less inclined than other donors to provide government officials with perquisites such as computers or training trips. This refusal, they said, dampened government support.

140. The World Bank also runs the Community Cash Transfer (CCT) program, which transfers funds to parents who send their daughters to school under UNICEF's Girl's Education Project (GEP). As this strategy suggests, donors in Kano today collaborate in what is referred to as a "twinning strategy," which links projects in

order to increase their scope and reach. As a further expression of this approach, donors are trying to move beyond annual planning by emphasizing State Education Sector Operational Plans (SESOPs) and Medium Term Sector Strategies (MTSS). Respondent U.

141. Some even say that school and teacher quality has declined since military rule as enrollment surged. Respondents X, V.

142. Respondent AA; Uchendu (1999).

143. For a historical survey of the walls and gates, see Barkindo (1983).

144. "The importance and legacy of the Sokoto empire for the development of the Muslim communities in present-day Nigeria cannot be overestimated," writes Roman Loimeier. "Until the present day, politicians of the North, religious scholars, and modern intellectuals claim the legacy of Usman dan Fodio for themselves in order to legitimate their political strategies and programs." Loimeier (1997), 3–4.

145. Hodge (2007).

146. Respondent D.

147. Respondent H.

Bibliography

Abdurrahman, A. M., and P. Canham. (1978). *The Ink of the Scholar: The Islamic Tradition of Education in Nigeria*. Lagos: Palgrave Macmillan.

Adamu, A. U. (2003). *Education in Kano State, Nigeria, 1999–2003*. Unpublished Consultancy Report. State Primary Education Board. Kano.

Bano, M. (2009). *Engaged yet Disengaged: Islamic Schools and the State in Kano, Nigeria*. Religions and Development Working Paper 29. DfID.

Barkindo, B. (1983). The Gates of Kano City: A Historical Survey. In Heinemann (Ed.), *Studies in the History of Kano*. Ibadan: Barkindo, 1–30.

Barkindo, B. (1993). Growing Islamism in Kano City since 1970: Causes, Form and Implications. In L. Brenner (Ed.), *Muslim Identity and Social Change in Sub-Saharan Africa*. Bloomington, IN: Indiana University Press, 91–105.

Bayly, C. A., V. Rao, S. Szreter, and M. Woolcock (eds.). (2011). *History, Historians, Development Policy: A Necessary Dialogue*. Manchester: Manchester University Press.

Brieger, W. R., and P .B. Ogunlade. (1997). *Process Evaluation of the Community Partners for Health Program of BASICS/Nigeria*. BASICS Technical Directive 000 NI 58 012; USAID Contract Number HRN-C-00-93-00031-00.

Chamberlin, J. W. (1975). *The Development of Islamic Education in Kano City, Nigeria, with Emphasis on Legal Education in the 19th and 20th Centuries*. PhD Dissertation: Columbia University.

Fafunwa, A. B. (1974). *History of Education in Nigeria*. London: Allen & Unwin.

Falola, T. (1998). *Violence in Nigeria: The Crisis of Religious Politics and Secular Ideologies*. Rochester: University of Rochester Press.

Ferguson, J. (1994). *The Anti-Politics Machine: Development, Depoliticization, and Bureaucratic Power in Lesotho*. Minneapolis: University of Minnesota Press.

Gubser, M. (2011). The View from Le Château: USAID's Recent Decentralization Programming in Uganda. *Development Policy Review* 29(1): 23–46.

Gubser, M., and J. Keilson. (2010). Retrieving the Past: History, Ahistoricism, and the Practice of International Development. *Monday Developments* 28(10): 27–8, 32.

Hill, P. (1970). *Population, Prosperity and Poverty: Rural Kano, 1900 and 1970*. Cambridge: Cambridge University Press.

Hodge, J. M. (2007). *Triumph of the Expert: Agrarian Doctrines of Development and the Legacies of British Colonialism*. Athens, OH: Ohio University Press.

Hogben, S. J., and A. H. M. Kirk-Greene. (1966). *The Emirates of Northern: A Preliminary Survey of their Historical Traditions*. London: Oxford, 184–214.

International Crisis Group. (2010). *Northern Nigeria: Background to Conflict*. Africa Report N°168.

Jerven, M. (2013). *Poor Numbers: How We Are Misled by African Development Statistics and What to Do about It*. Ithaca: Cornell University Press.

Kane, O. (2001). *Muslim Modernity in Postcolonial Nigeria: A Study of the Society for the Removal of Innovation and Reinstatement of Tradition*. Leiden: Brill.

Khalid, S. (2001). Nigeria's Education Crisis: The *Almajiranci* System and Social Realities. *Islamic Culture* LXXV(3): 85–103.

Kremer, M., and E. Miguel. (2008). The Illusion of Sustainability. In W. Easterly (Ed.), *Reinventing Foreign Aid*. Cambridge, MA: MIT Press.

Lewis, D. (2009). International Development and the 'Perpetual Present': Anthropological Approaches to the Re-Historicization of Policy. *European Journal of Development Research* 21(1): 32–46.

Loimeier, R. (1997). *Islamic Reform and Political Change in Northern Nigeria*. Evanston: Northwestern University Press.

Mildon, D., and G. Fournier. (2010). *Challenging Notions of Literacy: Testing in Nigeria*. Paper presented at the XIV World Congress, World Council of Comparative Education Societies (Istanbul).

Okoye, F., and Y. Zakari Yau. (1999). *The Condition of Almajirai in the North West Zone of Nigeria*. Kaduna: Human Rights Monitor.

Ostien, P. (ed.). (2007). *Sharia Implementation in Northern Nigeria: A Sourcebook*. Ibadan: Spectrum.

Ozigi, A., and L. Ocho. (1981). *Education in Northern Nigeria*. London: Allen & Unwin.

Paden, J. N. (1973). *Religion and Political Culture in Kano*. Berkeley, CA: University of California Press.

Royer, J. M. (2004). *Literacy Enhancement Assistance Program: 2002–2004 Student Assessment Final Report*.

Sachs, J. (2005). *The End of Poverty: Economic Possibilities for our Time*. New York: Penguin.

SBA Consultants. (1992). *The Sociocultural Analysis of the USAID Interventions in Nigeria*.

Smith, M. (1997). *Government in Kano, 1350–1950*. Boulder, CO: Westview.

Tibenderana, P. (2003). *Education and Cultural change in Northern Nigeria, 1906–1966: A Study in the Creation of a Dependent Culture*. Kampala: Fountain.

Uchendu, M. (1999). Kano Agog for U.S. Secretary. AllAfrica.com, P.M. News (Lagos), October 21, 1999. http://allafrica.com/stories/199910210252.html; accessed March 19, 2012.

Umar, M. S. (1993). Changing Islamic Identity in Nigeria from the 1960s to the 1980s: From Sufism to Anti-Sufism. In L. Brenner (Ed.), *Muslim Identity and Social Change in Sub-Saharan Africa*. Bloomington: Indiana University Press, 154–78.

Umar, M. S. (2001). Education and Islamic Trends in Northern Nigeria: 1970s–1990s. *Africa Today* 48(2): 127–50.

Umar, M. S. (2003). Profiles of New Islamic Schools in Northern Nigeria. *The Maghreb Review* 28(2–3): 146–69.

Umar, M. S. (2006). *Islam and Colonialism: Intellectual Responses of Muslims of Northern Nigeria to British Colonial Rule*. Leiden: Brill.

USAID. (1981). *Northern Nigeria Teacher Education Project*. A.I.D. Project Impact Evaluation Report No. 23.

USAID/The Mitchell Group. (2008). *An Evaluation of the USAID/Nigeria Social Sector Projects: ENHANSE and COMPASS*.

Zeller, S. (April, 2004). On the Work Force Roller Coaster at USAID. *Foreign Service Journal* 33–9.

Chapter 7

Practitioners Caught in the Middle

Evidence from the Democratic Republic of Congo

Nathalie Louge

Introduction

> The effectiveness of schools is seen not to lie in the specific list of characteristics of discrete additive elements, but in the creation of a whole efficient working system, which includes its people, structure, relationships, ideologies, goals, intellectual substance, motivation and will.
>
> (Lightfoot, 1983, cited in Association for the Development of Education in Africa, 1995)

Education in the Democratic Republic of Congo (DRC) has elicited great interest since the drafting of the Global Partnership for Education's (GPE) "All Children Reading" summit in Kigali in 2011. It receives attention not only from international funding agencies and implementing partners but also from local educators and the Congolese government (GDRC), who are renewing their efforts to improve student performance across the nation. The Ministry of Education's 2012 Education Sector Plan outlined steps to improve all aspects of the education system, from teacher training to infrastructure to student assessment, even as it took into account challenges like the DRC's enormous size, poor infrastructure, and lack of inspectors and properly trained teachers. This renewed attention gives hope for educational improvement in a country that has seen many failed initiatives. Still, significant challenges remain, including the country's deeply engrained corruption and its ongoing conflict. Conditions imposed by funders do not always take adequate account of these obstacles. As a result, projects struggle to address problems that exceed the resources and authority of practitioners. Donor, government, and practitioner failures to develop an approach that recognizes these challenges will result in projects that are unsustainable and ineffective.

This essay discusses the barriers to educational improvement in the DRC and recent steps taken to reduce their impact on project implementation. Following an overview of these challenges, the essay examines current approaches to educational development and the role played by practitioners in their application. It concludes by suggesting lessons drawn from the DRC and identifying actions that practitioners can take to improve projects in challenging policy and resource environments.

Fundamental Challenges in the DRC and Why They Matter to Projects

Development initiatives in the DRC's education sector face many of the same challenges as those in other sectors, as well as some that are unique. The broad challenges include the country's geography and lack of infrastructure, health and food insecurity, weak local capacity, conflict and instability, and poor governance; challenges specific to education include poor school infrastructure, few instructional materials, lack of trained teachers and inspectors, and inadequate cooperation and communication between central and provincial governments. Dire student performance is the result. Insufficient attention to these challenges at the planning stage means that projects are often set on a path to budget overruns, missed deadlines, and unachieved targets before the first staff members are even hired. Stakeholders who want their projects to succeed must recognize that they are being implemented in a country with problems that, at first blush, may appear unrelated to education and thus beyond project control. Yet the government, funders, and practitioners have begun to recognize the pernicious effects that fundamental national challenges have on education in particular, and they are taking steps to design context-specific projects that can succeed despite these challenges. Nonetheless, the scope and significance of the DRC's general problems, as well as the fact that they are disconnected from the work educators do on a daily basis, makes them difficult to address in the current development climate.

In this section, the fundamental challenges are described, together with the problems they pose for project design and implementation. Though funders often acknowledge these challenges in their solicitations, the targets they set may not take realistic account of their impact on project implementation. Yet ignoring them compromises the potential for project success.

Geography and Infrastructure

The DRC's massive size and lack of transportation, power, and communications infrastructure can immobilize projects. It is enormously difficult to serve geographically dispersed beneficiaries who live in inaccessible rural areas without water, electricity, roads, banks, phones, or other systems on which projects depend. Extending 905,567 square miles and covered by a dense rainforest, the DRC is slightly larger than Spain, France, Germany, Sweden, and Norway combined, yet it has the fewest miles of paved highways of any country in Africa—a total of 36,400 miles, of which only 1,864 are in good condition. The main mode of long-distance transportation is the airplane, but all local airlines are blacklisted due to a long history of crashes and poor safety records.

These challenges limit the safe and efficient transport of project personnel and materials to beneficiaries. Furthermore, lack of transportation options results in exorbitant shipping expenses. Projects can spend $20,000 on printing teachers' guides and another $10,000 to ship them to schools. Given the inefficiency at all levels, they may take half a year to be printed, loaded, and delivered. As a result, all materials distributed by projects must be finalized many months before they are meant for use in schools.

Electricity is also rare in rural Congo, which means that projects relying on electronic devices like radios and tablets need to plan for charging or powering. Internet connectivity is slow, unreliable, and expensive in all parts of the country, including the major cities, though a recent plan to install a fiber optic cable gives hope that internet access will improve.

One consequence of poor internet connectivity and unreliable electricity is the limited presence of rural banks. Projects need to plan for how per diem and other payments will be distributed. One potential solution is mobile banking—though it is not always available, especially in remote areas where there is no cellphone service. As a result, projects need to consider multi-faceted solutions that respond to different locations, taking into account the available infrastructure and online accessibility. Solutions require extensive planning, time, and money, often difficult within project constraints.

Health and Food Insecurity

Health conditions have long hampered development in Africa and pose a special challenge for education projects. HIV/AIDS, malaria, polio, cholera, typhoid, yellow fever, Ebola, and extensive insect-borne illnesses are constant threats to the livelihood of Congolese communities, dramatically affecting children's school attendance and teacher absenteeism. Parents whose children are sick must often divert money for school fees to pay for their treatment, thus reducing the child's attendance. Teachers who are sick will be absent from their jobs or lack energy to teach. Unfortunately, medical facilities are inadequate and medical supplies often unavailable, especially in rural areas. Payment for any medical service, which is invariably expensive, is expected in cash in advance of treatment, and those who cannot pay are refused treatment.

In addition to suffering frequent disease, nearly 75% of the nation's citizens confront food insecurity—a million women between the ages of 15 and 49 are undernourished, and 700 children under the age of five die each day (AFDB 2012).[1] Such insecurity contributes to the overall poor health of the population and has an impact on the country's potential for productivity. Major dietary deficiencies mean that children may lack the nutritional intake needed for brain development, and their potential to learn is jeopardized. A child with severe nutrition deficiencies will not fully participate in the classroom.

To mitigate these problems, projects that serve malnourished students need to partner with local health or food distribution organizations to ensure that their beneficiaries receive needed treatment, perhaps by mobilizing community resources to begin a school-feeding program. However, this is challenging in communities with sparse NGO presence and insufficient food.

Insecurity

Conflict and insecurity is a concern throughout the country, especially in the eastern provinces of North and South Kivu. The presence of numerous rebel groups and clashes over mineral extraction have left the population rattled by violent conflict, displacement and isolation, child abduction, gender-based violence, and frayed community ties. Though schools are often thought of as "safe spaces," some rebel groups recruit children to become soldiers by entering schools and forcing them to join their militias.

Heightened insecurity makes it unsafe for projects to send staff to some areas. As a result, those that need the most support receive the least. To confront this problem, education practitioners have partnered with organizations like the United Nations Peacekeeping Mission to arrange armored convoys into unsafe areas. In addition, communities have been mobilized to identify how to keep their schools safe from both rebel activity and gender-based violence. Even in urban areas like the capital Kinshasa, the high unemployment rate has led to spikes in crime.

Lack of Local Capacity

Projects in all sectors have great difficulty identifying qualified professionals to hire as staff members. The low skill level of the population is linked to the country's lack of employment systems or mechanisms to link job seekers with jobs (AFDB 2012). It is also due to the general degradation and inefficiency of the education system. Of the 9,000 graduates from Congolese universities each year, fewer than 100 find work. This is due both to a lack of jobs and to graduates' lack of qualifications. Those who are qualified are in high demand, contributing to turnover in development organizations and extensive expenditures to train new and underqualified personnel. Project beneficiaries also lack needed skills. The majority of teachers have received no formal training in pedagogy, and many have no more than a middle school education.

Facing these challenges, projects have hired young eager staff and paired them with experienced veterans. Though it takes time, their capacity grows. This, however, creates another problem: As staff members gain experience, it becomes difficult for projects to retain them. To increase teaching quality, projects need to provide teachers with a great deal of continuous training and support. Teacher trainers, however, are in short supply, which means that a training project must train teacher trainers as well as classroom teachers—requiring time and expenses that are not always accounted for in a project design.

Weak Governance

As in many conflict and post-conflict states, the administrative system in the DRC suffers from disorder and corruption. Composed of appointed officials, the Congolese civil service emulates its Belgian counterpart and is built on seniority rather than merit.[2] Once appointed, civil servants cannot be fired. Thus, those responsible for administering and managing public services are not always motivated to do so—sometimes they are not even present at their jobs. To compensate for low salaries, civil servants regularly search for opportunities to supplement their pay, including externally funded workshops that provide them a hefty per diem allowance. This leads to a notorious absenteeism. Officials who are absent from their work in order to attend workshops make it difficult for education projects to get government commitment and build a working and sustainable strategy. There are committed and hard-working civil servants in the DRC, but they are often dragged down by the bureaucratic weight of the system as well as its entrenched corruption. As a result, they grow frustrated and often resign themselves to playing the game and waiting their turn to be appointed to a position of power.

Those at the highest official ranks are not protected civil servants but political appointees. Because the political situation is volatile, these officials never quite know when they will be excused from their positions. As a result, many try to make the most of their time in power to accrue personal profit and promote their family members to positions of power, whether or not they are qualified. The reward for public office is not the chance to provide service or earn a decent salary but to use power and privileges to support family and friends.

Corruption is rampant, from the highest-ranking civil servants engaged in illegal logging that they are supposed to regulate to the ordinary farmer selling someone else's land for his own profit. This pattern dates back to the Mobutu Sese Seko's promulgation of "Article 15" in the 1980s, a legal clause that called for the population to do whatever it needed to survive. As Mobutu told the army: "you have guns; you don't need a salary." This *debrouillez-vous* (each for his own) way of working erased the lines between public responsibility and private interest (Stearns 2011).

In the face of this accepted norm for public service, funder-imposed accountability standards for local practitioners and government counterparts are inevitably misaligned. For example, U.S. funders disallow the payment of local government employees. However, due to their low salaries, officials rely on external funding in the form of per diems, transport reimbursements, and the like. Education practitioners expend great efforts trying to respect accountability regulations while still engaging government counterparts. They need to identify committed education officials from the beginning of a project and engage them continuously. These relationships, built over many years, can make a significant difference in project success and help shield projects from those who are uncooperative. Though this cultivation requires patience, time, and perseverance, it is well worth the effort to ensure smooth project advancement.

Challenges and Responses Specific to Education

In addition to the general challenges facing all Congolese development initiatives, there are problems specific to education. These include poor school infrastructure and lack of materials, lack of systematic teacher payment, lack of trained school inspectors, and poor coordination between central and provincial Ministries of Education. All of these exacerbate poor student attendance and performance, and they prevent students from completing school and mastering the curriculum. More than half of the children who enroll in the first grade drop out, and hardly more than 5% get to the university level.

School Infrastructure and Materials

Since the 2010 mandate for free primary education, student enrollment in the DRC has climbed. School buildings, however, are often unsafe—only 35% have solid structures (MEPSP 2010)[3]—and increased enrollment has led to overcrowded classrooms. Many children do not come to school when it rains because the roof leaks. Basic equipment like chalkboards and desks are often in poor condition or do not exist. Most schools are sparsely supplied with teaching and learning materials, perhaps having only textbooks provided by the Belgian foreign cooperation agency, UNICEF, and the World Bank. These books, though Ministry approved, do not always line up with student learning needs or levels. Although the national curriculum mandates that children in grades 1 and 2 learn to read in their local language, local language readers are not present in most schools. Most students therefore are taught in French, a language with which they and their teachers struggle. These conditions make it hard for students to learn the basic skills of reading, writing, and math. Partnerships with local organizations and the government-led Project for Support to Basic Education (PROSEB) (funded by the Global Partnership for Education [GPE]) and Quality of Education Enhancement Project (PAQUE) are important to ensure students' school environments are conducive to learning.

Teachers

Due to the poor banking system and flaws in the government's payroll and accounting procedures, many teachers are not paid their salary promptly. About a third never receive a government salary at all (Brandt 2014), especially at the provincial and sub-provincial levels, due to unsystematic teacher registration.[4] Real-time information on teachers is not readily available, so there are many "ghost" teachers—those who have retired, moved, or died but are still sent salaries. For the most part, teachers are not formally trained, though they may receive ad hoc training from external projects. Innovative attempts were made in 2014 to begin contracting the teacher payroll to a well-connected and far-reaching religious network (Caritas), but this system does not cover every teacher and may still be paying ghost teachers.

Yet in the face of these conditions, many teachers are motivated and resilient. A recent study on teacher motivation concluded that although the majority of teachers feel emotionally drained, physically exhausted, financially and technically unsupported, and bereft of teaching or learning materials, 80% say they stay in their job because they want their students to learn (Torrente et al. 2012).[5] They are, for the most part, motivated to improve the state of education in their country, a commitment that should not be underappreciated.

The poor quality of teaching is partly due to the general inaccessibility of pre-service and in-service training. Although many education projects have tried to reform in-service teacher training, it is still not available to all. And the training that is provided has mostly been limited to single short workshops with often unprepared teacher trainers.

This situation should improve due to a current policy that mandates continuous in-service training, with regular teacher meetings at the school and cluster levels or through coaching mechanisms. Whichever form of support is chosen, it is essential that continuous and coherent teacher training be incorporated in education project design and implementation.

Inspectors

School inspectors are lacking in both quality and number. As school principals are assigned a strictly administrative function, inspectors provide instructional support to teachers and are supposed to hold them accountable for their job performance. Unfortunately, the majority of inspectors in the DRC are reaching retirement age and not being replaced as needed—inspectors are only recruited and trained approximately every ten years. For projects that want to make a long-term impact, training soon-to-retire inspectors makes little sense. Older inspectors also tend to resist new instructional approaches, clinging to their beliefs about what quality teaching looks like. This may soon change, as the Ministry of Education administered a test in 2013 to select a new cohort of inspector candidates. However, because of the job's low salary and arduous work, many of those who qualify for inspector positions search for alternative employment.

To help the government combat losing newly trained inspectors, projects must capitalize on this new cohort of inspectors by training them in their roles and responsibilities and instructional approaches while attempting to work with the central government to devise incentive structures that keep them in their jobs. This strategy is essential to ensure coherence in the educational system.

Cooperation between Central and Provincial Education Authorities

Because of a decades-long history of conflict in the DRC, the education system is de facto decentralized, but in a manner that exacerbates inequity and poor quality. Decentralization is also current policy, prescribed as a constitutional provision and recognized in the Education Sector Plan (MEPSP 2011). The argument behind this policy is that decentralization ensures the input of all actors in a vast country. However, the implementation of decentralization through the division of the provinces, the distribution of responsibilities, and the allocation of resources remains a challenge that is subject to ongoing negotiation between the central government and provinces. The central and decentralized provincial Ministries of Education currently have no channels through which to reach schools with resources and to re-engage within the sector. At the base of the system, the absence of inspectors to support teachers and hold them accountable for good teaching severs the link between teachers and support systems. Although this fragmentation is widely recognized by the Ministry of Education (MEPSP 2011), a decentralized approach is still included as one of the strategic focus areas of the Education Sector Plan (ESP). Although logical for such a vast nation, tighter accountability systems and clearer communication channels need to be established for it to function properly. Until then, disparities in education quality and services across the nation will continue.

In order to facilitate communication between central and provincial Ministries of Education, projects must recognize the need to communicate their activities, data, and results at all levels. Although this may not resolve the problem, it demonstrates alignment with the Ministry vision for decentralization and can help breach communication barriers among local DRC stakeholders.

Student Performance and Attendance

As a result of inadequate infrastructure, poor facilities, untrained teachers, and weak support systems, student performance and attendance are poor. A 2012 Early Grade Reading Assessment (EGRA) sample from three of the DRC's largest provinces (Orientale, Equateur, and Bandundu) revealed that the average sixth grader can read only 28 words per minute (approximately 60 words per minute is expected for fluent reading of sixth-grade-level material in French, as defined by recently set DRC country benchmarks) and that 50% of second graders cannot read a single word from a grade-level text (RTI 2011). When differentiated by gender, girls dramatically underperform boys. Likewise, the results of the 2007 TENAFEP (DRC's primary school leaving exam) indicated that 35–43% of students in the sixth year of primary school had not mastered the foundational skills outlined in the primary curriculum; its results were confirmed by the Ministry's Directorate of Studies and Planning of the EPSP (Enseignement Primaire Secondaire et Professionel) (MEPSP 2010). Although these results are dismal, the presence of nationwide data is a positive step toward identifying the gaps in student knowledge and designing a teacher training program to meet them. Projects should exploit these results for the design of instructional materials.

Concerning attendance, DRC's gross enrollment rate for primary school in 2014 was estimated at 106%, up from 87% in 2007 due to a "free universal primary" education initiative launched in 2010. Practitioners attribute this demand to the public perception that education elevates one out of poverty. There is, in other words, a cultural recognition of the importance of education, an asset that projects can leverage. Nonetheless, the enrollment rate falls precipitously over the course of primary school as the primary completion rate is estimated at only 66.8% (World Bank, 2013).[6] This is largely due to late school entry which seems to be correlated with dropout. In addition, although primary school is said to be free, parents are asked to pay fees for school uniforms, quarterly testing, and other items that they cannot afford (UNICEF 2013).[7] At the secondary level, the gross enrollment rate drops to 43%—and then down to 7% for tertiary education (UNESCO 2015a).[8] Enrollment rates vary widely across the country. About 31% of children in the eastern provinces have never been in a classroom, even though the national percentage of children who have never attended school is lower than the average for Sub-Saharan Africa (INEE 2010).

Challenges Facing Practitioners When Implementing Education Projects

Using the author's experience in donor-funded projects in the DRC, this section discusses a range of challenges that confront practitioners during project implementation as a result of the tension between the local DRC context and external funder expectations. These include misplaced objectives, stringent requirements, short timeframes, abrupt interruptions, duplicative and conflicting efforts, and the misuse of resources. This section also discusses current efforts to address these challenges.

Narrowly Focused Objectives

Each international funding agency designs education projects within the framework of its country's foreign policy and its own organizational goals. Bilateral agencies are accountable to politicians and, ultimately, to the taxpayers who finance them. Thus, education projects, by design, must show impressive results and ensure a degree of accountability in order to justify the funds spent. This requirement has led in recent years to a narrowing of objectives to ones that can be measured, with aggregated results that show a global picture of progress. While in some cases the funding agencies' objectives may coincide with those of the government and people they are assisting, in others they do not.

A good example of the narrowing of objectives is the global push by funders to raise literacy rates of primary-school children. This is a widely accepted objective, as the failure to learn to read threatens later school success; reading and writing are critical skills in all subject areas. In the DRC, the stress on this single objective, however, causes some funding agencies to focus narrowly on curricula, materials, and teacher training, and to turn a blind eye to the absence of infrastructure, the lack of functioning systems for teacher payment, and numerous other deficits that have a direct effect on student performance. One cannot expect children to read when they must sit under leaking roofs and when their teachers do not come to school.

While any single foreign aid project cannot meet all the challenges faced by the DRC Ministry of Education, neither can it ignore the contextual constraints to improved reading. Fortunately, this myopia is beginning to change as funders are recognizing the multi-dimensional causes of poor reading performance (unsafe and dilapidated school environments, weak local and district level education governance, lack of sufficient and timely teacher salaries) and are starting to coordinate their efforts to address them. Practitioners have played an important role in raising awareness of these issues.

Too Many Requirements

In contrast—or sometimes in addition—to misplaced objectives, education projects are sometimes overwhelmed by a ream of specific requirements that lead to a loss of focus and overextended resources. One of the DRC's education projects has three broad objectives: teacher training, student performance, and community engagement. While these seem manageable, they are burdened with many varied sub-requirements, some of which, conceived in a resource-rich environment or based on anecdotal evidence, misunderstand what is needed and what is possible. Other requests are added by the Ministry for political reasons. While local design input may strengthen the project's relevance and local "ownership," it can also create logistical nightmares and unfulfillable promises.

Short Timeframes

Because they operate in an environment of fixed budgets and pressure to show results, funding agencies require project objectives to be accomplished in a strict timeframe. Yet it is well understood that genuine and systematic education reform does not follow lock-step schedules and that it takes time to come to fruition. This is especially the case when the country's needs are huge and wide-ranging.

Rarely have education projects been funded for more than five years. In many instances, they receive less than three. Five-year timelines are not sufficient to support a single child through primary school. And projects rarely effect change at the school level in their first year because of the time needed to hire qualified staff, set up offices, and establish a good working relationship with government officials. Until these officials trust the implementing agency and agree with them on common goals and strategies, there is little chance that they will take responsibility for sustaining activities once foreign funds disappear. Building this relationship does not happen overnight, and short schedules leave little time for activities at the school level, which are often the key to government buy-in and the ultimate opportunity for improvement.

In the DRC, where the complexities of the political climate take time to learn, projects may be required to move forward at an overly rapid pace. Practitioners are overwhelmed with a multitude of challenges and with insufficient time to reconcile them in order to meet contractual targets. This is especially important when education projects touch upon the national curriculum or other institutionalized practices. One project spent the entire first year designing learning modules and related activities that needed to reflect the curriculum while still following international best practices for improving student performance. The project schedule allowed for this process, but the instructional materials, which were procured overseas, were blocked in customs. Despite the delay, logistical difficulties, and costs associated with solving the customs problem, the project timeline was unforgiving and did not allow time for the full intervention. Such implementation problems are not atypical in DRC.

Duplicative and Opposing Efforts

The education sector in the DRC is flooded with private firms, foreign funding agencies, and foreign and local implementing agencies. Each has its own approach to improving schools. The government agents with whom they partner often accept all collaborators, since they benefit from such project perks as funded meetings and are happy to take as many as offered. Despite the good intentions of those involved, a failure of coordination among donors and practitioners leads to duplication of effort and wasted resources.

This is well illustrated by the NGO and for-profit support offered to the Ministry for improving and implementing the curriculum. Sponsored by many foreign governments, each of the numerous organizations has contractual or grant agreements with its funder that mandate a pedagogical approach and accompanying materials. The Ministry of Education, however, does not compare and choose from among them, but instead gives its blessing to the proposals of multiple organizations. For example, it validated the teaching practices and student learning standards for reading, writing, and math proposed by one project, and then proceeded to validate the standards of two others as well without informing any of them that it had validated all three. This is reasonable from the Ministry's perspective: It welcomes all resources. Yet it leads to confusion among practitioners, as they work with officials at the local level who are expected to carry out the central Ministry's dictates. When the central Ministry validates several standards for teaching and learning, it results in inspectors and teachers not knowing whom to believe or what to do. This is especially true in the more accessible urban and town centers, where projects are more numerous and overlapping.

Practitioners in implementing organizations have worked together to solve this problem by coordinating their activities, as in the 2013 harmonization and validation of teaching and learning standards for reading, writing, math, and other subject areas. They also share information through regular cluster meetings like the CATED (*Cellule d'Appui Technique a l'Education*). Yet they also remain in competition for Ministry attention and favors that position them for future funding opportunities. Despite organizational willingness to collaborate, NGOs end up providing similar interventions, often duplicating and sometimes working in opposition to each other. Some problems receive ample, though uncoordinated, attention, while others are ignored. Those who suffer the most are the teachers and inspectors, who do not receive a clear message on what they are expected to do. As a result, teachers often resort to the traditional methods of teaching with which they are comfortable.

Fortunately, major funders in the DRC have come to recognize that lack of harmonization results in inefficient resource expenditure and uncoordinated support. In 2014, funders began to coordinate their efforts through the provision of a large multi-million dollar project that pools funding. This cooperation may also allow donors to advocate more effectively for program priorities that they want the government to consider. Though there is still much to be done on this front, the willingness to work together for a common goal is a step in the right direction.

Unintended Consequences of Allowances for Workshops

The multitude of externally funded education programs in the DRC gives well-placed officials plenty of opportunity to attend workshops and other events. The general purpose of these workshops is to provide training for particular groups of educators. What actually happens is quite different. High-ranking civil servants make the rounds of most workshops, collect per diem allowances, and do not apply the knowledge or tasks imparted to them. While these officials may learn something, they are not the ones ultimately responsible for technical writing and curriculum development. Those for whom the training is intended are often not present. They come only when event organizers insist. In addition, because officials participate in these workshops fairly frequently, they are chronically absent from their jobs. Attendance at workshops and conferences is further complicated by the lack of uniformity in per diem rates for participants. Ministry officials understandably gravitate to the programs paying higher per diem. UN-funded organizations, for example, pay several times the per diem rate of U.S.-funded NGOs.

Fortunately, the issue of proper technical representation at trainings recently improved. The Minister himself appointed a Reading Commission to carry out technical work associated with the execution of a 2012 reading road map. This Commission is composed of not only technical personnel from the Ministry but also professors from the University of Kinshasa, school directors and teachers, and linguists who specialize in the four national languages. Among their responsibilities was the writing of a national reading and writing curriculum accompanied by performance standards and benchmarks, the identification and production of instructional materials, and the design of appropriate assessment materials to track student progress. Because these tasks were deemed the Ministry's "established vision" for the improvement of reading and writing in primary school, prominent education NGOs and the education clusters began working with reading commissions to assist them in their realization. Likewise, major funders chose to support this initiative and ensure that roadmap tasks were accomplished by the deadlines set. This promising change serves as an example of how progress can be made when political vision and will exist and when funders acknowledge and support official initiatives.

Abrupt Interruptions to Education Programs

Another threat to the successful delivery of education programs is that they can be brought to a dramatic halt when violent conflict erupts. When a crisis disrupts a program, funding may disappear. While the INEE standards developed for the DRC in 2012 see education as a humanitarian endeavor, not all agencies agree. U.S. humanitarian assistance provided after violent conflicts or coup d'états, for example, does not include assistance to schools. UNICEF, by contrast, does provide disaster assistance to schools, particularly those for vulnerable children, IDPs, and refugees. Undertaken through programs like the Rapid Response to Movements of Population (RRMP) Program established in 2012, these efforts aim to assist newly displaced or recently returned Congolese by providing essential items and social services such as emergency education programs, psychosocial support, and access to health services.[9] The education programs set up learning spaces, provide vouchers for school materials, and support teachers and principals through training. Nonetheless, this type of assistance is not sufficient to cover the enormous needs of the country, especially as education development funds flowing through ministries are curtailed when government functions break down, leaving schools to rely on their own communities or humanitarian programs.

A political crisis can also shut down an education development program. Following the 2009 coup in Madagascar, the U.S. government halted its aid until the government was ready to hold democratic elections, which took place four years later. A more dramatic case was U.S. cuts to foreign aid in Pakistan following that government's nuclear weapons test in 1998. Although some organizations have been able to respond to these situations, obtaining funding for education during times of crisis remains more difficult than for other sectors. While U.S. policy goals—to pressure governments to engage in democratic elections or comply with international bylaws—may be reasonable, they may not be achieved, and, in the meantime, schools suffer.

The DRC's politically volatile situation and history of general election disorder make it vulnerable to abrupt halts in foreign aid. As in other countries, the consequences could be crippling, putting tens of thousands of children and teachers out of school. This is particularly troubling as schools help instill a sense of normalcy for children and their communities in times of conflict. Aid is often denied just when schools need it most. Children who miss school for more than a year are likely not to return, creating uneducated cohorts and generations susceptible to economic degradation and political exploitation, increasing the likelihood of another cycle of instability.

Putting Our Best Foot Forward: Recommendations for Practitioners

The potential consequence to donors of flawed interventions is that they are ultimately wasting resources. As practitioners struggle to meet unrealistic goals or shut down abruptly due to political instability, problems are never resolved, and funders find further reason to invest in similar short-term fixes. This process is disorienting for local educators who understand what is needed yet must circulate through ever-new organizations, each with its own short-term objectives. In light of the challenges and responses discussed above, some recommendations are offered for practitioners based on recent experience in the DRC.

Work Collegially with Practitioners in Other Organizations

Practitioners serve as crucial communication channels, conveying information about local realities to donor agents who rarely visit the countries they fund. While practitioners cannot directly make policy or funding decisions, they can work with government counterparts and representatives of funding agencies to share data, best practices, experiences, challenges, proposed solutions, and materials. In the DRC, practitioners can see the need for updating the teacher database to ensure that money is not wasted on ghost teachers. Likewise, they can propose equal per diem scales across the board to stop the flight of officials from NGO workshops that cannot match the higher rates of other organizations.

Building on the reading road map experience described earlier, practitioners can also develop a cross-organizational road map and work plan that mirrors that of the government. These plans should establish how and where to create linkages among activities so that the efforts of implementing organizations can be mutually reinforcing. Practitioners should also engage Ministry counterparts in building a unified vision. For example, organizations supporting reading at home would benefit from a road map co-developed with those writing school curricula in order to make sure that parents support what their children are learning in school. Such small-scale collaborations, if useful, might lead to larger ones and eventually to cooperation among funding agencies as well as implementing organizations.

Keep in the Ministry's Favor

In spite of inevitable frustration, practitioners must gain and maintain the respect of their Ministry counterparts. Experience in the DRC shows that winning this respect takes considerable time and effort. The government now has a strong education strategy developed with stakeholder input. Still, constant rotation of Ministry personnel makes it difficult to complete tasks. The strategy and associated roadmaps should guide practitioners' efforts to engage Ministry officials in defining their roles.

Strengthen the Team and Make Full Use of Human and Other Resources

If a task appears too big to complete within the allotted time, the practitioner team must be creative in managing its resources. With some exceptions imposed by donor agencies, practitioners can generally decide how to make use of their resources. This means ensuring that every staff member is doing his or her job to the maximum effectiveness and is authorized to make necessary decisions. For example, staff members who are visiting schools for training or coaching sessions can find out from project managers which other tasks, such as collecting monitoring data, they might assist with on their visit. Sharing information within and among projects can avoid duplication of efforts and contribute to more efficient spending. Sharing materials with other organizations or adapting existing materials can help reduce expenditures. And coordinating the transport of materials and supplies can also minimize delivery costs, as bulk transport is cheaper than smaller parcels. This collaboration will also contribute to a coordinated approach for beneficiaries.

Document Progress and Challenges

It is important to document project challenges and successes. Thorough documentation provides the information funders need to make decisions about changing course in current projects and planning future ones. Documentation should include findings from rigorous monitoring and detailed memos that explain logistical and other challenges related to project delivery.

Implementing organizations are usually required to present regular, detailed work plans. Over time, experience and factual evidence reveal what is achievable within a given period. Setting short-term achievable targets along the spectrum of a long-term plan will allow for appropriate tracking and account for progress along the way. Ideally, this process should lead to adjustments in objectives, expectations, and resources, so that end goals are attainable.

Work plans and reports on progress should be consistently communicated to the funders, government officials, and local stakeholders throughout the project in quarterly or biannual reports. This is particularly important, as practitioners have the on-the-ground experience to present recommendations for future projects. Even if project outcomes are not overwhelmingly positive, challenges and pitfalls should be rigorously evaluated and communicated. If taken seriously by funders, this information may lead to more realistic project designs and timeframes.

Build the Case for Additional Resources

When project activities are well managed and lead to visible achievements, it is more obvious when there are genuine funding shortfalls and unanticipated opportunities. Though it may not be easy, practitioners can persuade funders to supplement the budget to achieve well-defined objectives when costs are clearly justified. Unsolicited proposals are often a good vehicle for proposing novel approaches.

Take Opportunities to Promote Policy Changes

Despite the DRC's recent history of insecurity and volatility, education programs have not been curtailed. Yet with the country teetering on the edge of conflict, particularly in the eastern provinces, the risk of schools closing is high. This would put many children at risk. Teachers can recognize signs of stress in children as well as impart vital information on personal safety and health. They can also promote tolerance and respect for human rights, utilizing education to help mitigate future conflict. Thus, when political instability increases the breakdown of government services, as is the case in the DRC, practitioners should take opportunities to lobby their funding agencies and persuade them not to abandon education. If foreign aid requirements associated with political coups result in aid cuts, donors should search for ways to keep funding available in the education sector, even if it means pulling back from a government that has lost its legitimacy to work directly with communities. The education of children should not suffer because the government fails.

Conclusion

The state of education in the DRC depends on the willingness of practitioners, donors, and the local government to work together. As this essay illustrates, such collaboration often poses serious challenges in practice, despite the best intentions of all parties. Practitioners should strive to work collegially with local counterparts and partners, no matter the difficulties, documenting challenges and best practices for the sake of future projects. This work is vital if we hope to improve education in the DRC as well as other unstable environments.

Notes

1. AfDB, OECD, UNDP, and UNECA (2012).
2. This system is also partially rooted in Mobutu Sese Seko's "Zaïrinization" program, which proclaimed that all farms, ranches, plantations, concessions, commerce, and real estate agencies be turned over to the "sons of the country," a select group of politicians and cronies of Mobutu's clan. Ulloa, Kast, and Kekeh (2009).
3. République Démocratique du Congo Ministère de L'enseignement Primaire, Secondaire et Professionnel (2010).
4. Brandt (2014)
5. Torrente, Aber, Johnston, Shivshanker, and Annan (2012).
6. UNESCO (2010).
7. UNICEF (2013).
8. UNESCO (2015)

9. The RRMP is a UNICEF-managed rapid response mechanism, co-led by OCHA (Office for the Coordination of Humanitarian Affairs), which pre-positions funds, supplies, and INGO partners in the conflict-affected provinces of North and South Kivu, Katanga, and Orientale to respond to population movements. RRMP conducts rapid multi-sectoral assessments and implements responses in Non-Food Items (NFI), WASH, and emergency education.

Bibliography

AfDB, OECD, UNDP, and UNECA. (2012). Congo, Dem Rep. Accessed November 20, 2013 at www.afdb.org/fileadmin/uploads/afdb/Documents/Publications/Congo%20Democratic%20Republic%20Full%20PDF%20Country%20Note.pdf.

Brandt, C. O. (2014). *Teachers' Struggle for Income in the Congo (DRC): Between Education and Remuneration.* University of Amsterdam. Accessed December 3, 2016 at https://educationanddevelopment.files.wordpress.com/2008/04/cyril-owen-brandt-master thesis-teachers-struggle-for-income-in-drc1.pdf.

République Démocratique du Congo Ministère de L'enseignement Primaire, Secondaire et Professionnel (MEPSP). (2010). Stratégie de Développement de l'enseignement Primaire, Secondaire et Professionnel (2010/11–2015/16). Accessed November 14, 2013 at http://planipolis.iiep.unesco.org/upload/Congo%20DR/CongoDRStrate gie20102016.pdf.

INEE. (2010). Democratic Republic of Congo. Found at: http://www.ineesite.org/en/education-in-emergencies.

RTI International. (2011). PAQUED: DRC, Baseline Report, Early Grade Reading Assessment (EGRA). Found at: https://learningportal.iiep.unesco.org/en/notice/T1427990758.

Stearns, J. K. (2011). *Dancing in the Glory of Monsters: The Collapse of the Congo and the Great War of Africa.* New York: Public Affairs.

Torrente, C., J. L. Aber, B. Johnston, A. Shivshanker, and J. Annan. (2012). Baseline Report: Results from the Socio-Emotional Wellbeing & Perceptions of School Context Data in Katanga Province, DRC. Accessed November 2, 2016 at http://stein hardt.nyu.edu/ihdsc/opeq/reports.

Ulloa, A., F. Kast, and N. Kekeh. (2009). Democratic Republic of the Congo: A Study of Binding Constraints. Accessed November 16 at http://siteresources.worldbank.org/INTRANETTRADE/Resources/239054-1239120299171/5998577-1254498644362/6461208-1300202947570/DRC_Growth_Diagnostic.pdf.

UNESCO. (2010). Primary Completion Rate, Total (% of relevant age group). Accessed December 10, 2016 at http://data.worldbank.org/indicator/SE.PRM.CMPT.ZS?locations=CD.

UNESCO. (2015a). EFA Global Monitoring Report. Education for All: achievements and challenges. Found at: http://unesdoc.unesco.org/images/0023/002322/232205e.pdf.

UNESCO. (2015b). Regional Overview: Sub-Saharan Africa. Accessed December 5, 2016 at http://en.unesco.org/gem-report/sites/gem-report/files/regional_overview_SSA_en.pdf.

UNICEF. (2013). Rapport de l'enquête nationale sur les enfants et adolescents en dehors de l'école. Accessed November 12, 2013 at www.uis.unesco.org/Education/Docu ments/OOSCI%20Reports/drc-oosci-report-2013-fr.pdf.

Chapter 8

Participation and Partnerships

Power Plays in Lowland Bolivia

Elizabeth Phelps

Introduction

In the 1990s, community development circles buzzed with the term "participation." Amid growing concerns about environmental impact and gender equality, the notion of local, grassroots participation, including women's participation, gained traction as a key component of sustainable development projects.

Today, similar enthusiasm is generated by the notion of *partnership*. In some ways, participation and partnership strategies share parallel aims: Both seek to foster horizontal power relationships, especially around decision-making. At the same time, however, whereas the concept of *participation* suggests individual actors, possibly but not necessarily acting as a group or collective, *partnership* implies that the primary actors are institutions working together in a formalized way.

In this essay, I examine the concepts of participation and partnership through a case study from the Bolivian lowlands, where four organizations partnered together in the late 1990s to implement a veterinary promoter training project. Because three of the four organizations valued stakeholder participation (at least in theory), decision-making was organized around consensus-building and consultation. However, specific decisions about resources and funding became highly fraught during the planning, and at times it appeared that the whole plan would fall apart. By 2001, however, the project was well underway, and the planners were able to overcome their differences, creating and implementing a successful project for the benefit of farmers. By examining the challenges and pitfalls of the process, we can gain insights into how a commitment to power equality through partnership and participation works out in practice.

A second question I explore in this essay relates to the use of donor funding. Although development practice today is almost universally financed by external donors, it is important—perhaps imperative—to consider the ways in which power is gained and lost through accessing donor funds. Grassroots movements and organizations are especially vulnerable to the dictates of donors, given the "power switch" donors can throw on an entire project simply by cutting off funding. Since the NGO workers featured in this case study shared strong commitments to power sharing through participatory processes and inter-institutional partnerships, the implications of accepting donor funding must be examined.

Background Context

The push for the project came about because of the needs of small farmers in the lowland colonization zone of Yapacaní for training in direct veterinary care of their animals.[1] Beginning in the 1960s, the Bolivian government had opened the tropical jungle areas for settlement, giving away 50 hectares of land to any farmer willing to join a syndicate and carve out a living from the rainforest. The basic motivation for this initiative was to ease population pressures in the highlands, where Quechua and Aymara indigenous communities—especially those involved in mining—were agitating for greater political power. Giving away free land seemed like a good way to pacify this restless population, as well as extend the reach and control of the government into the extensive lowland rainforests. Most of the colonizing farmers began by planting rice, eventually turning the land into pasture for cattle once soil productivity was depleted due to mono-cropping. The majority of farmers planted, cultivated, and harvested their crops by hand, and most developed diversified strategies for subsistence, which included keeping small animals (mostly chickens and pigs) near the home and raising tropical fruit and rice.

The town of Yapacaní, located on a wide, smooth river flowing out of the Amboró forest reserve, was the municipal center of a region included in this colonization effort. It was bisected by a major highway linking the lowland city of Santa Cruz and the central highland city of Cochabamba. In the 1990s, Yapacaní was the main market town for the surrounding rural communities. Farmers in the most distant communities might travel several hours by truck or motorcycle, mostly over dirt roads (most of them built by oil and natural gas companies operating in the area), to access the rice processing plants, agrochemical stores, and veterinarians. In addition, as the Santa Cruz–Cochabamba highway was completed, a slew of development organizations erected offices in Yapacaní, following the pattern Robert Chambers describes as "tarmac development."[2] From 1992 to 1999, the number of NGOs working in Yapacaní exploded from four to nearly 30.[3] Inevitably, they were compelled to find some way of working together, coordinating efforts, or at least avoiding open conflict over communities in which they implemented projects and programs. At times the municipality played a coordinating role, but more often than not the largest and most resource-rich NGOs simply dominated the development landscape in the region.

The Players

For several years, the Mennonite Central Committee (MCC) had been supporting a sheep-raising project with women's groups in the region.[4] Part of MCC's project involved sending representatives from each women's group to veterinary technician (vet-tech) trainings provided by World Concern in the zone of San Juan, a six-hour drive from Yapacaní. The formal partnership between MCC and World Concern revolved primarily around this project, although there were also friendly relationships between personnel from the two NGOs. In general, the two NGOs shared equal power: Both were professional faith-based NGOs with a mandate to work in community development, and both used funding from a North American constituency. Geographically, both had national offices in the city of Santa Cruz and implemented projects in similar and adjacent colonization zones.[5]

Along with the two international NGOs, two local, grassroots organizations also became involved in vet-tech project planning for Yapacaní: Central de Educación Popular de Yapacaní (CEPY, the Center for Popular Education in Yapacaní) and the Unión Nacional and Pequeños Ganaderos (UNAPEGA, the National Union of Small-Scale Cattle Farmers).[6] (See Image 8.1 for a diagram of the organizational relationships between the four participating partners.)

In the 1980s, MCC volunteers had facilitated the formation of UNAPEGA as a cooperative of small-scale cattle farmers, organized around a rotating loan of cattle on the Heifer Project model. UNAPEGA also supported their members in the production and marketing of milk, providing quality control and a central location for pasteurizing and storing the product prior to sale. Over the years, UNAPEGA was able to access grants from GTZ (Gesellschaft für technische Zusammenarbeit, or German Technical Cooperation Agency) and other donor organizations, although the director and core staff were elected in a general assembly of the entire membership and worked on a volunteer basis. At the time of the vet-tech project planning, MCC was in the process of transferring management of the sheep group project to UNAPEGA because of the similarity between the

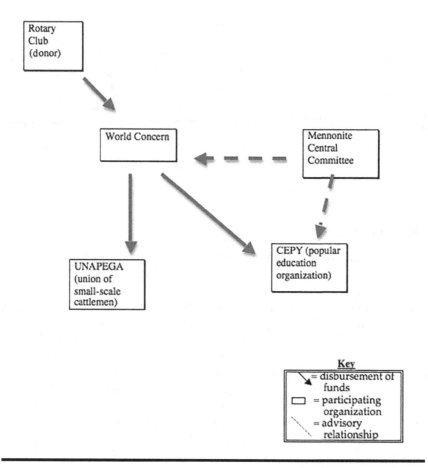

Image 8.1   Organizations Participating in Planning and Implementing the Yap-acaní Vet-Tech Project

sheep and cattle loan structures and UNAPEGA's interest in increasing women's participation.

CEPY, whose creation in the 1990s was also facilitated by MCC volunteers, was a group of ten small-scale farmers from the region who had been trained in popular education methodology.[7] Having obtained funding from Canada, CEPY educators traveled on bicycles to rural communities in the area, where they used colorful codifiers—drawings of community life and social reality designed to spark discussion—to engage farmers in reflection and social analysis, followed by a participatory needs assessment to determine what kinds of projects the community wanted to prioritize. The educators led the community in writing a formal project proposal and in seeking funding either through international channels (often facilitated by MCC) or through local government, which, thanks to the Law of

Popular Participation passed under president Gonzalo Sanchez de Lozada, had municipal funds that were designated through participatory processes involving the citizenry. CEPY capitalized on these trends in part by leveraging their cachet as an "authentically" grass-roots organization. Although CEPY and UNAPEGA had both emerged through MCC's work in the region, there was no formal relationship between the two organizations even though perhaps half of CEPY's members were also members of UNAPEGA, a byproduct of the fact that both drew from the same pool of farmers.

At some point, a fifth "shadow" participant joined the planning process: the donor, a Rotary Club in the nearby city of Santa Cruz, recruited by World Concern based on prior relationships (see Image 8.1). Although representatives from the donor agency did not attend planning meetings, they did communicate directly with representatives of UNAPEGA and World Concern. As we will see, the donor's power of the purse gave it final say on certain key decisions, regardless of what project beneficiaries preferred—and against the core premise of participation.

Although the time had not yet come when "partnership" was widely discussed as a solution to paternalism and colonial histories, the rhetoric of participation in some ways contributed to the formation of partnerships between more powerful international NGOs and less powerful but presumably more authentic "grassroots" organizations. A central concern in the partnership literature mirrors much of the 1990s rhetoric on participation: What one author (Fernandez 2016) explains as a concern for (1) solidarity and accompaniment, (2) mutuality and interdependence, (3) trust and respect, (4) humility and hospitality, (5) dialogue and openness, and (6) mutual empowerment, I prefer to rather inelegantly collapse into the single concept of "horizontal relations of power." A concept derived from the literature on social capital, "horizontal power relations" designates relationships where one partner does not dominate the other, especially to the extent that the subordinate partner is harmed in some way.[8] The extensive literature on participation echoes a similar theme, although even the earliest critics noted that participation is subject to limitations and controlled by the will of the most powerful partner.[9] The concern with control becomes increasingly relevant on projects funded by distant donors, who may have little local knowledge and certainly no "grassroots authenticity." A constant effort to mitigate power differences operated throughout the inter-institutional partnerships and planning processes of the Yapacaní vet-tech project.

The Project

The goal of the vet-tech project—as developed jointly by World Concern, MCC, CEPY, and UNAPEGA—was to provide small farmers in the Yapacaní area with training in basic veterinary techniques. The training was organized in a locally appropriate manner: Colloquial terms for diseases were accepted alongside scientific terminology; participants were encouraged to speak their native Quechua language, although the professionals guiding the workshops were usually Spanish speakers; and training facilitators did not assume that participants had access to high-tech surgical treatments for animal care but suggested instead low-cost and accessible options.[10]

Woven throughout the planning and implementation process was a concern for stakeholder participation, as both an ethical stance and a practical approach intended to promote long-term sustainability for the project by fostering local ownership and ensuring that decisions were contextually appropriate.[11] The commitment to participation was also reflected in the emphasis that World Concern, MCC, and CEPY placed on a popular education methodology. UNAPEGA did not share the same level of commitment, but it generally went along with these approaches since its members benefitted.

Project activities were primarily designed by World Concern and were never fundamentally contested by the other partner organizations. The project administration, in contrast, was hotly debated, almost to the point of thwarting the entire endeavor, a point I will discuss later. In terms of design, the Yapacaní vet-tech project replicated a project World Vision was already implementing in other regions that CEPY and UNAPEGA members had visited with MCC support. Structurally an agricultural extension initiative, the vet-tech project recruited a group of lay "vet promoters" from around the region (two from every community in the zone) to participate in a series of workshops on veterinary care for farm animals. Though attended by a licensed veterinarian, the workshop used local terminology and discussed "folk" cures as well as "scientific" treatment. Knowledge was supposed to be co-constructed by all the participants, who were respected as empirical experts even if they had only reached first grade. Workshops also included hands-on practice: Participants castrated goats and learned to vaccinate cattle. In the two months between workshops, vet-techs in training returned to their home communities to put their training to work.

One of the planners' favorite "success stories" from the vet-tech program involved Marcela Oropeza, a CEPY member who farmed 25 hectares about 20 kilometers from the town of Yapacaní. Marcela was cooking lunch for her family one day when two NGO workers came by and offered to vaccinate her cattle as part of a municipal campaign against various diseases. Although Marcela's land was too rocky and steep to make good pasture land, she did keep about seven or eight head of milk cows as well as a small herd of sheep and numerous chickens. She agreed to the vaccination and kept quiet about her own training as she watched a young man whom she deemed inexperienced vaccinate her cattle. Within a few days, the cows had all developed abscesses around the injection sites. Marcela was furious. When the NGO workers returned for a monitoring visit, she complained about their inadequate service and demanded that they pay restitution if any of her cattle died. Not only did Marcela have the knowledge she needed to take care of her own cattle, but she also had the self-confidence to speak up to men more highly educated, if far less experienced, than herself. In addition, she provided her neighbors with services such as livestock vaccinations and first-aid care. I observed her, for example, castrating a neighbor's pig for a very minimal fee, saving them a trip to town or a more expensive visit from a vet.

The biggest difference between the World Concern projects in other regions and the version developed in Yapacaní was the partnership structure. Elsewhere in Bolivia, World Concern designed and implemented projects on its own. In Yapacaní, three other organizations joined them. Because of the participatory process, every major decision and many minor decisions were subject to debate, negotiation, and at times threats and ultimatums. Sharing power in a substantive way makes any development project messier and more difficult, and it demands a great deal more time and commitment from project personnel. The tradeoff, however—at least in theory—is stronger local ownership, better contextualization, and greater sustainability. Nonetheless, a participatory approach is difficult to implement in today's climate of short grant cycles and demanding monitoring and evaluation structures. Twenty years ago, NGO personnel and local partners had far more time for the negotiations entailed in participatory decision-making. Today, donor demands for tighter planning, monitoring, evaluation, and reporting (PMER) timelines, as well as more technically sophisticated documentation, means less time for participatory deliberation.

The Negotiations

In order to manage the joint decision-making process, the four organizations involved created a coordination committee that discussed and negotiated project decisions. According to Ana Lopez, the project manager from World Concern, this arrangement was an unprecedented concession for her organization. In no other region and with no other project did it share decision-making power with local partners or beneficiaries in this way. Although World Concern consulted with beneficiaries through needs assessments, project design and implementation decisions were made exclusively by staff members. The other significant structural departure from previous World Concern vet-tech projects was to entrust CEPY's popular educators with the workshop planning and creation of educational materials ("codifiers," in popular education parlance).[12]

From the beginning, however, numerous points of design and administration provoked contention. First, because the original concept paper had originated with CEPY, the organization's members initially felt that funding secured from a Bolivian Rotary Club should be administered by them. UNAPEGA, however, also held a strong sense of project ownership—their narrative of project origins never mentioned CEPY at all, and it said that the concept paper had originated in their own office. They perceived CEPY as a rival or a threat. Because of early success in securing grant funding from a European donor agency, UNAPEGA leaders hoped to administer as much of the vet-tech project resources as they could; part of this interest stemmed from the fact that all the leaders worked on a strictly volunteer basis, with no remuneration for the hours they put into running the organization. Nicandro Zelaya, the president of the cooperative, felt so strongly about his organization's funding entitlement that at one point he threw down an ultimatum, threatening to withdraw completely unless project management funds were directly disbursed to UNAPEGA. He even went over the head of World Concern to meet directly with the funder and plead his case. Unfortunately for Nicandro, the funder denied his request, explaining that UNAPEGA did not have the administrative resources (e.g., a full-time accountant or paid staff to manage reporting) to manage project funds adequately. The grant would be disbursed to World Concern or not at all. Ultimately, UNAPEGA agreed to remain on the project and the coordinating committee but insisted on receiving copies of all financial reports. Furthermore, it extracted an agreement from World Concern that after a three-year implementation period, full project management would be turned over to UNAPEGA. This concession was fairly easy for World Concern to make since there was no guarantee that funding would continue at that point. Furthermore, given term limits in UNAPEGA's administration, Nicandro, the thorn in their flesh, would likely have moved on, and previous agreements would be easier to re-negotiate at that point.[13]

This dispute highlights important dilemmas of project management. First, UNAPEGA's insistence on receiving financial reports suggests an interest in transparency that project beneficiaries are not always empowered to demand. At the same time, its demand to manage the funds cast UNAPEGA's status as project beneficiaries in an ambiguous light. In the eyes of UNAPEGA leaders, the farmers who were members of the cooperative were the primary project beneficiaries; therefore, UNAPEGA itself fell under the "beneficiary" umbrella. Logically, then, at least in their minds, the beneficiary should receive the funds. From World Concern's perspective, however, UNAPEGA was another implementing organization, not a grassroots organization, and therefore not the intended beneficiary. The project had to pass all benefits disinterestedly to the "small farmers." Moreover, from World Concern's perspective, UNAPEGA was not even a very good implementing NGO, as it was run by uneducated farmers.

Similarly, CEPY had shown early interest in managing the fund but was told that it lacked the organizational structures to manage such a large grant. A small ten-person organization that lacked strong community membership or endorsement, CEPY was in a much weaker negotiating position than UNAPEGA, and it never contested the decision. Instead, CEPY relied on World Concern's appreciation for its popular education training to maintain a foothold in the project.[14]

By making decision-making more participatory, therefore, World Concern and MCC had courted conflict. Other disputes during the planning stages revolved around the rivalry between CEPY and UNAPEGA. When UNAPEGA, for example, discovered that World Concern had invited CEPY educators to join planning workshops and create educational materials, it demanded equal inclusion, even though its members did not have the same kind of training in popular education methodologies. And when it came time to select six community representatives to be trained as trainers for the vet-techs, more conflicts emerged. The initial plan called for rural community organizations to submit nominations in writing and let the coordinating committee choose the six most qualified. CEPY and UNAPEGA leaders, however, simply nominated their favorites from the communities and their own members. There was some concern that UNAPEGA nominees in particular were not qualified according to the agreed criteria, that they had been nominated for political reasons. At the same time, CEPY staff maintained—and the roots of this belief are obscure—that two of the six trainer spots "belonged" to their organization; they nominated two members who had previously participated in World Concern trainings in other regions. Despite its rivalry with UNAPEGA, CEPY held onto these spots because of a strong endorsement from World Concern, which resolved the issue by making it a non-negotiable point in the inter-institutional agreement.

Another heated debate revolved around the purchase of vehicles for the project. In other regions, World Concern personnel used four-wheel ATVs for transportation in rural communities on muddy dirt roads. UNAPEGA used two motorcycles. And CEPY members rode bicycles. In the original CEPY concept paper, the project budgeted for the purchase of several more bicycles; World Concern staff, however, revised the project to operate on a much larger scale and included a budget for the purchase of a double-cab HiLux 4×4 truck *and* a motorcycle. Several of my informants mentioned that Nicandro Zelaya talked incessantly about the vehicles. But when it came time for a collective decision, World Concern defaulted to proposing an ATV. UNAPEGA angrily protested that World Concern imposed its own criteria on the local partners, while World Concern staff objected that UNAPEGA was being ridiculous: Why look a gift ATV in the proverbial mouth? In the end, deeming it an irrelevant issue, World Concern conceded to the purchase of a motorcycle to be stored at UNAPEGA's office. When project activities required use of a truck (e.g., for transporting livestock), a local vehicle could be rented or a World Concern truck procured from Santa Cruz.[15]

Power Plays

These interactions reveal a struggle to level the unequal power relations. Each participating organization started from a particular point in the hierarchy, and each undertook different strategies for sharing, gaining, or ceding power under the ethos of participation and partnership. While World Concern and MCC, as long-established international NGOs, entered the partnership from a position of authority, UNAPEGA and CEPY had less structural and resource power but did enjoy a kind of legitimacy and leverage derived from their grassroots identities. Donor-funded projects, however, do not necessarily privilege grassroots authenticity, instead giving primacy to more traditional forms of power and capital—in this case, bolstering World Concern's position in particular. In the face of this reality, World Concern at times worked extremely hard to modify their typical processes and allow for greater power sharing; ultimately, however, professional grant management practices kicked in, pulling the project toward more typical NGO approaches. CEPY and UNAPEGA, although they both came from positions of relative weakness, approached the partnership very differently from one another. CEPY's approach was mostly passive, while UNAPEGA pushed aggressively to the point of nearly breaking the alliance.

Although the scope of this essay does not allow for a full historical analysis of power relations in Bolivia, the long history of domination and subjugation in Latin America bears some discussion at this point. The dynamics of the project partnership were shaped in part by the legacy of the colonial era; the farmers settling the Yapacaní region and the constitutive memberships of both CEPY and UNAPEGA were almost all indigenous Quechua people, whereas the professionals and volunteers in MCC and World Concern were white or *mestizo*. The Agrarian Reform that took place in Bolivia in 1952, when land ownership was re-distributed among peasant farmers, did not erase the deep history of patron/client relations running along ethnic lines. In other words, European-descended and Spanish-speaking families tended to be the owners of land, mines, and businesses, while indigenous and Quechua- or Aymara-speaking families tended to be unlanded workers, property smallholders, miners, and so forth. Ethnically mixed people occupied the middle range according to racialized physical markers and language use. That this pattern of power relations was recapitulated in an NGO donor-funded project—even when a participatory ethos is espoused—should not be surprising.

World Concern: Sharing Power by Fiat

A key irony in this process was World Concern's power sharing by fiat. Although it did incorporate participatory techniques in project planning, World Concern always had the power to decide when, how, with whom, and to what extent these techniques would be implemented, simply by virtue of holding the funds. Consider how, in a top-down, unilateral move, World Concern insisted on CEPY's continued participation in the vet-tech project, imposing this condition, without negotiation, on UNAPEGA in spite of the latter's attempts to exclude its rival. World Concern used undemocratic means (primarily ultimatums, threatening to pull the funding from the project) in order to secure a more democratic and participatory process for planning and implementation.

At the same time, World Concern was quite intentional about sharing power through participatory processes and institutionalizing those processes. An initial needs assessment was carried out with all stakeholders using participatory methodologies, and the method for selecting trainers was structured along democratic lines. The specific steps taken to ensure stakeholder involvement can be found carefully detailed in World Concern's project reports; it shows deliberate planning and intention. One UNAPEGA member, Vicente, described the needs assessment to me as highly participatory: "We had all the requests of the *compañeros*, that they suggested. . . . [W]e had a spirit of collaboration and understanding the suggestions and requests of the farmers themselves."[16]

Additionally, World Concern created new structures for project management—notably the coordination committee—that reflected its strong commitment to participation and partnership. Although UNAPEGA decreased its involvement over time by missing more and more planning meetings, there was a space for consultation and an opportunity to engage in decision-making.

Donor Funding and Its Discontents

Even though the external funding of development projects is often assumed to be the only way to practice community development, my experience on the Yapacaní vet-tech project led me to see donor funding as disempowering, especially with respect to local, "grassroots" partners. Most development practitioners consider the acquisition of outside funding as a means of gaining power and influence. However, relying on donor funds also means relying on the donor, and that inevitably places restrictions on how funds can be spent. Every donor has an agenda or driving interest, and if that interest does not match the recipient's interests, then these will be thwarted or undermined. By resorting to external funding, development practitioners give a great deal of power to donors, and grassroots input and control is lost in some measure.

This loss of power can be seen clearly in CEPY's case. Despite early hopes that funding for the vet promoter project would be channeled through CEPY, World Concern took over the project after CEPY handed it the original concept paper. Such a takeover does not always occur; but the situation was complicated when World Concern chose to expand the project and sought to ensure its professional quality. As a donor, it functioned as a power switch for the project. All projects proposed to donors require money by design in order to be implemented. If the donor refuses to invest, the project will not happen. Ana Lopez, World

Concern's manager for the vet-tech programs, clearly understood this power and used it when she threatened to cut funding unless UNAPEGA capitulated to her agenda. Fortunately for CEPY staffers, her agenda incorporated them. But CEPY's involvement reinforced the fact that it was at the mercy of World Concern's agenda.

World Concern, too, gave up some measure of power by turning to a higher donor agency—the Rotary Club in Santa Cruz—for funds. During its disputes with World Concern, UNAPEGA shrewdly went over Lopez's head by going to the Rotary Club to advocate for its organizational interests. Although this strategy was not wholly successful, it shows their understanding of the hierarchy. The one who holds the purse strings holds the power; resorting to donor funding automatically signs over a measure of control.

The belief shared by all three of these organizations—that acquiring donor funding is necessary for implementing community development projects—actually led to a loss of power for all of them and did not enhance democratic structures or participatory processes. While one can ask how the project could have been carried out without funds for transportation, pedagogical materials, and professional expertise, a different question might be more appropriate: How could the goals of the project have been reached on a smaller and more local scale without the need for external funds? CEPY's initial proposal offers one option: relying on human and material resources already present in the region, using bicycles instead of ATVs, and offering per diem compensation at a scale low enough that it would be within reach for the beneficiary communities collectively to remunerate the vet promoters.

At the same time, given the reality that development projects almost always rely on external donors, perhaps the most important point for practitioners to recognize is that accepting donor funds is always a negotiated process that takes place within relations of power. Donor funding is never power-neutral or value-neutral. It behooves development practitioners to be aware of these power dimensions, and grassroots organizations to accept funds with care and circumspection.

Conclusions

Today, the entire process surrounding the vet-tech project would likely look quite different. Although interest in participation and partnership continue, the increased "professionalization" of the field—especially surrounding planning, monitoring, evaluation, and reporting—means that drastically less time is available for participatory consultation and decision-making. The democratic deliberation that World Concern and MCC sought to institutionalize in the Yapacaní program would be severely shortened by today's project timelines.

Given how challenging and difficult it was even 15 years ago to carry out participatory partnerships, I wonder where the spaces might be today for this kind of grassroots inclusion. If the rationale for participation and partnership is to appropriately contextualize development initiatives in order to ensure local ownership and sustainability, what effect will the acceleration of the project cycle have in the long run? Donors may like the quick turnaround in reporting, with tables of measurable impact and outcomes, but if local-level partners—including intended beneficiaries—are not involved in design and implementation, then those impacts may be fleeting.

The Yapacaní vet-tech project was a real-world effort by dedicated and committed individuals to respond to the needs of a rural population. As such, it was fraught with conflict, disagreement, power struggles, and rivalries. But given the ethical commitments of the participating organizations, it was not the top-down development juggernaut that it might have been. This was one of its fundamental strengths.

Notes

1. Although individuals' names have been changed, I use the real names of places and organizations.
2. The full term is "tarmac and roadside biased development," indicating the tendency of development organizations to orient their work along lines of convenient access (paved roads) instead of prioritizing locations based on need. The hardest-to-reach places are often those where goods and services are weakest (Chambers 1983, 23).
3. Jantzi 2000.
4. From 1995 to 1999, I worked in Yapacaní as a volunteer with MCC under the rubric of "women's promotion and economic development," primarily with the sheep group program.
5. There are obvious questions to consider regarding the environmental impacts of development work in these lowland colonies. Were NGOs actively promoting the destruction of the rainforest by supporting farmers in these areas? One of my colleagues at the time remembers flying over the region and seeing enormous tracts of land cleared for cattle farming—though these belonged to a powerful politician in the area. Immediately adjacent to this politician's land were patches of diversified small farms in a colonization zone, where fruit trees provided shade and habitat for birds and animals. MCC's assumption at the time was that people would settle in these areas regardless of our presence, and that our work emphasizing low-input, small-scale agricultural technologies could help mitigate the most severe environmental degradation by encouraging people to maintain forest patches on their land. At the same time, farmers themselves often had a vision of their own development that included mechanized rice farming and large-scale cattle ranching. Defining a vision for development that took into consideration environmental factors was a continual conversation between development workers and small-scale farmers in Yapacaní.

6. The term "grassroots" can be used to describe a broad range of organizational structures and mandates. Two dimensions that are relevant here are membership and accountability. "Grassroots" often functions as a proxy for a Marxist understanding of the peasant class, defined by engaging in small-scale food production (in other words, close to literal roots of plants). In industrialized societies, "grassroots" is often extended to include the working class in general, as opposed to owners (of property, capital, and the means of production). A grassroots organization, then, owes its legitimacy either to peasant or working-class membership, or direct accountability to these classes. UNAPEGA, a cooperative whose membership and lines of accountability were wholly tied to small-scale farmers, could be seen as legitimately grassroots. One World Concern worker I talked with questioned CEPY's grassroots legitimacy because members were not elected (and therefore not accountable to the rural communities) and because their funding came from Canada, which tied accountability to an external donor. In this sense, CEPY may have had grassroots membership but not accountability.

7. Popular education is a philosophy and methodology for adult education (originally adult literacy) developed by Paulo Freire in Brazil in the 1970s, based on the idea that (1) adults are not empty vessels to be pumped full of knowledge but have knowledge and ideas of their own and (2) adult education necessarily includes "conscientization," becoming aware of social reality (e.g., power and resource inequalities and structures of oppression). Freirean popular education uses drawings called "codifiers" that reflect these structures and systems of oppression in order to prompt discussion and analysis.

8. See for example Flora 1995.

9. See also Cohen and Uphoff 1980.

10. Popular education purists would categorize the approach described here as "*appropriate* adult education" rather than *popular* education, because the vet-tech program did not engage in a critical analysis of structural power relations or seek to form a grassroots-based movement for social change. In that sense, they would not consider the vet-tech program to be truly liberatory.

11. They did not, for example, assume that participants always had access to potable water or electricity.

12. See Freire 1970.

13. I should note that although the account here is rendered dispassionately, there was in fact considerable shouting.

14. MCC, it should be noted, began reducing its personnel midway through the planning process, motivated primarily by the steady increase in NGOs in the Yapacaní region. Thus, its role in negotiations steadily decreased.

15. MCC stayed on the sidelines and CEPY remained silent throughout the dispute.

16. Personal interview. November 1999. Yapacaní, Bolivia.

Bibliography

Chambers, R. (1983). *Rural Development: Putting the Last First*. Harlow, UK: Longman.

Cohen, J., and N. Uphoff. (1980). Participation's Place in Rural Development: Seeking Clarity through Specificity. *World Development* 8: 213–235.

Fernandez, E. A. (2016). Theology of Partnership in a Globalized World. *World Development* 113 (1): 23–31.

Flora, C. B. (Fall, 1995). Social Capital and Sustainability: Agriculture and Communities in the Great Plains and Corn Belt. *Research in Rural Sociology and Development: A Research Annual* 6: 227–246.

Freire, P. (1970). *Pedagogy of the Oppressed.* New York: Seabury Press.

Jantzi, T. (2000). *Local Program Theories and Social Capital: A Case Study of a Non-Governmental Organization in Eastern Bolivia.* PhD dissertation, Cornell University, Ithaca, NY.

Chapter 9

Accompanying Reparations in Colombia

Mampuján and Las Brisas

Anna Vogt

"During the armed incursion, they assassinated people, generated evictions and displacements from our lands and communities, but they have never killed our dreams and desires to leave, nor our desires to defend and demand our rights, among which is return, with guarantees to our communities and return to work the land," stated Colombian community leader Juana Alicia Ruiz Hernandez in 2013, referring to the internally displaced community of Mampuján. "We are Colombian *campesinos*. Our grassroots associations, our organizational processes and the positive spirits of our leaders are proof."[1]

Unlike the majority of the almost 7 million internally displaced people (IDPs) in Colombia, Ruiz Hernandez spoke in the context of a specific opportunity for community change. In 2010, the first court ruling of the Justice and Peace Law ordered the Colombian state to engage in reparations, resettlement, and guarantees for the non-repetition of armed conflict for a group of 1,016 IDPs in Colombia's Montes de Maria region. This court order set a historic precedent for transitional justice in the midst of an ongoing conflict and provided an opportunity for the state to address internal forced migration through a new model of reparations-funded development that would supposedly bring victims back to a pre-displacement level.[2] Reparations included individual monetary sums for each displaced person and community-level provisions, including a health center, school, potable water and sewage systems, agricultural projects for small farmers, and a return to the community's original site. The court order was historic not only for the level of reparations promised but because it was the first and only time that the courts issued such an order on a collective level.

In Mampuján, the implementation of the state's court order—even if only in limited fashion—can be attributed to the determination of the IDPs themselves and their ability to organize and present their story in a way that generated popular support and built relationships with national and international institutions, including a long-term relationship with the Colombian NGO Sembrandopaz. Mampuján residents took advantage of the arrival of multiple organizations to advocate directly for community change, including their rights as IDPs and the collective reparations laid out in the court order.

Based on my experiences with Sembrandopaz in Mampuján, this essay examines the role of development practitioners in 'accompanying' or supporting displaced peoples as they advocate for their own rights and development. It argues for the value of an accompaniment model of development practice, while also recognizing the tendency of this model to marginalize disorganized communities.

As a development practitioner, I moved to Mampuján in September 2011 for two years, working with the Canada- and U.S.-based Mennonite Central Committee's (MCC) Seed program for young adults.[3] Each MCC participant was seconded to a local Colombian partner organization in order to work with communities across the country. While our main tasks were to carry out the objectives of the partner, we did so as community "accompaniment" workers, learning from community members and leaders, supporting daily work as we became immersed in local contexts. We were encouraged to build personal and professional relationships and learn about community dynamics before creating formal work plans, even as we searched for practical ways to support the community development already underway. I was seconded to Sembrando Semillas de Paz (Sembrandopaz), a small, local peacebuilding and development organization founded by the Mennonite lawyer Ricardo Esquivia in 2005.[4] Sembrandopaz is headquartered in the city of Sincelejo, on Colombia's Caribbean coast, and it works in a number of rural communities in the Montes de Maria region, including Mampuján, to build a culture of peace and reconciliation and to link local civil society organizations with relevant Colombian state agencies through local-level advocacy. The organization defines development as much more than simply reducing poverty. Instead, it espouses what it calls 'holistic development,' caring for the needs of a whole person or community: spiritual, emotional, physical, mental, and social. Part of this mandate is social justice, examining the structures and systems that keep people from accessing their rights and opportunities.

I moved to Mampuján with the goal of accompanying a women's sewing project launched in 2006 and expanding it from a trauma-healing initiative to an income generator for participants. It was unclear, however, what this effort would entail in practice, especially as the community was already in the midst of complicated court order proceedings regarding reparations. I arrived to a community in waiting, yet also one faced with a sense of urgency, in which normal daily activities, such as sewing, were on hold. Due to its small size and limited capacity, Sembrandopaz was not in a position to implement specific projects beyond offering legal advice to Mampuján leaders and providing an accompaniment worker (me). In contrast to the many state-based organizations then starting to visit the community, Sembrandopaz was a non-state entity. It did not have a vested political stake in ensuring that reparations benefited the organization itself in terms of either fees or other charges typically imposed by outside organizations; this flexibility gave its staff more freedom to respond to community needs than many state agencies. Instead of working with the quilters, my job became simply accompaniment, working with leaders to understand their vision for the community. Rather than pushing a specific development agenda, I was able to support the needs of the moment and therefore allow Mampuján to advocate more fully for its own vision of local development.

One of my tasks was to keep track of visits and meetings with outside, mainly governmental, organizations. This record, which I consolidated at the end of each week, included events that had never been scheduled in the first place. It revealed a community frantically trying to keep track of changes and activities that threatened to overwhelm it. Banks, the United Nations, the Colombian Victims' Unit, the Organization of American States, USAID, the Colombian President, and journalists and film crews came through the community in a steady stream, each trying to promote a new vision of development and of a state that was eliminating poverty and encouraging post-conflict reconciliation. How can non-governmental development organizations that wish, as Ruiz Hernandez states, to promote grassroots associations and community efforts support sustainable change in the midst of such chaos and anticipation?

"In such an environment, transitional justice measures can camouflage premature attempts to close the books on displacement, while the rhetoric of transitional justice can marginalize rather than empower the displaced, whose persistent problems are out of step with the notion of post-conflict Colombia," writes Megan Bradley.[5] The same charge can be made against the technical language of development as well. Thanks in part to capacity building from outside organizations like Sembrandopaz, Mampuján had an organized leadership and a community story that aligned with the hopeful rhetoric of a post-conflict Colombia. The rhetoric of transitional justice and development, however, can work in the other direction as well. The neighboring community of Las Brisas was marginalized in the legal proceedings, their struggles rendered invisible, as they did not fit the image of a developed Colombia that the state wanted to portray and did not receive the same level of support from development organizations.

This essay compares the experience of the IDPs in Mampuján with those in Las Brisas, included in the same court order. The comparison provides insight into how development organizations can support the forcibly displaced in exercising their agency and promoting their own development in times of rapid change. By understanding IDPs as important advocates of their own rights and acknowledging their perception of events, development practitioners can work fruitfully with displaced communities, placing their needs at the center of organizational goals and activities. I argue that an accompaniment model that recognizes clear political realities but does not impose an outside agenda can function well but can also overlook populations that do not have sufficient political and organizational capacities. Accompanying local communities during times of rapid change is more effective than imposing strict, external objectives, but, if it relies only on support from local leaders, it risks overlooking communities that are not as well organized.

Colombian Context and Conflict

The recent half-century of conflict in Colombia often came down to land: who owns it, who controls it, and who has the right to eke out an existence on it. Many of the roots of current violence and conflict in Colombia center on territorial claims. The Armed Revolutionary Forces of Colombia (FARC) and the National Liberation Army (ELN), Colombia's main guerrilla groups, were born after the Cuban revolution and sought to establish land reform and reduce inequality, yet, according to the World Bank, Colombia remains the second-most unequal country in Latin America, after Honduras.[6] The Gini coefficient for land concentration is one of the highest in the world: 52% of arable land lies in the hands of 1% of the population, according to the United Nations Development Program.[7] Forced displacement of civilian populations has been a strategic tactic for maintaining territorial control. As of January 2016, the UNHCR had registered 6.9 million internally displaced persons; non-governmental sources report even more. All armed groups in Colombia have used the forced displacement of civilians as "part of their military strategies to take control of or maintain a presence in certain territories. The practice involves expelling people considered to be an actual or potential part of the social base of the enemy, in order to ensure control of territories and populations."[8]

In the late 1990s and early 2000s, right-wing paramilitary activity generated a new wave of violence and displacement. A group of drug traffickers, ranchers, and large-scale landowners formed self-defense units across the country in response to earlier guerrilla tactics of kidnapping for ransom.[9] In Cordoba, on the Caribbean coast, the unit led by brothers Carlos and Fidel Castaño began to expand, and, toward the end of 1996, leaders announced the creation of a national coordinating paramilitary body, the United Self-Defense Forces of Colombia (the *Autodefensas Unidas de Colombia*, or AUC).[10] Paramilitaries targeted civilians and presumed guerrilla sympathizers and, often with the implicit support of state forces, stigmatized communities as guerrilla supporters and violently forced them off their land.[11] *Campesinos* ended up either selling their land or abandoning it as they left for urban centers or fled the country.

Montes de Maria and the Route of Death: Mampuján and Las Brisas

The Montes de Maria is a small mountainous region located between the departments of Sucre and Bolivar on Colombia's Caribbean coast. Due to its geographical position as a natural corridor between the sea and the interior, it is a strategic location for moving troops, arms, and illicit drugs, as well as for transporting cattle and farming merchandise. The surrounding lowlands have fertile soil, perfect for small-scale subsistence farming or large-scale palm oil production.[12] Many of the region's inhabitants, including those in Mampuján and some in Las Brisas, are Afro-Colombians, a historically marginalized group that comprised large numbers of armed conflict victims across the country.

On March 10, 2000, a group of paramilitaries from the AUC front Heroes de los Montes de Maria displaced the township of Mampuján. Paramilitary commanders rounded up the inhabitants, 245 families, into the central plaza, accused them of belonging to the guerrillas, and threatened them with death. In the end, they did not kill anyone, but they did kidnap seven people and ordered all of Mampuján's inhabitants to leave their land by morning. The entire community fled to the nearby municipal center of Maria la Baja.

According to AUC testimony, the paramilitaries also knew of an armed guerrilla encampment seven kilometers up the road from Mampuján, in the neighboring hamlet of Las Brisas. They ordered the kidnapped men to guide them there.[13] Although they found no weapons, the paramilitaries this time massacred 12 *campesinos*, torturing them and burning some of the bodies beyond recognition. The families and neighbors of the massacred men fled to the nearby towns of San Juan and San Cayetano. Community members recount the complicity of the nearby military base in the atrocities. One of the displaced men testified, "[A] soldier from the battalion asked what had happened, and I responded that there were 12 people assassinated, and he replied that according to his information, there should be about 25 dead people in Las Brisas."[14] In total, the AUC displaced over 1,200 people from Mampuján, Las Brisas, and surrounding areas.

In contrast to millions of other IDPs in Colombia, Mampuján residents managed to maintain community cohesion. Although some members of the community left to seek work in urban centers, and despite what many refer to as the destruction of their social fabric, the community stayed together, both physically and emotionally. Mampuján is a majority evangelical Christian community; its narratives from that day center on God's protection. Church members claim to have seen the hand of God covering the moon and angels in the surrounding hillsides. Following the displacement, many community members, whether evangelical or not, cite a prophecy that was declared in church in the weeks before the displacement: "Mampuján will be famous one day throughout the world." After the displacement, new leaders arose among the youth of the evangelical Church of the Open Doors (Puertas Abiertas). The young leaders started to advocate for the victims almost immediately, interacting with the Red Cross, the mayor's office in Maria la Baja, and other arriving humanitarian organizations. Leaders spent hours arranging for emergency relief, passing out food, and visiting other organizations to plead for help.[15]

The stigma of being accused of guerrilla activities, along with overcrowding in Maria la Baja, generated understandable fear and conflict.[16] Yet after three years in Maria la Baja, the 245 displaced families built a new community on a farm plot nearby, called Rosas de Mampuján. Purchased with the assistance of an Italian Catholic priest, it is now commonly known as Mampuján, seven kilometers down the road from what is now Old Mampuján. The Catholic Church provided each family with a subsidy to buy a small piece of land on the plot, where they built new homes, often out of materials from the houses they had fled. Despite better living conditions, high levels of poverty, unemployment, and trauma continued to plague the community. Without state assistance, residents viewed moving back to Old Mampuján as impossible. Despite fear of paramilitary retaliation, however, the men of the community began to journey to Old Mampuján every day to farm their former land, returning to Rosas de Mampuján in the evening. The majority of the community's women and children, however, shunned Old Mampuján completely.

From the first days of displacement and through the establishment of their new community, Mampuján leaders had a strong vision for their development. It was through their advocacy that the community connected with Sembrandopaz in 2005. At the time, Sembrandopaz was working with local non-Catholic churches, and it encouraged the Puertas Abiertas church to organize a social ministry, the ASVIDAS, or Asociación para la Vida Digna y Solidaria—Mampuján's only legally registered organization. The ASVIDAS could manage small-scale development initiatives, such as small loans to raise farm animals or install water tanks. Despite these efforts, most community members agreed that the initiatives did not reach many people.

In 2006, the arrival in Mampuján of Teresa Geiser, a psychologist from the United States who collaborated with MCC, established a new basis for Sembrandopaz's activities. At the insistence of Mampuján leader Juana Alicia Ruiz Hernandez, Sembrandopaz decided to support trauma healing among displaced women. Instead of focusing on poverty, Geiser taught a group of women from the Puertas Abiertas church how to quilt as a strategy to encourage them to share their experiences. During the displacement, many of the natural community gatherings, such as washing laundry at the creek, had disappeared. As is common in many Colombian displaced communities, members rarely processed the trauma they had experienced, and the continued presence of paramilitaries in the area engendered persistent fear and silence. Although the women at first met reluctantly, they soon started to talk about what had happened to them, cutting out fabric figures to represent community members and stitching them to cloth as a form of trauma healing. As part of these meetings, they decided to quilt their own oral history as an Afro-Colombian community, tracing their ancestral lives from Africa to enslavement in Colombia, rebellion, arrival in Montes de Maria, displacement, and the current quest to return to their land. Quilting allowed them to construct a shared community narrative, linking past and present. During this activity, they reflected on cycles of violence and examined their own responsibility for promoting peace.[17] While the men did not participate directly, they sometimes played the drums, a traditional instrument, and accompanied the women as they sewed, thereby contributing to reflections on community history. The women ended, as the last quilt in the series, with a tapestry that represented their hopes for the future: a return to life in Old Mampuján and a community living at peace. This vision included housing, land, education, health care, and human rights protection.

This intervention would have lasting ramifications. The women's quilting began to draw national attention; the quilts were exhibited in Bogotá and in universities in Ireland and the United States, generating high levels of attention for Mampuján and providing a way for the IDPs to form a cohesive self-narrative.[18] Their faith and forgiveness story also garnered attention from a state wishing to promote a peaceful vision of post-conflict Colombia. The ASVIDAS became a focal point for outside organizations seeking to enter the community, especially during the court order and reparations process that began in 2008.

A strengthened relationship with Sembrandopaz was another result of the project. In 2009, Mampuján invited my predecessor, Torin Thomas Schaafsma, to live in the community after Geiser left. He entered Mampuján just as the Justice and Peace proceedings began in earnest, after two years of initial investigations by the state. One of his main roles was to support the community as it decided how to engage with the courts. After consultation with Esquivia and local leaders, Schaafsma designed a survey to determine how many community members were interested in moving back to Old Mampuján and the needs that would have to be met to enable a return. The completed survey listed the families who wished to return and identified conditions they needed: electricity, sewage, a school, health center, land titles, police presence, and cellphone service. As I illustrate below, Sembrandopaz's determination to accompany residents in pursuing their goals, rather than impose an outside agenda, would become crucial during the years of the court order.

In contrast, IDPs from Las Brisas did not have an assertive leadership or a cohesive social fabric. Displaced residents did not move to one central location, such as María la Baja in the case of Mampuján. Even before the displacement, they lived further apart, on separate farms. On the day of the displacement, therefore, paramilitaries did not round up all community members in one location. Rather, each family made the decision to flee on its own. Las Brisas residents fled to several places—the municipalities of San Cayetano, Cartagena, and San Juan. Community leaders moved to the nearby city of Cartagena or otherwise distanced themselves from former neighbors. The displacement and violence caused a complete disintegration of community ties. Las Brisas also lacked the strong church ties that bound so many Mampuján residents. The majority of Las Brisas residents were Catholic, but there was no local congregation. As a result, IDPs from Las Brisas and surrounding farms faced greater instability, poverty, and isolation than those from Mampuján. There was also no trauma healing process, although the IDPs suffered from the impacts of massacres as well as displacement, leading to even higher levels of institutional distrust and rending of social fabric. In fact, the military forbade mourning at the funerals of the massacred victims and continued to question displaced family members about their links to guerrillas. While local authorities did harass Mampuján to some extent, especially when the community was still living in María la Baja, Mampuján's unity shielded it from the threats faced by dispersed IDPs. For those from Las Brisas, recovery was more difficult.[19] Like the majority of IDPs in the Montes de Maria, Las Brisas did not receive attention from the media or development organizations. The community was scattered and alone.

Demobilization and Sentencing Process

In 2005, the government of President Alvaro Uribe formalized negotiations to demobilize the AUC, and the Colombian Congress ratified the Justice and Peace Law (Ley 975), the first transitional justice law in Colombia's history.[20] The law stipulated that paramilitary members would receive reduced sentences of eight years in exchange for telling the truth about serious human rights violations. It included a special prosecution mechanism and established a Justice and Peace Tribunal.[21] The law also established mandatory reparations for the victims, to be paid out of a newly created National Reparations Fund. As part of the reduced sentence, paramilitaries were required to hand over goods gained through illegal activities, which would be stored in the fund.[22] The law also created the National Reconciliation and Reparations Commission (CNRR), responsible for guaranteeing the participation of the victims and producing a report about events that had taken place. Despite the more than 30,000 members of the paramilitaries who went through demobilization ceremonies, the law was more rhetoric than reality.[23] The process is generally referred to as a failed demobilization that respected neither victims' rights nor international law. In 2006, the Colombian Supreme Court and the Constitutional Court modified the law after ruling that it provided impunity for those guilty of crimes. The revised law was limited in its ability to provide justice, however, partly because of the difficulty of implementing its measures in the midst of ongoing conflict and the lack of political will. Many demobilized paramilitaries formed new armed groups and continued illegal activities under different names.

In 2007 and 2008, two of the demobilized commanders, Edwar Cobos Tellez and Uber Enrique Banquez Martinez, confessed their involvement in the displacement of Mampuján and the massacre in Las Brisas, initiating a state investigation process into the damages suffered in the two communities. They were the first applicants (*postulados*) to embark on a process of truth-telling and eventual sentencing as part of their demobilization. The majority of their victims, however, remained onlookers in the proceedings, even though they could technically participate, especially in the verification of the applicants' confessions.[24] Since paramilitaries continued to operate in Montes de Maria, victims were afraid of retaliation if they took part in legal proceedings. Rumors circulated, for example, that anyone who participated would have their photo handed to paramilitaries, who would then harm members of their families.[25]

Based on conversations with attorneys from the Justice and Peace Unit, Mampuján leaders understood the sentencing and hearing process to have the goal of returning the community to Old Mampuján and providing for its development, including individual and collective reparations to be used for basic services.

> Dr. Yolando Gomez, Justice and Peace Attorney 11 indicated that the goal was to achieve justice and to provide reparations for the victims. We understand this to mean a return to conditions before, the avoidance of new victimizing acts, re-establishment of rights, and regaining the trust of the state in the Justice and Peace process. They explained a bit of the law to us, that it was their job to investigate the activities of the paramilitaries, Edward Cobos Tellez, alias Diejo Vecion and Uber Enrique Banquez Martinez, alias Juancho Dique, who had demobilized in July of 2005.[26]

Sembrandopaz's interventions supported Mampuján's participation in the process. While Sembrandopaz was not an active participant in the legal proceedings, the organization—and especially its founder, Ricardo Esquivia—played a supporting role by encouraging Mampuján in its involvement. Esquivia provided advice on how to engage with the state, and the presence of a foreigner, at this time Schaafsma, living in Mampuján also contributed to greater confidence. Community members felt that if anything were to happen, international attention would be drawn to Mampuján. In a PowerPoint presentation put together at the request of the U.S. Embassy,[27] community members reflected on the fear felt by many and the difficulty of participating in the proceedings due to the lack of financial resources. The majority of the first hearings were held in Bogotá, an hour's flight. According to community members, there were no security or logistical guarantees for their participation, yet there was excitement about the promise of reparations and a return to Old Mampuján. State entities, such as the CNRR, arrived in the community in 2008 to investigate the impact of displacement. Community excitement, combined with an already cohesive social structure and the support of Sembrandopaz, ensured that Mampuján became one of the few communities whose leaders actively participated in the depositions, when the Justice and Peace Unit invited them to do fact checking, present questions, and ask for testimony clarification. In part thanks to the quilting project, Mampuján leaders were clear about the community's vision for the future and comfortable interceding with outside organizations. Participating in the Justice and Peace process was seen as one way of meeting future goals.

The Mission of Peace of the Organization of the American States (MAPP-OEA)[28] also monitored the proceedings and advocated for Mampuján. It provided some funding for travel to the city of Barranquilla when events took place there. During the hearing to verify and accept charges, only two community members were able to attend, and they complained of a lack of honesty on part of the paramilitary commanders on trial. "They kept all of the important information reserved for themselves," reported a community leader after his experience during the deposition, expressing a common sentiment among residents. "We remember that one victim asked how the [paramilitaries] had been able to pass from El Palmar to Mampuján, if the state had put in place military and administrative structures? There was a five minute silence and the attorney insisted that Enrique Banquez respond, but he avoided answering."[29]

In contrast, IDPs from Las Brisas received much lower levels of institutional and NGO support. Mampuján was centrally located and well-organized, but the Attorney General's Office did not search for more dispersed IDPs, despite testimony from the applicants about the crimes committed elsewhere.[30] During the investigation of community damages, members of the Attorney General's office refused to travel to the location of the Las Brisas massacre, stating that they had already heard the story.[31] It was easier for the state to promote its own success with an organized community, rather than locate more marginalized IDPs. Due in part to the intervention of Sembrandopaz and legal advice from Esquivia, Mampuján was ready to respond to state requests, providing names of community members when asked, using the ASVIDAS structure to issue receipts for meals purchased by states officials and official documents needed for the process. In contrast, victims from Las Brisas did not receive funding to travel or participate in preliminary hearings, nor did they have much support from an outside organization.[32] Many IDPs from Las Brisas were not included in the final court order, because they lacked knowledge of the proceedings until a week before the final hearing, when the Attorney General's office made formal contact with them.[33] As Patrick Lefkaditis, a lawyer from the Spanish NGO ILSA, stated, "It is worth noting that all of the interventions, as the pilot project, social mapping, workshops about collective damages and the visits of the magistrates, investigators, and the Vice Attorney General, took place with the community of Mampuján."[34] The same was not true for Las Brisas.

Despite this marginalization, Sembrandopaz support did allow Las Brisas residents to observe the final hearing and presentation of charges in Bogotá, livestreamed in Mampuján in April, 2010. The state invited all the IDPs named in the final court order—from Las Brisas as well as Mampuján—to watch the proceedings. Sembrandopaz supported the logistics at a grassroots level, and Schaafsma, along with other Seed members who came to the event, worked with local leaders to organize logistics and suggested that community members provide food so that local families would benefit financially from the events. Mampuján succeeded in contracting local women to cook nine days' worth of meals for 400 people from Mampuján and Las Brisas. The UNDP also provided funding (including the food money paid to local cooks), logistical support, and transportation for the victims in the court order. It also funded 20 residents of Mampuján and Las Brisas to travel to Bogotá to participate directly. The advocacy before and during the hearing, supported by Sembrandopaz, ensured that at least some of the events during the Justice and Peace proceedings would have positive repercussions in Mampuján, including the strengthening of local leadership and the financial remuneration of cooks and their families.

Sembrandopaz's interventions in the community, especially around trauma healing, also bore fruit within the court. During the hearing, Alexander Villareal, a Mampuján leader, presented the two paramilitary commanders with Bibles and publicly forgave them for their actions, a gesture that thrust Mampuján even more into the spotlight. Media and government institutions heralded the community as an example of Colombian reconciliation and a new direction for the country. The clear decision of community members from Las Brisas not to forgive was never mentioned by the media, nor was the community held up as an example of a new Colombia. Yet the different backgrounds of the communities were rarely considered: Facing displacement but no massacres, Mampuján residents stayed together and enjoyed external support. Las Brisas had a different story: Massacres and displacement dispersed families and leaders. As a result, many IDPs were unprepared to meet the perpetrators in court, nor had they gone through a healing process similar to Mampuján's quilting experience. While Sembrandopaz cannot claim responsibility for Mampuján's decision to forgive, the community received external support to make that decision, support Las Brisas did not have.

Court Order

On June 29, 2010, the Justice and Peace Tribunal sentenced Edwar Cobos Téllez and Uber Enrique Banquez Martínez, alias Juanco Dique and Diejo Vecino, to 38 and 39 years in prison, respectively, for their involvement in the displacement and massacre of Mampuján and Las Brisas. Due to provisions in the Justice and Peace Law, the court reduced their sentences to eight years each.[35] The tribunal also ordered reparations, to be carried out by state entities using the money collected from paramilitaries in the National Reparations Fund, including individual payments for the crime of displacement, symbolic signs that the state was guaranteeing the non-repetition of conflict (including a commemoration and public declarations that the IDPs were not guerrillas), and collective reparations to return the community to a pre-displacement level. The latter included a new school, a health center, a police station, formal land titles, agricultural projects, housing, improved roads, a sewer system, an ambulance, and a return to Old Mampuján. It is important to highlight the collective nature of most of the reparations. This order marked the first time that a Colombian court recognized collective damages caused by displacement and ordered the state to make amends.[36] These measures represented not only development possibilities for the victims but also a chance for the state to demonstrate its ability to meet the needs of IDP communities. The IDPs of all the communities appealed the first court order in an attempt to increase the amount of individual reparations, and the Supreme Court of Justice issued a second version on April 27, 2011. While the eight-year sentences remained the same, the second order downgraded calls for collective reparations from orders to exhortations, removing the timeline that had been established in the previous document. This change made it more difficult for IDPs to access their dues. The court, however, did uphold the need for both collective and individual reparations. The IDPs welcomed the news that reparations would take place but acknowledged that they never received the truth about who had actually given the orders for their displacement and massacre, making promised guarantees of non-repetition difficult. From the beginning, the ruling did not match expectations.

After the court order, many national and international institutions, including the Justice Department of the U.S. Embassy, began to build relationships with Mampuján leaders and invite them to share their story of healing. These invitations, by organizations with a vested interest in presenting a new Colombia, announced to the public that the country was developing, even as the IDPs had yet to witness the implementation of the court order. Mampuján leaders, however, took full advantage of the opportunities to create real change, accompanied and assisted by Sembrandopaz.

Community Implementation and Accompaniment

After the tribunal issued the court order and sentence, the difficult process of enforcement and implementation began, providing additional spaces for Sembrandopaz accompaniment as the IDPs began to navigate new territory. The order listed the different state entities responsible for the articles, but Mampuján leaders observed a lack of political will and decided to act on their own behalf. The only reparations to take place by that point had been symbolic: On August 28, 2011, the Colombian state issued a public statement declaring the innocence of the displaced communities and clearing their names of any association with guerrillas. The statement also cleared the names of the 12 men tortured and killed by the AUC in Las Brisas. Yet nothing had actually changed for the IDPs, besides entering a state of administrative limbo: The majority of the victims continued to live in poverty and uncertainty. An additional hurdle involved the creation of the Victims and Land Restitution Law, in 2011. The government of President Juan Manuel Santos viewed the new law as a legal avenue to provide reparations and land restitution for Colombia's victims, replacing the Justice and Peace Law and its institutions, including the Justice and Peace Tribunal and the National Reparations Fund.

It became clear that in order for IDPs to see any of the court-mandated changes, they would have to continue their self-advocacy. But in order to do so, they needed to learn about the court order and the rights contained within it. In this context, external development organizations could play a crucial role. Internally, Sembrandopaz staff dedicated time to learning about the new law and understanding its ramifications in the region so that they could help communities navigate the legal landscape. To build local capacity, the organization printed a copy of the 462-page court order for each Mampuján leader and hosted informal meetings to explain it, encouraging them to dedicate time for study and to formulate questions for the various state entities responsible for implementation. Organizations such as the MAPP-OEA also led official workshops in affected communities. Sembrandopaz's director, Esquivia, also hosted meetings with community leaders and suggested avenues for action. Despite excitement over the promised changes, however, the document itself was received with trepidation due to its length and legal language.

> In a survey that [community leaders] did in May of 2013, due to the complexity of the court ruling, the educational level and the daily

occupation of the inhabitants, the majority of people still have not understood the ruling and the dynamics of its implementation. Only a few of us [leaders] understand that the process did not end with the ruling, but rather, that we had to continue working, up to even educating state institutions so that they would understand the ruling, assume it as an obligation and assume their obligations that went beyond the ruling, to restitute the dignity of the victims as rights bearing subjects.[37]

As the leaders noted, this "understanding has been difficult." Nonetheless, with time and study, community leaders in Mampuján became familiar with the court order, quoting from it and pulling it out at meetings to show state institutions their numerous responsibilities. Las Brisas did not have similar success: Because Sembrandopaz and other organizations did not have a strong relationship with their leaders, IDPs from Las Brisas received less support.

Accompanying Advocacy

It was at this point of uncertainty—after the two court orders had been issued, their articles awaiting implementation—that I moved to Mampuján in the fall of 2011 ostensibly to support the quilting project. The women had finished their series of history tapestries and, in discussion with Sembrandopaz, had expressed interest in moving the project from a memory exercise to a small business. It became clear during my first month, however, that specific projects would be impossible due to the uncertainty within the community. Instead, my role was defined by accompaniment, as illustrated by the first major activity I participated in. The community invited Esquivia to facilitate a meeting on nonviolent movements in October 2011 as a way to encourage action around the lack of reparations. As a result of this meeting, Mampuján residents decided to march as a community to the departmental capital of Cartagena, a distance of 78 kilometers, in order to bring attention to their case. Community leaders invited their counterparts in Las Brisas to take part, but Mampuján took the organizational lead. Due to their Sembrandopaz-supported logistical work during the sentencing hearing, Mampuján leaders felt confident in organizing this march. They recruited the same women to cook, this time free of charge. I provided support that external organizations could not: As the only person in the community with internet and a computer, I spent most of my time emailing requests for support, constructing logistical spreadsheets (e.g., for food preparation), and visiting community members to glean their perspectives and worries. My role as a practitioner-accompanist, in other words, was to provide simple services that were not available in the community.

The title of the IDPs' public statement, written with the support of Esquivia, was "Non-violent action campaign for JUSTICE and PEACE for the victims of armed conflict" (emphasis in the original).[38] It spoke to the victims' feelings of powerlessness in a process that was supposed to benefit them. They were determined to raise awareness of their status by walking to demand collective, and not simply individual, reparations—including infrastructure inputs and a return to their original village. As the communities noted in their demands, the second court order contained no dates for implementation, and it issued exhortations, not orders, for completion. Marchers asked to learn the maximum dates for the completion of the court order and also demanded that President Santos be present during the commemoration of 12 years of displacement to preside over the successful delivery of individual and collective reparations. Communities also demanded clarity about new institutions created under the Victims' Law of 2011 and the roles of the municipal, departmental, and national governments.

The march demonstrated the importance of development practitioners accompanying local communities. The Sembrandopaz team, including myself and three other Seeders, helped as organizers, and we also actively accompanied marchers, alternating between walking with the IDPs and hurrying ahead to assist with meals and lodging. A Seed colleague held the megaphone as community leaders took turns encouraging the marchers and shouting slogans as they walked. Every evening, Esquivia sat down with leaders to help them articulate their demands for the day, while the Seeders helped organize cooking groups, keep track of receipts, document activities, and provide other logistical services. By helping take some of the pressure off the leaders, these support activities enabled the march to proceed smoothly. Esquivia's presence provided the community with legal support and advice as they negotiated with the governor and other state institutions.

Mampuján residents described to me their feelings as they left before sunrise on the day of the march, explaining that it felt like the day they were displaced because they could only bring what they could carry. This time, however, they were leaving of their own volition, to make their lives better. Throughout the three-day march and subsequent meetings in Cartagena, community pride was palpable. Every time I return to Mampuján, people reminisce with pride about their actions, whether they participated in the march or not.

During the rest of my time in Mampuján, residents brought up the march as proof of the community's willingness to demand its rights—and the presence of foreigners, the Seeders, was evidence of international support for their demands and part of the fulfillment of their prophecy that the community would become famous. This support encouraged residents to continue to advocate; they were not alone in this process. As Lefkaditis states, the march not only served to empower and bring community members together, but it "obligated inter-institutional communication to make visible the orders of the court ruling and allowed the victims to participate in scenarios that were destined to facilitate implementation.

As was solicited by the victims, a permanent working group for the inter-institutional coordination and articulation of reparations was created, called the follow-up working table (*mesa de seguimiento*)."[39] For the first time, authorities began to take the communities, especially Mampuján, seriously in their demands for implementation. The newly established working group called for monthly meetings on how to move forward, and the Justice and Peace Tribunal held a follow-up hearing about the court order in Mampuján the following January. State institutions began to set specific timelines for reparations.

Moving toward Reparations?

During and after the march, my role shifted even further from economic projects toward support for community leaders and local accompaniment. Due to my active participation in the march, most residents trusted me as someone "on the side of Mampuján." At the invitation of local leaders, I started traveling with them to meetings with officials. In the community, I spent my days documenting changes and visiting residents, including maintaining a community meeting schedule as state institutions, universities, journalists, and other organizations descended on the Mampuján for multiple daily visits. My position as an insider-outsider enabled me to translate information from meetings with leaders to community members not present at official gatherings. It allowed me to dispel rumors and misinformation, including claims that reparations had already taken place or that they would never happen. While the majority of the community trusted its leaders, communication lines were not clear, and leaders spent more time in meetings with state entities than with residents, creating an information gap. I served as a bridge between outside organizations, community leaders, and residents. My computer—and, by extension, my home—became the organizational space of community advocacy, where we printed documents, created surveys, sent emails, verified the reparations status of community members, and provided a space for residents to express their concerns. Over countless cups of coffee and informal conversations with neighbors, I became familiar with the community as a whole and the uncertainties residents felt about their future. My documentation and writing was included in advocacy reports in an effort to provide critical input regarding the role and promises of the state.[40] I continued to focus on the desired return to Old Mampuján, re-doing and expanding Schaafsma's earlier survey of community residents so that leaders could use it as a tool to pressure officials. Yet even during this post-march period, the work of Sembrandopaz focused on Mampuján alone. Support for leaders from Las Brisas was offered only in spaces where Mampuján was also involved, such as large events and commemorations. I interacted with Las Brisas residents only if they were at the same meetings as Mampuján or visiting the community. They were not included in any of my documentation or writing.

Accompaniment became more challenging as the process garnered more attention. Symbolic reparations (the acknowledgement of the harm suffered among the IDPs), such as the public commemoration of 12 years of displacement on March 11–12, 2012, should have been the easiest policy for state institutions to implement, yet it was full of challenges.[41] Sembrandopaz hosted community planning meetings, inviting leaders from both Mampuján and Las Brisas to their office, encouraging the communities to decide how they wanted to be commemorated and then inform the state. On March 11, each community would celebrate internally, in their original locations of Old Mampuján and Las Brisas. The state would provide a logistical operator to purchase food and deliver it. The main event would then be held jointly in Old Mampuján on March 12, with the presence of institutions, international guests, and a long-anticipated visit of President Santos, followed by a trip to the massacre site in Las Brisas. The event was structured as a symbolic return to Mampuján. Despite these plans, the commemoration was a disaster. The Colombian government's Victim's Unit did not have the budget or capacity to follow through on its promise of logistical and financial support. I worked with local leaders to send emails, organize spreadsheets, and figure out budgets, but no amount of preparation could compensate for the lack of state support. The food for both communities only arrived in Mampuján on the 11th, and, instead of enjoying the commemoration, community leaders and I spent the day trying to organize the delivery. Las Brisas received its food late that night, after their celebration had ended. Also on the 11th, before the joint commemoration, government staff informed the communities that the president would not be able to attend due to a previous engagement. Expectations for monetary reparations were very high, but civil servants announced that they were postponed, causing dismay among residents who had taken out loans based on the promises. It was a disappointing day for everyone except state representatives, who received favorable media coverage and used the event to promote country-wide transitional justice and community development, ignoring the hungry and upset community members behind the scenes. In the end, there was no time to visit Las Brisas. In preparation for the event, Mampuján had contracted bus drivers to transport the IDPs, a service to be paid by the Victim's Unit. Yet after the government operators had left, the drivers had stopped in the middle of the road and refused to budge without payment, leaving Sembrandopaz and community leaders to solve the crisis. Ultimately, Sembrandopaz lent emergency money to Mampuján leaders to cover transportation, as the Victim's Unit had not paid the drivers to take residents of Las Brisas home. As a result, they felt forgotten and marginalized.[42] Not only did Mampuján have to ensure their return, but the entire ceremony focused on Mampuján, without the visit to the site of the massacre.

By the end of the event, rumors circulated that community leaders had already received their reparations, as breakdowns in communication and obstacles to participation hindered their ability to advocate and act. In contrast to other events, such as the march, when leaders had controlled the finances and logistics, during the commemoration, control had been removed from Mampuján's hands. Yet for residents, that change was unclear, and several members of the community claimed that the leaders must have kept the money for themselves. Leaders invited everyone to community meetings, which I helped to organize, but it took several meetings and subsequent visits before tension calmed. While the community leaders were not at all certain about what had occurred, uncertainty was even higher among residents. In this situation, accompaniment required that I remain aware of community anger at the process and talk to residents to understand their frustrations. In an interview I conducted as part of the documentation process, a resident complained: "When we were displaced, it was really scary. But we all thought that we would be back in our homes in a couple of days. We didn't ever imagine that 12 years later we would still be waiting. Sometimes, I feel like this process is harder on us as a community than the actual event of displacement." This statement became a common refrain in Mampuján. The director of the Victim's Unit (Paula Gaviria) and the magistrate (Uldi Jimenez) both said that peace would be possible only with the participation of the victims. That participation, however, was difficult to guarantee without persistent community advocacy ensuring that all residents could engage in the process. Following the march, state institutions invited only community leaders to participate in meetings—often at the last moment. Established timeframes for implementation were ignored or delayed, leading to confusion and monetary loss.[43] Ruiz Hernandez stated, "We didn't allow our tears to fall because we are strong . . . sometimes we would laugh saying that these spaces for participation were really so that the victims would get frustrated and decide not to participate."[44] From my home, we continued to send emails and try to ensure the best channels of communication possible, often by simply using my phone since I was the only person locally with an ample supply of minutes. Yet information was difficult to glean, and the community was often the last to know about events related to the court order. The accompaniment model of development enabled me to respond flexibly to these uncertainties without being hamstrung by project targets and objectives.

Accompaniment was also important when dealing with the legal snags surrounding implementation of the newly created Victims and Land Restitution Law of 2011. Mampuján's leaders did not know how to proceed and whom to trust. The Supreme Court ruling had stipulated reparations payments totaling more than $32 billion Colombian pesos for the 1,016 victims included in the court order. The National Reparations Fund, however, claimed they had only been able to collect 1.5% of the total amount from paramilitary goods; there would be no remaining funds for the rest of the Colombian IDPs if the 1,016 IDPs in the court order received full reparations. The Colombian State Council declared that the demobilized paramilitaries should make up the difference, despite a legally binding court order holding state entities responsible for reparations. This created a legal loophole: According to the Justice and Peace Law, funds were to come from the National Reparations Fund, but the court order named the state as the responsible party. Without informing IDPs, the state offered to pay the victims using the lower amount in the Victim's Law, even though the reparations available were still under half of the amount needed. News of the reduced reparations filled my inbox, thanks to a Google alert, and community leaders quickly began calling their contacts in the Victim's Unit to verify it. Community leaders called an emergency meeting to discuss options, including contacting the jailed paramilitaries and asking them to intervene in the community's favor, either by giving over more resources gained through illegal activities or by using their contacts with local authorities to advocate against the changes. A day after the news broke, leaders invited Esquivia to the community to explain the legal dilemmas. As one option, he suggested petitioning the state and demanding more information. Residents filed in and out of my home to sign the petition against the changes. Esquivia encouraged them not to contact the paramilitaries and instead to use their legal avenues. Organizations such as the MAPP-OAE and the U.S. Embassy Justice Department were also willing to advocate on behalf of Mampuján. Their interventions, and the extremely negative press that the situation generated, ensured that all IDPs in the ruling would be paid according to the original court order; however, subsequent cases would be dealt with administratively, with lower reparations and less specialized attention. Collective reparations, the most highly praised aspect of the ruling and the main prospect for community-level development, would not be provided to other Colombian communities.[45] Again, even as the ability of Mampuján to advocate for its needs was strengthened due to Esquivia's advice, members of Las Brisas were not consulted, and IDPs from the area were not sure what was occurring.

I was present in Mampuján for the August 2012 launch of individual reparations payments, overseen by the Victim's Unit. At the request of local leaders, I documented the event and helped community members register before they received their checks. One of my key tasks after the reparations was to document the use of the money and the changes it effected. Residents built new homes, bought motorcycles, opened small businesses, gifted money to each other, and celebrated their change in fortune.[46] Stores in nearby Maria la Baja ran out of refrigerators, a popular item for new homes. Community roads were impassable, due to the clutter of building materials and the constant delivery of new furniture and goods. I continued to take photos and visit families as they toured me around their new Rosas de Mampuján homes. Leaders used the photos to advocate for continued implementation, demonstrating the changes taking place. We continued to put together PowerPoint presentations and work on spreadsheets and documents regarding the remaining reparations. I also continued with the community survey for the promised return to Old Mampuján, and I accompanied leaders to meetings. Finally, I spent time with illiterate members of the community, explaining how to open bank accounts to cash their reparations checks. By the time I left Mampuján in June 2013, 60% of those included in the court order had received payment; the Victims Unit distributed the remaining checks in the following months. Follow-up meetings for collective reparations continue even today. A school is being built, there is a health center, and the state has built new homes in Old Mampuján, yet work still remains to be done. Colombia's land titling agency issued titles for many of the informal plots in Old Mampuján to the residents who used to live there, and a few families have returned. The majority, however, continue to wait for conditions to improve: There is no electricity, running water, health center, or schools in Old Mampuján. Sembrandopaz, in its continued encouragement for a return to Old Mampuján, has supplied the first two returning families with solar panels, but there is no other infrastructure. There has been little progress or change in the lives of thousands of IDPs not included in the court ruling. Paramilitaries and other illegal armed groups continue to operate, even after a peace deal signed in 2016 between the state and the FARC guerrillas.[47] Juancho Dique was released from prison after serving his eight-year sentence. Mampuján's fame continues to grow because of its quilts and reconciliation work, originally encouraged by Sembrandopaz. The women's sewing group was awarded the National Peace Prize in 2015, yet no mention was made of Mampuján's political advocacy or the lack of implementation of the court order. The community is heralded as a sign of a new Colombia, without critical examination of the process itself.

It is not surprising that the courts and the Colombian government have made Mampuján their poster child for transitional justice, reconciliation, and community development. From a featured cover story in the *New York Times* to helicopter visits from the head of USAID, Mampuján was used to demonstrate the changing conditions for IDPs in Colombia. Its unity, the relative ease of access, the ongoing processes of social healing, a cohesive narrative, effective local leadership, and a coherent faith-based language—all of these factors symbolize a supposedly changed Colombia.

Nonetheless, IDPs from Las Brisas remain absent from public dialogue. It was easy for institutions to ignore the thousands of communities lacking Mampuján's many assets. Even today, Las Brisas residents report threats of violence after receiving individual reparations payments. "Sadly, in contrast to Mampuján, in Say Cayetano, those who have received reparations and community leaders are once again receiving threats. Ludis Monroy, a leader in the justice and peace process, has received so many threats that she now has a bodyguard."[48] At a meeting in 2012 in the battalion of Malagana, community members of Las Brisas living in San Cayetano described being threatened by armed men at a nearby palm plantation, throwing into question the guarantees of non-repetition included in the court order.[49] Community members assume that the threats come from previously demobilized paramilitaries, often contracted by large land owners as private security forces. Armed groups in the area also extorted members of Las Brisas for reparations money, threats that did not take place to the same extent in Mampuján because the community had developed a closer relationship with local police. In the end, Mampuján residents developed more trust in state institutions because they were able to garner favorable responses from them—and thanks to Esquivia's advice and Sembrandopaz assistance, they knew how to interact well with its agencies.

In the conclusion of his survey, Lefkaditis states:

> There are significant differences in the levels of satisfaction between those of Mampuján and those from Las Brisas and in San Cayetano. The satisfaction curve of those in San Cayetano presents significantly lower grades in all aspects of the reparations than the curve of Mampuján, except regarding satisfaction of collective reparations, where both curves present very low levels of satisfaction. . . . Las Brisas has expressed their nonconformity with the execution of the court order, the exclusions and the differentiated treatment they received during the implementation of the ruling.[50]

The case of Mampuján shows the importance of recognizing and supporting local leaders and responding to community-determined needs. The limited successes achieved as a result of the court ruling can be attributed to the commitment and dedication of the local families and leaders, who used pressure, public actions, complaints, and official demands to secure their rights.[51] However, Sembrandopaz's role in community support before, during, and after the court proceedings points to the important role development practitioners can play in fraught political circumstances. The flexibility provided by an accompaniment model allowed Sembrandopaz to support the political agency of local residents; sometimes, the most important assistance is a willingness to follow the community's lead.[52]

Sembrandopaz, however, also failed to recognize the marginalization of Las Brisas. The community remained isolated throughout the process and did not consider the proceedings a success. While accompaniment works in communities with organized structures, cohesive leadership, and sufficient capacity, it is difficult to support communities that lack these characteristics. In this regard, Sembrandopaz's work exemplified the common complaint that development practitioners tend to focus their attention on easy-to-access populations, ignoring more remote and needy communities. In fact, Sembrandopaz's interventions encouraged the state to focus almost solely on Mampuján.[53] Las Brisas's lack of satisfaction highlights some of the challenges of 'accompanying' IDPs, who often lack the very characteristics that accompaniment requires to be effective. A lack of organization should be expected from groups of people who have suffered displacement and other rights violations. The building of trust that is required by accompaniment is a long-term project that demands more than simple accompaniment, although NGOs can still play a role in documentation, communication, and bridge-building between state and community, attending to those on the outside of such processes.

Organizational coherence and community cohesion should not be determining factors in state compliance or development support. In displaced communities, part of the goal of social and economic development must be to restore the torn social fabric. How do our development interventions strengthen cohesion and ties among populations with whom we work? We must not fall into the temptation of either depoliticizing demands for reconciliation or strengthening a narrative where 'good victims' receive more attention than IDPs that are not as easy to reach. Accompaniment can play a crucial role in supporting local actors, but it must also entail a critical examination of those who fall outside the reach of interventions.

Notes

1. Ruiz Hernandez et al. (2013), ii. *Campesino* is a Spanish term meaning small-scale farmer or peasant.
2. In 2011, all remaining cases under the Peace and Justice Law were absorbed by the newly created Victims and Land Restitution Law, administered not by the courts but by the Victim's Unit, a new government department. Under this law, reparations payments, both individually and communally, are much lower, and IDPs do not have access to a special tribunal, as was established in the Justice and Peace Law. The 2016 peace accords between the Colombian government and the FARC aim to push development even further by focusing on the root causes of the conflict and rural and agricultural development, along with the rights of conflict victims.
3. MCC's program consisted of three components built around the three facets of Brazilian educator Paulo Freire's pedagogy: reflection, service, and action. Reflection included a three-month orientation period, with lectures and discussion on Colombian history, economics, politics and peacebuilding, as well as workshops and reflection space throughout our two years. Service referred to our time living and working in local communities. Advocacy was done through writing about our experiences and connecting with MCC advocacy staff in Canada and the United States.
4. The full organizational name in English is Planting Seeds of Peace.
5. Bradley (2015), 2.
6. Alsema (2016).
7. Semana (2011).
8. Andreu-Guzmán (2012), 4.
9. Kirk (2003).
10. Tate (2015), 92.
11. Tate (2015), 93.
12. Colombia, Comisión Nacional De Reparación Y Reconciliación (CNRR) and Organización Internacional Para Las Migraciones (OIM) (2011).

13. Corte Suprema De Justicia (2011).
14. Ruiz Hernandez et al. (2013), 30.
15. Ruiz Hernandez et al. (2013), 22.
16. Ruiz Hernandez et al. (2013), 21.
17. Lederach (2015); Vogt (2015).
18. Lederach (2015).
19. Lefkaditis and Gomez (2014), 69.
20. International Crisis Group (2006), 1.
21. International Center for Transitional Justice.
22. International Crisis Group (2006), 5.
23. Human Rights Watch (2010).
24. Andreu-Guzmán (2012), 13.
25. Ruiz Hernandez et al. (2013), 45.
26. Ruiz Hernandez et al. (2013), 44.
27. The Department of Justice invited community leaders to travel and meet with other IDPs to share their experiences with the Justice and Peace Law.
28. MAPP-OEA is the Spanish acronym for the Mission of Peace of the Organization of the American States, or Misión de Acompañamiento del Proceso de Paz de la Organización de los Estados Americanos.
29. Ruiz Hernandez et al. (2013), 45.
30. Lefkaditis and Gomez (2014), 79.
31. Lefkaditis and Gomez (2014), 80.
32. MAPP-OEA provided limited assistance.
33. Lefkaditis and Gomez (2014), 79.
34. Lefkaditis and Gomez (2014), 79.
35. In exchange for truth-telling and turning over goods to the Reparations Fund, the Justice and Peace Law established maximum sentences of eight years for paramilitaries who participated in the Justice and Peace process.
36. Lederach (2015).
37. Ruiz Hernandez et al. (2013), 67.
38. "Campaña de acción no violenta por JUSTICIA Y PAZ para las víctimas del conflicto armado."
39. Lefkaditis and Gomez (2014), 125.
40. Haugaard, Castillo and Romoser (2012).
41. Symbolic reparations included not only the commemoration but also a public apology from the state and a clearing of the names of the IDPs from accusations of belonging to the FARC, as well as a public monument dedicated to the victims in Mampuján and Las Brisas.
42. Lefkaditis and Gomez (2014), 116.
43. Loans acquired on the assumption of coming payments had to be repaid.
44. Ruiz Hernandez et al. (2013), 139.
45. Interview with UNHCR in Mampuján. Anna archives.
46. While motorcycles may appear frivolous, they play an important role in the coastal economy. There are no public transportation systems, so many young men use their motorcycles as taxis, transporting people and goods around the area for a small fee.
47. Human Rights Watch.
48. Ruiz Hernandez et al. (2013), 37.

49. Anna archives—community meeting at the Marine Infantry base in Malagana, July 2012.
50. Lefkaditis and Gomez (2014), 142.
51. Lefkaditis and Gomez (2014), 134.
52. As James Ferguson notes, technical development programs tend to supplant, rather than support, local political initiatives, often by imposing outsider perspectives on both the problem being addressed and the solution. Sembrandopaz's accompaniment model provides a way to practice development without suppressing local political initiatives. See Ferguson (1994).
53. This tendency was famously noted by Robert Chambers.

Bibliography

Alsema, A. (2016). Colombia Is Latin America's 2nd Most Unequal Country After Honduras. Colombia Reports, March 10, 2016. http://colombiareports.com/colombia-latin-americas-2nd-unequal-country-honduras/. Accessed March 30, 2016.

Andreu-Guzmán, F. (2012). Criminal Justice and Forced Displacement in Colombia. *ICTJ-Brookings*. www.ictj.org/sites/default/files/ICTJ-Brookings-Displacement-Criminal-Justice-Colombia-CaseStudy-2012-English.pdf. Accessed September 20, 2015.

Bradley, M. (2015). *Forced Migration, Reconciliation, and Justice*. Montreal: McGill-Queen's University Press.

Colombia. Comisión Nacional De Reparación Y Reconciliación (CNRR) and Organización Internacional Para Las Migraciones (OIM). (2011). *Proyecto Piloto De Restitución De Tierras De La Comisión Nacional De Reparación Y Reconciliación. Corregimiento De Mampuján, María La Baja- Bolívar*. Bogotá: Dígitos Y Diseños.

Corte Suprema de Justicia, CSJ. (27 de abril, 2011). *Sala de Casacion Penal, Sentencia 34547 de Segunda Instancias de Justicia y Paz, en contra de Edwar Cobo Tellez y Uber Enrique Banquez Martinez. MP Maria Del Rosario Gonzalez de Lemos*. Bogota, DC.

Ferguson, J. (1994). *The Anti-Politics Machine: Development, Depoliticization, and Bureaucratic Power in Lesotho*. Minneapolis, MN: University of Minnesota Press.

Haugaard, L., Z. Castillo, and A. Romoser. (2012). Still a Dream: Land Restitution on Colombia's Caribbean Coast. www.lawg.org/storage/documents/Still_a_Dream.pdf. Accessed March 12, 2016.

Human Rights Watch. (2010). Paramilitaries' Heirs: The New Face of Violence in Colombia. *Human Rights Watch*. www.hrw.org/report/2010/02/03/paramilitaries-heirs/new-face-violence-colombia. Accessed April 10, 2016.

International Center for Transitional Justice. Transitional Justice Mechanisms in Colombia. ICTJ | Transitional Justice Mechanisms in Colombia. www.ictj.org/colombia-timeline/index_eng.html. Accessed April 15, 2016.

International Crisis Group. Colombia: Towards Peace and Justice? International Crisis Group, March 14, 2006. www.crisisgroup.org/latin-america-caribbean/andes/colombia/colombia-towards-peace-and-justice. Accessed February 10, 2016.

Kirk, R. (2003). *More Terrible than Death: Massacres, Drugs, and America's War in Colombia*. New York: Public Affairs.

Lederach, A.J. (2015). *We Need Memory: Practices of Living Memory in Colombia*. (unpublished).

Lefkaditis, P., and F.O. Gomez. (2014). *El Derecho a la Reparacion Integral en Justicia y Paz*. Bogota: ILSA.

Ruiz Hernandez, J. A, T.R. Maza Julio, G. Pulido Contreras, A. Vogt, and A. Villareal Pulido. (2013). *Vivensias, Narraciones comunitarias de la historia, los apredizages y el desarrollo de la ruta juridical en el marco de la sentencia 34547 de Justicia y Paz, a partir de las experiencias de Mampuján*. Colombia: Departamento de Justicia de los Estado Unidos de America.

Semana. (2011). Tierra Concentrada, Modelo Fracasado. *Semana.com*, September 25, 2011. www.semana.com/nacion/articulo/tierra-concentrada-modelo-fracasado/247010-3. Accessed March 25, 2016.

Tate, W. (2015). *Drugs, Thugs, and Diplomats: U.S. Policymaking in Colombia*. Stanford, CA: Stanford University Press.

Tribunal Superior del Distrito Judicial de Bogota, Sala de Justicia y Paz. (2010). *Sentencia de primera instancia en contra de los postulados Edwar Cobos Tellez y Uber Banquez Martinez, Sala de Justicia y Paz*. MP Uldi Teresa Jimenez Lopez, 29 de junio.

Vogt, A. (2015). Quilts of Hope | The City Paper Bogotá. *The City Paper Bogotá*, February 14, 2015. https://thecitypaperbogota.com/features/quilts-of-hope76778/8413. Accessed March 23, 2016.

Chapter 10

Development and Peacebuilding

Disparities, Similarities, and Overlapping Spaces

Carl Stauffer

Definition of terms

- **Development**: The unfolding growth and expansion of human and material capital, capacity, and resources over time.
- **Peacebuilding**: The social construction of harmonious relationships and just societal structures that serve to mitigate destructive conflict and violence.

Introduction: Peace before Development or Development before Peace?

The unexpected assassination of Prince Mhlambi in an internal leadership 'coup' sent shock waves through the community of Phola Park; 1992 was a turbulent year, and South Africa was lurching toward democracy in hopeful yet painful starts. Dreams of freedom and fears of violence punctuated the political transition unfolding in the wake of apartheid. Prince, a grassroots leader, was a member of the Resident's Committee of Phola Park, a squatter settlement situated on the east side of Johannesburg. My peacebuilding colleagues from Wilgespruit Fellowship Centre (WFC)—an ecumenical NGO working for peace, justice, and development—had worked closely with Prince, and they were caught off guard by the news of his death.[1] Reeling from the shock, they began to ask searching questions about the nature of their work. How could a community living in such squalor and insecurity sabotage its own development? Why would a community violently undermine its only prospects for a durable peace? Why did the valiant efforts of 'progressive' development and peacebuilding practitioners seem to be failing?

The Phola Park community represented a microcosm of the complicated metamorphosis of South Africa. An archetypal 'informal settlement' (as shack communities are termed in South Africa), Phola Park pulsated under the dizzying effects of the long-awaited unbanning of resistance movements, the release of Mandela in 1990, and the dissolution of the apartheid regime that had imposed a structural racism for over 40 years. Suddenly, the many social conflicts long frozen in amber (over identity, culture, power, land, labor, and livelihoods) were freely aired and bartered in the market place—the 'public square' of this transitioning nation. These debates sometimes turned violent, and, as a consequence of the high levels of insecurity, Phola Park became a deeply politicized and heavily armed community.

At the time, Phola Park consisted of approximately 15,000 to 20,000 residents who lived in 4,000 temporary structures made of tin, wood, plastic, and other forms of fabric canvass. From its inception in 1987, when it encompassed 150 families, the community struggled to survive in the face of questions over its legal status and regular external threats. The residents faced three attempts at forced removal by white local government officials in its first year of existence alone.[2]

Phola Park quickly became emblematic of the violence and complexity that characterized the transition from authoritarian to democratic rule in the new South Africa. By August 1990, clashes erupted between Phola Park residents—aligned with the United Democratic Front (UDF), a coalition of political parties led by the African National Congress (ANC)—and the residents of adjacent single-sex hostels for migrant mine laborers, who predominantly aligned with the Inkatha Freedom Party (IFP), the chief opposition to the UDF.

What followed was a low-scale war that quickly caught the attention of the apartheid government security forces, resulting in a series of violent, state sanctioned reprisals designed to quash the so-called "black-on-black" violence in the name of "law and order." However, multiple primary and secondary sources (including the final report of the Truth and Reconciliation Commission) have indicated that much of this violence was fueled by 'third-force' elements—in this case, the white security apparatus that helped to arm the IFP against the UDF in order to make the country appear ungovernable by a black majority.[3]

This intermittent violence proved a formidable hurdle to peace and development in Phola Park until early 1995. Starting in 1991, numerous development endeavors attempted to foster peace in the community. The first was initiated between May and September of 1991 with a grant of R23 million secured from the Independent Development Trust (IDT), an established South African development agency.[4] The blueprint for this program was drawn up outside Phola Park and presented to the community with high expectations. Facilitating the project was a Johannesburg-based urban consulting firm, Planact, which boasted the 'best practices' in people-centered urban planning and development, practices that engaged beneficiaries as co-analyzers, co-designers, and co-partners (including joint decision-making and community ownership) in the implementation of local development activities. Planact represented the young and racially diverse metropolitan professionals of the new South Africa, who espoused liberal values and global-cultural competencies. Nonetheless, it seemed like every development initiative launched by the IDT and Planact in Phola Park was hijacked by violence.

Bremner and Visser, peacebuilding facilitators in the community, described the program as follows:

> The year is 1991, and the residents of Phola Park seem to have won the lottery. The IDT has blessed them with R23 million for development, to include houses, water, sewerage, electricity, jobs, recreation facilities, health facilities, schools, and a community centre. Planact has designed a model project that is going to revolutionise urban development in South Africa. The community is highly organised and motivated to make the best of their good fortune. Negotiations between the IDT, Planact, the Phola Park residents' committee, the TPA, and another half dozen actors are proceeding apace . . . *not quite.* Some residents' committee members were assassinated and the rest replaced in a "coup" in 1992. The new committee chased away all developers, lawyers, NGOs, and other outsiders. Not one house has been built. Only about thirty water taps service 15,000 people. There are no toilets, electricity, or facilities. Not only was the negotiated development process for Phola Park unsustainable, it was absolutely devastating.[5]

By early 1995, due to these eruptions, the infrastructural development of Phola Park was at a standstill despite the initial promise of the Planact strategy. The R23 million remained in trust with IDT, and Planact withdrew from the project. WFC, which had not worked directly with IDT or Planact, remained engaged with the community, accompanying and coaching local partners as they negotiated new projects.

After the implosion of the IDT and Planact effort in Phola Park, critics were quick to point out what appeared to be another disastrous development program imposed on an African community by external actors. At this point, the African communities were deeply politicized and entrenched in Liberationist, neo-colonialist ideology. Anything white-run or owned (especially if South African) was met with a great deal of suspicion. The IDT, after all, was founded in 1990, still considered the white apartheid era in the eyes of many.

In response to this criticism, Winnie Mandela, the estranged wife of Nelson Mandela, offered to subsidize a radical housing scheme for Phola Park starting in 1995. Working through the Coordinated Anti-Poverty Programs (CAPP), a development agency she founded in 1993, Mandela appeared to be vying for a share in the $25 million housing program proposed by the ANC government. A key political promise of the ANC was to provide affordable, government-subsidized housing for South Africa's poorest. Mandela promised the people that she would not hire white-owned and operated subcontractors, and she claimed that for the same $1,400 housing subsidy per household promised by the government, she would give people four-room houses with internal plumbing rather than two-room houses with outdoor plumbing. Mandela's plan supposedly involved not only houses but schools and clinics as well. To the amazement of many involved, this effort also failed and ended in a political controversy over police accusations of corruption on the part of Mandela herself.[6]

What Went Wrong in Phola Park?

While it is tempting to analyze this scenario from a historical context, citing the political economy of colonial racism, the legacies of institutionalized racism, and the power dynamics of liberation movements—and while it would be both stimulating and profitable to debate the effects of political turf battles, third-party spoilers, and the easy access to small arms on the multiplication of violence in South Africa—I maintain that these would serve as distractions from what I believe is the core lesson for development workers from this experience: that underneath the drama surrounding the Phola Park conflicts, there were essential human needs that were neglected by development and peacebuilding programs implemented in the community. Unless our interventions were reconfigured to address these needs, we would continue to work at parallel with—or, worse, at cross purposes to—these critical areas of need.

Those of us working in the Phola Park community needed to retreat from the frontlines and ask a different set of questions. First, we needed to clarify what we meant by the notion of 'community.' What is community? How is it defined? How does it function? Second, we needed to re-think the processes of development and peacebuilding that were being used. What were the worldviews imposed by our efforts? What were the values and ethics that drove our programs? How could even our best intentions 'bite back' with grave unintended consequences? Third, we had to come to terms with the realization that our development efforts were not objectively benevolent—that 'good' development practice could just as easily be a source of violence as it could a resource for peace, depending on the circumstances surrounding its application.

Conflict Sensitive Development

At the foundation of WFC's reflective analysis on the seeming development 'failure' of Phola Park were the multiple discourses of 'community' and the meanings given to collective unity, representation, participation, and mobilization. For us, Prince Mhlambi and the Resident's Committee represented the legitimate spokespersons and leadership of the community. After all, they were democratically elected, and they were what appeared to be the voice of reason in the midst of a chaotic transition beset by political violence. As Bremner stated:

> To the outsider organisations, Phola Park presented itself as a well organized and highly unified community—having withstood threat after threat, attack on attack, from various authority structures, political rivals, and the security forces. And in the face of common enemies and major attacks, Phola Park *was* unified for its defense.[7]

In addition, the Resident's Committee was responsible for attracting the IDT contract for the development funding:

> The Residents Committee . . . worked tirelessly to take advantage of the efforts of Planact, a group of urban developers, who were promoting an upgrading and development project for the community. The residents committee and Planact together put a proposal to the Independent Development Trust (IDT), which secured a grant of R15million (which was then increased to R23 million), for building houses, water-borne sewerage, water, streets, electrification, and recreation facilities.[8]

Once WFC paused to analyze what we thought was the representative community of Phola Park, however, and listen to the myriad 'feedback loops,' or informal social networks, that we had *not* heeded before, it became clear that beyond the Resident's Committee, we were dealing with at least four additional communities that had conflicting interests, disparate priorities, and competing power bases. Against the backdrop of high levels of politicization and a heavily armed community, these competing subgroups provided fertile ground for dissension, sabotage, and violence.

The first and most obvious of these groupings was the **political parties**, who in the wake of their official unbanning and the impending all-inclusive elections were vying for votes and wanted to appear as if they were responsible for the material and physical development of the community. The Resident's Committee, which represented the civil society, posed a threat to the political parties' attempts to find favor among the citizenry. A second, less obvious group was the **migrant laborers** who had come to the city in search of jobs but had left land, homes, and kin back in rural homesteads. They had no interest in using their hard-earned pittance to upgrade the transient city shacks and community plots they lived on. Their goal was to make as much money as possible in the urban mines and factories and send funds home to their families whenever possible. The third and even less visible subgroup was the **foreigners** from surrounding countries who lived in South Africa illegally. Phola Park provided shelter for many of them to go about their daily lives unnoticed by authorities. They were opposed to community development because as undocumented immigrants they did not want to be exposed, and they were unable to benefit legally from the proposed IDT development plan. Lastly, and probably the most hidden of all Phola Park community members, were the **criminal elements**. These syndicates found cover in the dark, cramped shack settlement, inaccessible to larger vehicle movement, where they could avoid close surveillance by police and security forces. For obvious reasons, criminals benefitted from this underdevelopment. Infrastructural development would disrupt their livelihoods and sources of income and profits.[9]

With these layers of community interest and lines of conflict unearthed, it became clear that we had failed the unarticulated litmus test of "Do No Harm" as well as the call to promote conflict-sensitive development.[10] In the first place, we had not sufficiently comprehended our role as 'outsiders.' The foremost rule of the Do No Harm (DNH) framework is the realization that once development practitioners enter into a conflict zone, we become part of the conflict. We become *actors* in the context in either constructive or destructive ways, and the sooner we acknowledge that circumstance, the more readily we will be able to act with sensitivity. Despite our good intentions, WFC did not realize that in our support of external material development we had awakened the latent divisions already existing in Phola Park and inadvertently contributed to violent conflict. In the words of the late Rev. Dale White, Executive Director of WFC from 1965 to 1995, "In the development process, we want the communities to divide the money, but instead the money divides the community."

Second, we realized that infrastructure development was not the immediate need of the citizens of Phola Park. There were *intangible needs* that had to be addressed before the *tangible* development gains could be shared by all. In particular, most of Phola Park did not feel secure, and until they did it would be futile to try to disarm them or ask them to work together.[11] Beyond the issue of safety and protection, the needs for participation, freedom, production, and ownership were also suppressed as the police and security forces continued to enforce remnants of apartheid law. Addressing these fundamental human needs and enabling people to make choices about their future was an essential precondition to sustainable development and peace in Phola Park.

This meant that WFC abandoned its dutiful obligation to produce some form of material development and focused instead on the long-term strengthening of the *social fabric* of Phola Park community. How do we create, form, and encourage community? How do we engage all the segments of a divided community? How do we assist the community as it negotiates identity, interests, ideology, and power while trying to build unity? How do we measure our progress, and—of even more immediate concern—how do we persuade our donors to fund sustained dialogue as a precursor to building peace?

Re-imagining Our Work—Implications for Practice

With the support of progressive donors who encouraged us to think and act creatively with regard to peacebuilding, we embarked on a process intervention that we believed would sustain what we termed "interlocking spheres of dialogue" across varied sectors and stakeholders in Phola Park and the surrounding township of Thokoza.[12] Using innovative means of social engagement, we attempted to build a people-centered relational foundation for both the peacebuilding and the development work that ensued. For peacebuilding, this meant providing spaces where former 'enemies' could meet to talk, reconcile, or negotiate interests. For development, this meant building the capacities of people so that they could in turn develop the necessary, satisfying material aspects of life for the sake of the 'common good.'[13] There were multiple facets and dimensions to this combined intervention.

Conflict Containment

First and foremost, we remained critically engaged with the various peace and conflict resolution mechanisms that were being put in place to manage political violence. These included the Thokoza Peace Coordinating Committee (TPCC) established by the local town council in March 1991; the National Peace Accords (NPA) signed into effect in September of that same year; and the Thokoza Local Dispute Resolution Committee (TLDRC), the on-the-ground structure in Thokoza that grew out of the NPA in November 1991.[14] We also continued to monitor and facilitate the relationship between the security forces and the community on an informal basis from 1991 to 1995—and then on a formal basis with the establishment of the Community-Policing Forums (CPFs), the first major piece of legislation enacted by the newly elected ANC in September 1994.[15] With varying degrees of efficacy, these peacekeeping mechanisms assisted in maintaining open channels of communication among all parties to the conflict and in preventing further violence and bloodshed through public negotiations and solidarity-building.

Peace Education

WFC was known for its training programs in peacebuilding skills, and in this capacity we remained engaged in training community groups, political parties, police, and other groups in Phola Park and Thokoza. Through a United States Institute of Peace (USIP) three-year funding grant and a partnership relationship with the Harvard Negotiation Project (1991–1994), we offered workshops on basic and advanced skills in Principled Negotiation.[16] We also facilitated educational seminars about the Truth and Reconciliation Commission and its structures, goals, and functions, and we conducted training in public participation and deliberative democracy. The latter emerged as a need after the ANC had introduced a rigorous process of soliciting input from ordinary citizens. Every new piece of legislation was first released to the public in the form of white and green papers that allowed citizens to give input before a law was enacted. Also, national development funds were designated for local development forums consisting of both politicians and community leaders who were to decide together how that money was going to be spent in their communities.

Sustained Collective Dialogue

From 1996 to 1999, with funding from the Red Cross (ICRC), WFC embarked on a Video Dialogue project in the Kathorus area, encompassing the three adjacent communities of Katlehong, Thokoza (including Phola Park), and Voslorus (located in the East Rand of the city of Johannesburg).

This project was based on a pioneering initiative undertaken in the Cape Town community of Crossroads, then engaged in a bitter war. In 1992,

> the regional peace committee, formed under the National Peace Accord was at a loss to bring the parties together in a forum to discuss the violence. The Media Peace Centre, a Cape Town based NGO, used the filming of a video as a way to get parties to state their positions and reasons for fighting. This material was shared across the 'enemy' lines and a consensus was built that the film product would be useful if viewed by the adversaries together. This step introduced the notion of "video dialogue"—the making of a video product as a stimulus to bring parties together to talk, first to the camera and secondly to each other in a facilitated process.[17]

The relative success of the Crossroads experiment gave rise to the same idea in Kathorus, another of the most violent areas in South Africa. The resulting project, called "Simunye (We Are One) Dialogues," was launched in 1997 by the WFC, the Media Peace Centre, and Simunye, a local community-based organization serving the ex-combatants of the East Rand. Video cameras were given to two former commanders of the militarized youth wings from opposing political groups. They were to tell, or "diarize," their own and their community's story through video. This was a difficult and taxing process as each of the commanders had to play down his own prejudices in order to produce a joint video that was acceptable to all.

The product of this effort was a 1.5-hour video that candidly outlined past and current conflicts and solicited solutions from all stakeholders. It was screened publicly for community leaders in April 1997. Following this, various public viewings were conducted for different segments of the community, after which participants were divided into committees to engage in facilitated dialogue. This follow-on process used community resources—facilitators, video machines, church and school halls, and caterers—to interact with groups who otherwise would not have talked to each other. The overarching aim of the project was to promote a broad-based unity, restore a sense of "community," and assist the Kathorus community to recognize its divisions. As Project co-coordinator Philip Visser explained:

> Through this process of visually recording the past, interlocking spheres of dialogue are constructed—slowly building understanding, restoring humanity and initiating a process of reconciliation towards peace, respect, tolerance and a joint future.[18]

In the first mid-term evaluation of the Video Dialogue program, a number of salient insights emerged.[19] First, the medium of video provided a much less threatening channel for communication than dialogue with political leaders. Had we tried to bring in high-profile speakers or outside facilitators, it would have been difficult to find a mediator acceptable to all. Second, the video outlined 11 possible roots of the conflict that were particularly relevant to the local communities involved. As one community member put it, "This [the video dialogue] was *our* truth commission!" Third, these dialogue processes increased the trust and connection among formerly divided community members. It opened up direct conversations between rival political parties who up to that point had relied on third-party mediators to facilitate any conversations regarding local governance, including community development projects.

Psycho-Social Trauma Recovery

The transitional violence in South Africa led to an enormous need for psycho-social healing. Due to the magnitude of the societal trauma coming from both the oppression of the apartheid system and the direct violence that accompanied it, the individualized therapeutic counseling model was untenable. In partnership with the National Peace Accord Trust (NPAT) and the Centre for the Study of Violence and Reconciliation (CSVR), WFC offered an array of embodied trauma treatment services for policing units, youth ex-combatant organizations, and the Khulumani Support Service, a self-help group organized to assist people who were victims and survivors of political violence.[20] Through the holistic healing mechanisms of a low ropes course built on our organizational conference grounds, guided wilderness experiences, and free trauma clinic services, we were able to provide forms of therapeutic self-help that accomplished four goals: (1) the provision of a safe-space to identify, name, and grieve traumatic shock and loss; (2) the normalization of relationships and everyday living tasks; (3) the increased ability to develop personal coping mechanisms; and (4) the opportunity to build and nurture familial and social support networks for resiliency.[21]

Linking the Business Sector and Our Peacebuilding Efforts

The Catholic Church actively advocated for the well-being of Phola Park from its inception in 1987. When the community was under threat of forced removal, a Catholic social worker brought the plight of the squatters to the attention of local industry leaders through the Alberton Industries Association (AIA), which became increasingly concerned about the dire living conditions of its Phola Park employees. As a result, the AIA funded water taps and established a health clinic.[22]

In addition, the owner of a neighboring AIA brick factory that was continually vandalized opened negotiations with Phola Park community leaders that led to an unlikely alliance.

> The manager made it clear that he accepted the rights of Phola Park residents to live where they were. . . . The community asked whether rubble and broken bricks from the factory might be used to repair roads inside Phola Park. He offered the bricks and the front-end loader, and the work was done to improve the roads. The manager made it a point to hire short-term and piece job employees from the community whenever possible.[23]

Synergistic Peacebuilding and Income Generating Projects

Finally, WFC continuously looked for opportunities to meet our goals of reconciliation and development. One of the ways we did this was by investing in income-generation schemes that could improve income and build stronger relationships at the same time. For instance, we encouraged the building of a peace monument in Thokoza as a symbolic gesture of reconciliation and memorialization, and then we linked the construction with the increasing tourism business.

We proposed training young unemployed ex-combatants to become paid community tour guides, offer theater performances about the political struggle, and open local businesses like restaurants to attract external clientele. While the program never received the full funding we desired, WFC was able to use portions of its flexible funds to train many of the ex-combatants in community development, income-generating skills (e.g., sewing), and permaculture (urban gardening). We also played a supportive role in the formation and implementation of the ANC-led program of Local Development Forums (LDFs), through which local governments were required to consult and make joint decisions with the community on the use of development monies allocated by the national government.

These varied activities were able to establish and strengthen bonds among groups with different interests—what scholars call 'social capital'—in order to foster durable peace and sustainable development in Phola Park and Thokoza.[24]

Tracing Movements in the Fields of Development and Peacebuilding

In Phola Park, development and peacebuilding intersected at the point of human needs. In order to explain this assertion, I intend to briefly trace important worldview shifts in both the development and the peacebuilding disciplines and to make the argument that human needs theory is where the two fields currently meet. I will do this by highlighting the ideas of two leading theorists of human needs: John Burton in the fields of conflict resolution and peacebuilding, and Manfred Max-Neef in development and economics.

Vernon Jantzi, a veteran development worker and professor, has argued that the development field utilized four different paradigms to approach its work: modernization, growth-with-equity, liberation from dependency, and global interdependence.[25] The Modernization (or neo-classical) approach is still the most prevalent framework, although it was dominant in the 1950s and 1960s. Taking its blueprint from the rebuilding of Germany after World War II, the modernization vision of development holds fast to the idea of unidirectional progress. Proponents of modernization explain the disparity in global development as an evolutionary process—some nations are ahead of others, but everyone is heading in the same direction. They have considerable faith in the nation-state and the institutions of government, economics, science, and education. The modernist development mindset accepts that each sovereign nation stands on its own and has an array of economic choices that determine its path to poverty or prosperity. The global modernization agenda calls for 'more developed' countries to assist 'less developed' countries to achieve macro-economic growth.[26] In many ways, the 23 million rand development plan proposed for Phola Park by the Independent Development Trust (IDT) was a good example of the modernization approach—external design, large scale, and focused on physical infrastructure with little regard for the conflict context in which development was to occur.

In the 1970s, through the seminal work of Frank Schumacher and his book *Small Is Beautiful* (1973), another development trajectory was birthed—what is termed the 'Growth-with-Equity' (GWE) approach. The GWE paradigm provides a clear critique of the failures of the modernization framework, giving voice to less-advantaged communities who experienced modernization as politically alienating, culturally patronizing, and economically wasteful. The GWE movement emphasizes local place and appropriate technology as the nucleus of sustainable development. Its advocates were strong proponents of decentralization, putting an emphasis on context, cultural specificity, and the particularity of community customs and practices. GWE had faith in societal institutions as a whole but remained suspicious of the giant economic and political monopolies. GWE put emphasis on capacity building, or training, and it rewarded low-cost technological innovation and economic entrepreneurship. Critics of GWE maintain that its central fallacy is its failure to denounce the economic order that propagates modernization theory, making it an unwitting tool of the liberal machinery that provides a conduit for the poor to enter and assimilate into the global economic system.[27] In Phola Park, the Planact group—after realizing the sizable gap in language, culture, and values between the IDT and the informal settlement—attempted to position itself as a 'bridge,' translating IDT's development scheme into acceptable political parlance and a local practice that would be sensitive to the dimensions of local conflicts. It employed a form of the 'Growth-with Equity' approach.

As opposed to modernization and GWE, the 'Liberation from Dependency' paradigm received its energy from the historically less-developed or economically marginalized countries located in the southern hemisphere. In this theory, global poverty is the result not of the choices of individual states or government leaders but of systemic exploitation by economically powerful nations of less prosperous economies, sometimes referred to as the "core and the periphery."[28] Proponents of liberation-from-dependency thinking are quick to cite unfair trade agreements, usurious global lending practices that cause inordinate debt, and the highly uneven flow of funding and natural resources from south to north. In other words, the wealthy nations, they argue, maintain their level of prosperity by keeping other nations poor. Liberationists have a general suspicion of societal—and especially global—institutions because all structures carry the potential to oppress the less powerful. In dependency theory, the cure for underdevelopment is not reform, assimilation, or capacity building, but transformation—a cutting off of the economic relationship between rich and poor nations. Liberation-from-dependency practitioners work at advocacy campaigns, mobilize people's movements for change, and attempt to set up alternative institutions and structures. While the liberationist approach has attracted many articulate spokespersons, they tend to be global in their critiques, and thus few have offered viable, concrete plans to counter the dominance of the current economic order.[29] Many would say that Winnie Mandela's intervention in the development of Phola Park was by far the most promising of all the efforts. It was a prime example of the 'Liberation from Dependency' approach. Mandela was a champion of the poor, gave credence to radical leftist revolutionary ideologies, and garnered a strong following among impoverished urban communities across the country. However, her socio-political capital and liberationist rhetoric did not provide her with the necessary legitimacy to pull off a successful development intervention in Phola Park.

Jantzi proposes that the next development paradigm will stress Global Interdependence. In this view, globalization is seen as inevitable and comprehensive, affecting access to information, mass communication, travel, and technological advances. At the core of this theory is an unprecedented opportunity. As barriers between people and nations break down, development practitioners should seize the moment to speed up and enhance development.[30] Key to this program is the effective utilization of relationships and people-to-people networks across the globe. While there is an inherent suspicion of institutionalized geo-political structures and borders in this post-modern development approach, there tends to be a benign disregard or even acceptance of monolithic economic corporations and their role in the global power dynamics. While it would be nearly impossible to have a development discussion today without talking about 'globalization,' it remains debatable whether globalization constitutes a paradigm in itself or simply an environmental phenomenon that has cross-cutting impact on all the development processes. In this case, globalization should be seen not as a separate approach but instead as an inescapable variable to be reckoned with in the contemporary development equation (Korten 1990).[31]

Although the peacebuilding discipline is younger than development, it has followed a similar path in thought and practice.[32] The field emerged in the 1960s and 1970s with the rise of Alternative Dispute Resolution (ADR) practices, which tried to provide an option for solving conflict and crime outside of the conventional legal process through informal processes such as arbitration, negotiation, and mediation. In the 1980s, the mediation movement grew out of the ADR field, offering various forms of problem-solving mechanisms embedded within local, community-based programs. The mediation movement led to new applications in the criminal justice system (victim-offender meetings), schools (training students and teachers to handle in-school conflict with mediation as opposed to punishment), and the workplace (organizational policy that requires conflicting colleagues to use mediation processes before resorting to legal action). The field's emphasis, in other words, was on conflict management. The relative success of these experiments in micro-level problem solving was soon translated into applications for large groups and institutional change (increased use of formal diplomacy and informal civil society arbitration, negotiation, mediation, and dialogue before resorting to military intervention at the international level). However, it became increasingly clear that the notion of 'conflict management' had its limitations: It was too concerned with containment alone. In response, the field adopted the idea of conflict resolution, which focused on uncovering the 'roots' of conflict and making structural adjustments to resolve it.

In the early 1990s, with the end of the Cold War, the global conflict landscape became even more complex, and deep-rooted conflicts became increasingly difficult to resolve. Out of this concern came another language shift, from conflict resolution to conflict transformation.[33] The notion of 'transformation' implies that the goal is *not* the elimination of conflict as such, which will always be part of our reality, but the transformation of its energy into a constructive force. Conflict transformation takes its cues from the natural sciences and complexity theory, which show that networked systems can change with the infusion of just one new factor. Thus, conflict transformation provides the conceptual framework for understanding peacebuilding practice as an inter-sectoral, multi-dimensional, long-term shift in the relationships and systems of conflict.

What can we observe from this brief account of the evolution of development and peacebuilding? First, we see that both fields are moving away from underlying

Table 10.1 Movements in Theory and Practice

Development	Peacebuilding
■ *Modernization Approach* (Large-scale resource capital + specific values + institution-building = growth) ■ *Growth-with-Equity Approach* (Small-scale local entrepreneurship + appropriate technology = sustainable livelihoods) ■ *Liberation-from-Dependency Approach* (Break-off dependency + raise awareness + redistributed power = world systems change) ■ *Global Interdependence Approach* (mobilized people + social networks + use of mass technology = global change)	■ *Dispute Management Approach* (Conflict prevention through the application of specific human relations skills-sets, communication techniques, and decision-making procedures) ■ *Conflict Resolution Approach* (Conflict mitigation through structural reform by the application of intensive problem-solving processes and uncovering the deep-seated 'root' causes of the conflict) ■ *Social Transformation Approach* (Conflict metamorphosis through a process of re-directing relational energy and re-channeling of emergent systems for social change)
The Common Denominator: Progression of Human-Centered Focus Fundamental Human Needs Conflict Theory (John Burton) and Human-Scale Development Theory (Manfred Max-Neef)	

worldview assumptions that are singularly configured around economic, technical, and material realities. Second, both are moving toward a people-centered approach to societal change. Their common theme is the pivotal focus on the satisfaction of foundational and fundamental human needs.

Human Needs Theory—John Burton and Manfred Max-Neef

John Burton (1915–2010) is one of the founding voices in the contemporary peacebuilding field. With a background in diplomacy, political science, and international relations, Burton is best known for his conceptions of deep-rooted conflict and his development of a complex system of problem-solving processes aimed at addressing them. For Burton, the seedbed of deep-rooted conflict was unmet basic human needs:

> We believe that the human participants in conflict situations are compulsively struggling in their respective institutional environments at all social levels to satisfy primordial and universal needs, needs such as security, identity, recognition and development.[34]

Burton identified four primary human needs in relation to conflict theory: identity, recognition, security, and belonging.[35] He also wrote about drivers such as self-esteem, cultural security, freedom, distributive justice, and participation. For Burton, conflict resolution could not rely on a set of skills or technical instruments applied at a surface level; it required a systematic deconstruction of the conflict with human needs as the primary motivating and organizing principle:

> Human needs are a powerful source of explanation of human behavior and social interaction. All individuals have needs that they strive to satisfy, either by using the system, 'acting on the fringes', or acting as a reformist or revolutionary. Given this condition, social systems must be responsive to individual needs, or be subject to instability and forced change (possibly through violence or conflict).[36]

Burton's framework reveals that all four of the primary needs in Phola Park were under considerable strain. Staggering from apartheid's divisive racial categorization and structural ranking, the **identity** of the black African in this new order was tenuous at best. With the unbanning of political formations of the liberation struggle, public and political **recognition** was a highly contested terrain. **Security** problems were paramount as the Phola Park community faced an onslaught of life-threatening confrontations with insidious third-force operatives of the fading white regime as well as other black opposition parties struggling to find their ideological space. Finally, it was notoriously difficult to find a place of **belonging** for informal dwellers in the country's transitional period as the legal standing of communities like Phola Park remained under threat. I use the notion of 'belonging' here in the sense of a place where the community could be permanently 'rooted' and generationally networked, and in juxtaposition to the experience of migration due to lack of access to land, labor, livelihoods, and locations.

By the end of the 1980s, at the same time that Burton was publishing his pivotal thinking on human needs in conflict resolution, Manfred Max-Neef, a Chilean economist, was bringing together a multi-disciplinary group of thinkers to elaborate alternative development paradigms from the perspective of the southern hemisphere. This effort resulted in a framework that Max-Neef (1991) and his team termed Human Scale Development (HSD). HSD proposes nine fundamental human needs that appear to be universal in nature: subsistence, protection, affection, understanding, participation, idleness (leisure), creation, identity, and freedom. In order to meet these needs, Max-Neef proposed different forms of "satisfiers," including pseudo, violating, and inhibiting satisfiers (destructive); and singular, multiple, and synergetic satisfiers (constructive):

> Any fundamental human need that is not adequately satisfied reveals a human poverty. Some examples are as follows: poverty of subsistence (due to insufficient income, food, shelter, etc.); of protection (due to bad health systems, violence, arms race, etc.); of affection (due to authoritarianism, oppression, exploitative relations with the natural environment, etc.) of participation (due to marginalization and discrimination of women, children, and minorities); and of identity (due to imposition of alien values upon local and regional cultures, forced migration, political exile, etc.). But poverties are not only poverties. Much more than that, each poverty generates pathologies.[37]

Max-Neef (1991) was deeply interested in the evolution of human satisfaction from the need of 'having' to the needs of being, doing, and interacting. In his own words,

> Satisfiers are not the available economic goods. . . . Satisfiers may include, among other things, forms of organization, political structures, social practices, subjective conditions, values and norms, spaces, contexts, modes, types of behavior, and attitudes, all of which are in a permanent state of tension between consolidation and change.[38]

The ideas of Burton and Max-Neef overlap in several ways. First, both differentiated their thinking from Maslow's groundbreaking 1954 work on needs theory in two important ways: They moved analysis beyond the organizing principle of the psychological individual and into the collective social realm, and they refused to rank human needs in a hierarchical fashion.[39] This difference was critical for the peacebuilding field—in particularly as it relates to the models that guide current interventions, which are characterized by collaboration among multiple levels, sectors, and actors.[40]

Second, both Burton and Max-Neef influenced their respective disciplines to move from tangible (material) toward non-tangible (social) units of measurement for human development and progress. This shift allowed for progress beyond the 'zero-sum' game or 'limited pie' outlook of competition for scarce resources to the novel idea of the unlimited production of social capital and networking for the purposes of peace and human development. As Burton (1990) put it: "The more security, identity, and development one party experiences, the more and not the less are the opportunities for the satisfaction of these same needs by others."[41]

Third, both Burton and Max-Neef suggested systems that were holistic and cohesive—aligning theory, praxis, and structures with corresponding values and ethical processes—in order to ensure broad societal application.

The integrated concerns of Burton and Max-Neef have been reflected in the gradual shift away from GNP as a measure of human development and toward more people-centered indices such as the Human Development Index (HDI)[42] and the Inequality-adjusted HDI (IHDI)[43] that emphasize 'quality of life' indicators such as Health (life expectancy at birth), Education (mean and expected years of schooling), and Living Standards (gross national income per capita).

One of these indexes, based on the Capabilities Approach of Harvard economist and Nobel Laureate Amartya Sen, appeared in 2008. I postulate that the Human Security Index (HSI),[44] launched with the support of the United Nations Development Program (UNDP), is the best index currently available to assist us with integrating peacebuilding and development. The very designation of 'human'

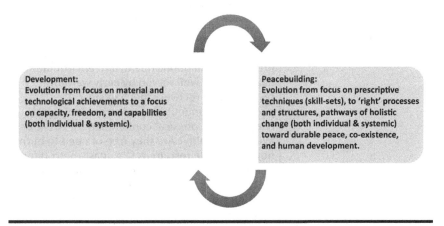

Development:
Evolution from focus on material and technological achievements to a focus on capacity, freedom, and capabilities (both individual & systemic).

Peacebuilding:
Evolution from focus on prescriptive techniques (skill-sets), to 'right' processes and structures, pathways of holistic change (both individual & systemic) toward durable peace, co-existence, and human development.

Image 10.1   Overlapping Spaces in Development and Peacebuilding

security immediately places the human being at the core of what it means to live in peaceful development. The intersection between peacebuilding and development is well articulated in the tagline of "Freedom from fear, freedom from want, freedom to live in dignity."[45] The HSI is concerned with multiple dimensions of human security: economic, food, health, environment, personal, community, and political. There have been varied iterations of the concept of human security, but in essence it can be summarized in the following five components:

Table 10.2 Summative Overview of Components of Human Security[46]

Components	Guiding Questions
Component One: Information Empowerment	*Are people connected and empowered through the diversity of traditional and modern means of information exchange?* Do they have access to each other in person, by telephone, and the internet? Do they have access to uncensored, unbiased, and effective people-centric (rather than self- or ideology-centric) information through print, broadcast, and internet sources?
Component Two: Corruption Control and Good Governance	*Do people feel safe that human security is a focus of government leaders, and that businesses are customer-focused?* Although businesses may be entitled to a fair profit, are corporate leaders getting huge salary packages while the average people receive wages that do not allow them to live above the poverty line? Are bribes and lobbying co-opting decision-makers away from public service and toward the individual interests of a few?
Component Three: Environmental Protection	*Do people feel safe and comfortable in their environment?* Is the community relatively well protected from public health and environmental hazards—and well served by early warning response and recovery mechanisms? Are people and communities safe from biological, chemical, and physical contamination? Are they living sustainably? Are they free of need to burn non-renewable resources (e.g., gas—petrol) for transportation, heat, or cooking? If they have electricity, is it from renewable sources? Is their housing a sustainably low resource and energy consumer?

Components	Guiding Questions
Component Four: Peace and Safety	*Do people feel safe in their homes, communities, nation, and the world?* Is crime a threat? Are power groups (from foreign or domestic individual, institutional/corporate, or governmental forces) disrupting human security? Is one's community or country involved in domestic or foreign conflict, conscripting community residents and spending scarce resources on disruptions?
Component Five: Protection of, and benefitting from, diversity	*Are people at ease, or not, because of their gender, age, place of origin, religion, other beliefs, educational status, economic status, so-called disability, or other characteristic that they are not abnormally pushing on others?* This is not an opportunity for people to attempt co-option of or hegemony over others' equally valued situations or belief systems.

The HSI components outlined above present a framework that can encompass the human needs models of both Burton and Max-Neef, with their systematic theories of change and practical applications for program design, monitoring, and evaluation.

Conclusion

If my colleagues and I in South Africa had had the framework of the HSI and the benefits of systems change theory, how would we have changed the way we approached the Phola Park community? First, we would have been increasingly wary of the traditional development paradigm that is neatly packaged in a linear, prescriptive, end-focused equation. I also believe we would have moved more readily into a process approach that valued the cyclical, participatory, and means-focused nature of human development. Second, we would have sought a new language to describe our role as third-party interveners in order to accomplish human scale development for the future. I could imagine at least three different role identities and functions.

Third, we would have identified our "Theories of Change"[47] and would therefore have been more intentional in aligning our 'means' with our 'ends' in the overall intervention design. The following chart combines the intervention activities that we embarked on in Phola Park with their attending "Theories of

Role Identities:	Role Functions:
1.) The Seer: Native American peoples define this role as the "vision-catcher" who is able to see the signs of the times and know what to do.	Prioritize engagement in joint analysis and future scenario building with the community to nurture common vision as the seed for any intervention.
2.) The Catalyst: A catalyst is a substance that when introduced to other substances can radically change the form of those substances without altering its own.	Prioritize relationships and trust building through sustained dialogues for the purposes of increasing empathy, learning, and understanding across community divides.
3.) The Tracker: Borrowed from indigenous Southern Africans, the term tracker refers to traditional hunters who used their embodied senses and knowledge of nature to locate wild game.	Prioritize networking, linking external ideas, people, and organizations with community actors to provide new energy, resources, and partnerships.

Image 10.2   Re-imagining Our Intervention Roles in Phola Park

Table 10.3   Integrating Intervention Activities and Theories of Change[48]

Intervention Activities	Theories of Change
1.) *Conflict Containment—* support National Peace Accord structures, local peace committees, and community-police forums.	*Transitional Institutions Theory*: If support is provided to temporary institutions that assist in the transition from a violent to a peaceful society, then the likelihood of violence re-emerging in the future will be reduced. *Problem Solving and Dialogue Theory*: If people from both sides of a conflict engage in unofficial dialogue at the Track 2 and 3 levels, then these efforts will ultimately strengthen official negotiation processes.
2.) *Peace Education—* trainings in principled negotiation, transitional justice, reconciliation, and deliberative democracy processes.	*Improving Skills and Processes Theory*: If parties have skills and good processes for resolving conflicts, then they will be more successful in negotiating peace and dealing with underlying causes of conflict.
3.) *Sustained Collective Dialogue—*Video Dialogue Project.	*Social Contact Theory*: If groups from conflicting societies participate in joint activities, then this contact will lead to increased understanding of the other and will reduce inter-group conflict. *Cooperation and Mutual Interest Theory*: If groups from similar sectors of conflicting societies work together on issues of mutual interest, then they will learn to cooperate and, through cooperation, develop increased trust.

Intervention Activities	Theories of Change
4.) *Linking Business Sector and Peacebuilding*	*Changing Choices about Violence Theory*: If incentives for violence are changed because violence seems more costly and non-violence more attractive, then key actors will pursue peace and reject violence.
5.) *Synergistic Peacebuilding and Income Generation Projects*	*Capabilities Approach to Development Theory*: If we increase the capacity of people living in poverty to make choices that will improve their circumstances, then human development and peaceful co-existence will more likely be sustained.

Change." These Theories of Change represent both the assumptions behind our activities and the outcomes that resulted from them.

In the end, this re-imagining of roles and the application of theories of change is precisely what my colleagues and I did, although at the time we did not have the language outlined in this chapter. Nonetheless, the outcome was ultimately the same. The Phola Park and Thokoza communities were eventually able to move in the direction of durable peace and joint ownership of their own development. Human needs were met, and human scale peace and development took hold, though multiple challenges remained. After all, development like peacebuilding is not an *end* state but a *means* toward advancing a better way to live.

Notes

1. WFC supported church and civil society efforts in the resistance against the apartheid system for 30 years. For more information, see: http://wilgespruit.com.
2. Douwes-Dekker et al. (1995): 8–9.
3. Douwes-Dekker et al. (1995): 24–25.
4. Douwes-Dekker et al. (1995): 33.
5. Bremner and Visser (1994): 1–2 (emphasis in original).
6. Keller (1995).
7. Bremner (1994): 5.
8. Douwes-Dekker et al. (1995): 33.
9. Bremner (1994): 5–7.
10. Anderson (1999); Ceretti 2009. In her 1999 book *Do No Harm*, Anderson pioneered the concept of conflict-sensitive aid by articulating the DNH framework. It called for an in-depth, contextual analysis of conflict "connectors" and conflict "dividers" in any aid locale. Ceretti proposes six crucial elements of conflict-aware development: demilitarization; targeting the most deprived; non-segregated resettlement; rewards for cooperation; limiting private foreign investment; and truth and reconciliation processes.

11. It was over this same period that Gun-Free South Africa launched a campaign to disarm communities like Phola Park in order to reduce violence, but they were not successful. Why? Not because this was a bad idea, but because, as human needs theory tells us, unless people feel secure needs are met in an alternative way, they will continue to hold on to the protection they have, including lethal weapons.

12. This phrase came from Philip Visser, the Coordinator for the Letsema Conflict Transformation Program at WFC, Johannesburg, South Africa. The Swedish International Development Association (SIDA) and the International Committee of the Red Cross (ICRC) funded most of our intervention in the Thokoza/Phola Park communities.

13. Manfred Max-Neef put it simply: "Development is about people, not objects."

14. Douwes-Dekker et al. (1995): 122–129.

15. This legislated act required all police stations across the country to establish a legally registered entity to promote collaboration between the police and the communities. These forums were to work out how to handle public safety and security, budgets and resource allocations, and civil society-government cooperation in their local communities.

16. Principled Negotiation espouses a set of collaborative, problem-solving skills instead of the competitive, adversarial strategies often employed in political, legal, and labor negotiation frameworks. The seven primary elements of Principled Negotiation are: relationship, communication, interests, options, legitimacy, commitment, and re-negotiation.

17. Wilgespruit Funding Proposal (1998): 2.

18. Visser (1998).

19. Stauffer (1998).

20. The use of the term "embodied" here refers to whole body (physiological) treatments, not just psychological or what is often referred to as "talk therapy" (counseling alone).

21. What we now know about trauma healing is that negative emotions (fear, paranoia, anxiety) as well as physical reactions (pain, tears, sweating, sleeplessness) are trapped inside the body and mind of a person who has experienced trauma, and they need release both psychologically and physically. For instance, trauma may make a person feel powerless. We once took a group of female activists who had suffered imprisonment and rape through the low ropes course; one of the elements of the course was a 12-foot high wall that they were to help each other climb. They succeeded. One woman said that the sheer physical accomplishment of getting over the wall empowered her in a new way—she realized that she was able to make decisions for herself, that she had the agency to change her life.

22. Douwes-Dekker et al. (1995):12–14.

23. Douwes-Dekker et al. (1995): 21–22.

24. Flora and Flora (2008).

25. Jantzi (1990).

26. For further reading on modernization theory, see Rostow (1960); Morganthau (1962); Rogers (1969); Inkeles and Smith. (1974).

27. For further reading on 'Growth with Equity,' see Shumacher (1973); McGinnis (1979); Yunus (1999); and Davis (2004).

28. Gunder-Frank (1966).

29. For further reading on the 'Liberation from Dependency' theory of development, see Illich (1968); Freire (1970); Eglitis (2004).
30. Of course, it goes without saying that there may be new barriers stemming from globalization, such as internet accessibility, that exacerbate the divide between richer and poorer nations.
31. Jantzi's work is mirrored in the thinking of David Korten (1990) who outlines four generations of development work: (1) *Relief and Welfare* (focus on the task), (2) *Community Development* (focus on who does the task), (3) *Sustainable Systems Development* (focus on who defines the task), and (4) *People's Movements* (focus on connecting people to decide jointly, and act on the most important tasks).
32. Jantzi and Jantzi (2009): 65–80.
33. Lederach (1995). This perceived or actual tension is highly contested in the field as many of my professional colleagues still use the concept of conflict resolution. Those who prefer the descriptor of 'transformation' would argue that history has revealed that there are few, if any, conflicts that are completely resolvable and that destructive conflicts tend to recur cyclically and resurface at unexpected locations in unexpected ways—what experts have termed 'wicked problems' or 'intractable conflicts.'
34. Burton (1988): 13.
35. Burton (1990); Hicks (2011): 27.
36. Coate and Rosati (1988): Preface–ix.
37. Max-Neef (1991): 19.
38. Max-Neef (1991): 24.
39. Psychologist Abraham Maslow is probably best known for his pyramid (hierarchy) of human needs, which starts at the base with the need for physiological sustenance (food, water, and shelter) and moves up through safety, love/belonging, esteem, and finally, at the tip of the triangle, "self-actualization."
40. Lederach (1997).
41. Burton (1990): 15.
42. For more information see: http://hdr.undp.org/en/.
43. For more information see: http://hdr.undp.org/en/statistics/.
44. For more information see: http://unocha.org/humansecurity/.
45. Ibid.
46. Adapted from: www.humansecurityindex.org.
47. Babbitt et al (2013).
48. All the 'Theories of Change' presented in this diagram (except for the last one under #5 listed as Capabilities Approach) are directly quoted from Babbitt et al. (2013): 18–21.

Bibliography

Anderson, M. (1999). *Do No Harm—How Aid Can Support Peace—or War*. Boulder, CO and London: Lynne Rienner Publishers.

Babbitt, E., D. Chigas, and R. Wilkinson. (2013). *Theories and Indicators of Change Briefing Paper—Concepts and Primers for Conflict Management and Mitigation*. United States Agency for International Development (USAID).

Bremner, D. (1994). *Phola Park: Worst of the Worst or Signs of the Times* (unpublished paper). Johannesburg, South Africa: Negotiation and Community Conflict Programme, Wilgespruit Fellowship Centre.

Bremner, D., and P. Visser. (1994). *Negotiation, Conflict Resolution, and Human Needs: Social Transformation for a Sustainable Future in South Africa* (unpublished paper). Johannesburg, South Africa: Negotiation and Community Conflict Programme, Wilgespruit Fellowship Centre.

Burton, J. (1988). *Conflict Resolution as a Political System* (Working Paper No.1). Washington, DC: Institute for Conflict Analysis and Resolution, George Mason University.

Burton, J. (1990). *Conflict: Human Needs Theory*. London: Palgrave Macmillan.

Burton, J., and F. Dukes. (1990). *Conflict: Practices in Management, Settlement and Resolution*. New York: St Martin's Press.

Ceretti, J. (2009). Hurdles to Development: Assessing Development Models in Conflict Settings. *Peace & Conflict Review* 4(1): 11–17.

Coate, R., and J. Rosati (eds.). (1988). *The Power of Human Needs in World Society*. Boulder, CO: Lynne Rienner Publishers.

Coleman, P. (2011). *The Five Percent: Finding Solutions to Seemingly Impossible Conflicts*. West Hartford, CT: Public Affairs.

Davis, M. (2004). Planet of Slums. *New Left Review* 26: 5–35.

Diamond, L., and J. McDonald. (1996). *Multi-Track Diplomacy: A Systems Approach to Peace*. West Hartford, CT: Kumarian Press.

Douwes-Dekker, L., A. Majola, P. Visser, and D. Bremner. (1995). *Community Conflict— The Challenge Facing South Africa*. Cape Town: Juta & Co., Ltd.

Eglitis, D. (2004). *The Uses of Global Poverty: How Economic Inequality Benefits the West*. Washington, DC: George Washington University. www.gwu.edu/~soc/docs/Eglitis/Global_Poverty/pdf

Flora, C.B., and J.L. Flora. (2008). *Rural Communities: Legacies and Change* (2nd ed.). Boulder, CO: Westview Press.

Freire, P. (1970). *Pedagogy of the Oppressed*. New York: Seabury Press.

Gunder-Frank, A. (1966). *The Development of Underdevelopment*. New England: Free Press.

Hendrick, D. (2009). *Complexity Theory and Conflict Transformation: An Exploration of Potential and Implications* (Working Paper 17), Bradford University: Department of Peace Studies.

Hicks, D. (2011). *Dignity—The Essential Role It Plays in Resolving Conflict*. New Haven and London: Yale University Press.

Illich, I. (1968). The Hell with Good Intentions: An address presented to the Conference on Inter-American Student Projects (CIASP) in Cuemavaca, Mexico. www.swaraj.org/Illich_hell.htm.

Inkeles, A., and D. Smith. (1974). *Becoming Modern: Individual Change in Six Developing Countries*. Cambridge, MA: Harvard University Press.

Jantzi, T., and V. Jantzi. (2009). Development Paradigms and Peacebuilding Theories of Change: Analyzing Embedded Assumptions in Development and Peacebuilding. *Journal of Peacebuilding and Development* 5(1): 24–51.

Jantzi, V. (1990). Helping Developing Nations: Social Political Paradigms of Development. In C. Desanto, Z. Lindblade and M. Poloma (Eds.), *Christian Perspectives on Social Problems*. Indianapolis: Wesley Press.

Keller, B. (March, 1995). Real Winnie Mandela: Benefactor or Grafter? www.nytimes.com/1995/03/03/world/real-winnie-mandela-benefactor-or-grafter.html.

Korten, D. (1990). *Getting to the 21st Century—Voluntary Action and the Global Agenda.* Boulder, CO: Lynne Rienner.

Lederach, J. P. (1995). *Preparing for Peace—Conflict Transformation Across Cultures.* Syracuse: Syracuse University Press.

Lederach, J. P. (1997). *Building Peace: Sustainable Reconciliation Across Divided Societies.* Washington, DC: USIP Press.

Maslow, A. (1954). *Motivation and Personality.* New York: Harper Publishers.

Max-Neef, M. (1991). *Human Scale Development: Conception, Application and Further Reflection.* New York: Apex Press.

Max-Neef, M., A. Elizalde, M. Hopenhayn, et al. (1989). Human Scale Development: An Option for the Future. *Development Dialogue* 1: 5–80.

McGinnis, J. (1979). *Bread & Justice—Toward a New International Economic Order.* New York: Paulist Press.

Morganthau, H. (1962). A Political Theory of Foreign Aid. *The American Political Science Review* 56(2): 301–09.

Ramsbotham, O., T. Woodhouse, and H. Miall. (2011). *Contemporary Conflict Resolution* (3rd ed.). Hoboken, NJ: Wiley, John and Son, Inc.

Rihani, S. (2002). *Complex Systems Theory and Development Practice.* London: Zed Books.

Rogers, E. (1969). *Modernization among Peasants.* New York: Holt, Rinehart and Winston.

Rostow, W. W. (1960). *The Stages of Economic Growth.* Cambridge, MA: Cambridge University Press.

Rubenstein, R. (2001). Basic Human Needs: The Next Steps in Theory Development. *International Journal of Peace Studies* 6(1): 51–58.

Sen, A. (1999). *Development as Freedom.* Oxford: Oxford University Press.

Shumacher, E. F. (1973). *Small is Beautiful: Economics as if People Mattered.* London: Harper & Row.

Stauffer, C. (1998). *Video Dialogue: An Innovative Tool for Story-Telling, Problem-Solving & Conflict Transformation.* (Unpublished paper). Johannesburg, South Africa: Wilgespruit Fellowship Centre. www.academia.edu/4915739/Video_Dialogue_An_Innovative_Tool_for_Story-Telling_Problem-Solving_and_Conflict_Transformation

Visser, P. (December, 1998). *The Media as Conflict Intervener: Using Video Dialogue in Thokoza.* Track Two Newsletter Publication. Cape Town, South Africa: Centre for Conflict Resolution.

Wilgespruit Fellowship Centre. (1998). *Participation in Kathorus Media Dialogue Process.* Funding proposal to the International Committee of the Red Cross (ICRC).

Yunus, M. (1999). *Banker to the Poor—Micro-lending and the Battle Against World Poverty.* New York: Public Affairs Press.

Chapter 11

Education for Development

Theoretical Perspectives and the Nigerian Situation

Abdalla Uba Adamu

The 'education for development' (EfD) paradigm has long shaped perceptions of education as a primary tool for the social and economic advancement of developing countries. Based on a human capital theory that sees the production of qualified manpower as the main resource for development, state and international efforts have focused on the production of qualified students and other personnel as the mainstay of their EfD work.[1] Increased enrollment, higher retention, and even higher transition from one level of education to another is heralded as the most effective way to achieve development because it produces more and better manpower. Accordingly, from the early 1960s to the mid-1970s, governments in developed and less-developed countries encouraged investment in education to enhance the quality of human productivity and thereby spur development.

By the late 1970s, however, the lack of economic growth in most parts of the world slowed investment in education, and researchers started to question the feasibility of human capital theory as a basis for development strategy.[2] Researchers no longer accepted that expenditures aimed at increasing enrollment rates were enough to enhance economic productivity.[3]

Criticism of the EfD paradigm typically centered on its core assumptions. First, the theory assumes that there is a perfect market for labor, and that better-educated and more-skilled people will obtain better jobs and become more productive—conditions that do not hold in the real world. Second, human capital theory does not consider factors other than education, such as job satisfaction and working conditions, that could contribute to higher worker productivity. Third, human capital theory fails to recognize education as a screening or filtering device.[4] That is, employers may use schools to identify workers with superior ability even if education does not directly improve worker skills and productivity. Finally, as Fagerlind and Saha propose, education exists in a dialectical relationship with society. It is at once a product of society and acts continually upon that society.[5] The contribution of education to the development process, therefore, depends upon the nature of other dimensions of development in a given society at a particular time. By late 1980s, in other words, it was becoming increasingly clear that the education industry should aim at more than making sure children enroll in school and pass with good grades. The search for additional dimensions and inputs led to the emergence of a new paradigm: Education for Sustainable Development (ESD).

Sustainable development is a difficult and evolving concept. One of its original definitions is credited to the Brundtland Commission: "Sustainable development is development that meets the needs of the present without compromising the ability of future generations to meet their own needs."[6] It is generally thought to have three components—environment, society, and economy—each of whose well-being is intertwined with the others. For example, a healthy, prosperous society relies on a healthy environment to provide food and resources, safe drinking water, and clean air for its citizens. The sustainability paradigm rejects the contention that casualties in the environmental and social realms are inevitable and acceptable consequences of economic development. Thus it is a paradigm for thinking about a future in which environmental, societal, and economic considerations are balanced in the pursuit of an improved quality of life.

Since the Earth Summit in 1992, there has been increasing recognition of the critical role of education in promoting sustainable consumption and production patterns. What eventually became fashionable as 'Education for Sustainable Development' entailed two distinct approaches in developing countries. The first called for the heavy involvement of domestic and international organizations in planning and implementing educational policies and programs. The aim was to create a socially equitable and politically accountable process of education provision as an agent for development on a global standard. In Nigeria, international partners such as the World Bank, UNICEF, and UNESCO, and national agencies such as the Federal Ministry of Education, all pushed the new perspective—though as we will see they often continued to implement programs based on old EfD approaches. The Sustainable Development framework called for education planners to consider more indigenous perspectives on education. Sustainable development education carries with it the idea of implementing programs that are locally relevant and culturally appropriate. As Olsen noted, "We define 'sustainable' development as development which respects the balances provided by political stability, social equity, economic stability, and development in harmony with nature."[7] As a result, programs must be created for each region. Rather than searching for curricular models to adopt throughout a country, ministries of education and school districts should invest their resources in processes by which communities of different sizes and traditions can define their own programs.

As these distinct approaches suggest, there is little agreement about the meaning of sustainable development and whether or not it is attainable, a discord that has stymied efforts to develop new policies. The holistic nature of sustainable development opens it to a broad range of interpretations and misinterpretations depending on the particular lenses of practitioners. Economists and 'developers,' for example, view it in terms of economic sustainability, whereas environmentalists see it as environmental sustainability. These discrepancies often result in conflicting scenarios at the operational level.

In addition, there is the lack of clarity regarding the practical goals of ESD. In simple terms, educators want to know: "What am I to do differently? What should I do or say now that I didn't say before?" These apparently simple questions perplex most experts. Each country must decide whether its educators are being asked to teach about sustainable development or to go further by changing the goals and methods of education to achieve sustainable development. Those that elect to teach only about sustainable development may find that it comes across as simply an abstract concept that does not give students the skills, perspectives, values, and knowledge to live sustainably in their communities.

In addition, while it is a good idea to bring together the economic, social, and environmental dimensions of sustainability, the concept of sustainable development itself faced the major contradiction of having to exist in global capitalism, which is rooted in the exploitation of natural and human resources and informed by an ideology of economic growth and modernization. Development seen as economic growth often becomes a top-down process in which experts impose their own perception of development on local people considered backward and ignorant. Although this approach has fueled the growth of most developed countries, it has led to major environmental, social, and economic problems that the world is trying to address today.[8]

In sum, EfD explores the relationship between education and development through strategies such as teacher competencies, use of new technologies, gender equality, and infrastructural provisions in education at both formal and non-formal levels—all designed to produce greater human capital. Education for Sustainable Development, on the other hand, is learner and outcome focused. It purports to allow every human being to acquire the knowledge, skills, attitudes, and values necessary to shape a sustainable future. It also requires participatory teaching and learning methods that motivate and empower students to change their behavior and take action for sustainability. Thus, it promotes competencies like critical thinking, imagining future scenarios, and making decisions in a collaborative way.

Education and Development Efforts in Nigeria

Nigeria offers many examples of the quandaries of education for development. The country itself presents a paradox. It is rich in resources, yet its people are poor. Despite Nigeria's strong economic track record, poverty is endemic due to heavy reliance on oil wealth and a corresponding de-emphasis on non-oil growth. As a 2013 report argued:

> Despite a plethora of natural and human resources, relatively strong growth, and its ranking as a middle-income country, Nigeria has struggled to make progress on key development indicators. About 68 percent of Nigerians are living in poverty (below $1.25 daily) . . . while the illiteracy rate for adults (both sexes) is approximately 61 percent. Nigeria is also currently failing to provide education to many of its primary-school-age children.[9]

Some of the hindrances to enhanced growth include the investment climate, infrastructure, incentives, the lack of articulated agricultural policies, and the low quality and irrelevance of tertiary education. From 2009, security challenges caused by an extremely violent insurgency compounded these problems.

The attainment of independence from the British in 1960 led to a condemnation of the objectives of colonial primary education. The clamor for an education system that reflected Nigerian realities reached a crescendo during the oil boom of the 1970s. In 1976, the quest to design something indigenous, coupled with the need to observe the right of the child to education, led to the declaration of the Universal Primary Education (UPE). This policy ushered in a tremendous increase in enrollment as well as extensive community efforts to develop primary education. There was so much enthusiasm that primary education became the major sector for extending government presence to many villages, towns, and communities. However, with it came increased costs and funding needs.

In 1977, the Nigerian government promulgated a National Policy on Education to provide the basis for an improved curriculum to meet the nation's development needs. Many lofty ideals were laid down without adequate planning on the assumption that funds would be available indefinitely to meet the needs of the sub-sector. When policy implementation commenced in the 1980s, however, economic recession had set in. As the economy declined, the school population and number of schools grew. As a result, classrooms became over-crowded; structures fell into disrepair; and teaching facilities were grossly inadequate. In addition, the dearth of data for effective planning and management became acute as teachers' competences could not meet the needs of increased responsibilities. Finally, constant changes in government created political insecurity.

Additional problems arose due to government outlays for other sectors of the economy. At the dawn of independence, the government devoted as much as 40% of its annual budgets to education. But as pressure for other social and economic services mounted, particularly investment in roads, secretariats, pipe-borne water, agriculture, and industries, the share of annual budgets allocated to education declined, with the lowest figures recorded in the 1990s. The government could no longer bear the financial burden for education alone. Although education continued to attract a huge share of national budgets, the gap between estimated expenditure and actual allocation widened, leaving several needy areas, including teacher's salaries.

To address these problems, the federal government set up the National Primary Education Commission (NPEC). The same decree also established the State Primary Schools Management Boards (PSMB) to perform a similar function in each state, and the Local Government Education Authorities (LGEA) to manage schools within their respective districts. While this framework held, a great deal of improvement was recorded in primary education funding and management. Salaries were paid regularly, and workshops were held for inspectors and head teachers.[10]

It was in the midst of this transition that the World Bank first intervened in Nigerian education. In 1989, a World Bank study asserted that Nigeria, along with many developing countries, had not met the objectives set by them for the primary education sub-sector. Schools had been ineffective in developing in pupils the core skills stipulated by the national curriculum. Above all, it had not been able to provide all school-age children, particularly girls, access to primary schooling. Consequently, national efforts to develop a human capital base for development had been seriously jeopardized.

World Bank concerns, focused as it was on educational capacity and infrastructure, fell directly within the purview of EfD, despite a growing worldwide interest in ESD, an interest that the World Bank also held. To assist Nigeria in improving overall performance in primary education, the Nigeria Primary Education Project was approved by the World Bank in 1990 and ran from 1992 until June 1997. It became the first in a series of interventions in Nigerian education targeted at achieving the 'education for development' objective. Yet by the mid-2000s, a series of think-tanks, workshops, and conferences revealed that major challenges persisted:

- Low enrollment, completion, and progression rates at all levels of education
- Inequities in terms of gender, geographical zones, states, local governments, and schools

- Poor quality of learning outcomes
- Inappropriate curriculum for the needs of a growing economy
- Inadequate attention to the learning needs of adults and youth in non-formal settings
- Poor teacher training and development at both pre-service and in-service levels
- Weak system of staff deployment leading to large numbers of unqualified or under-qualified teachers.
- Poor infrastructural facilities for teaching and learning
- Weak institutions and poor management systems leading to weak planning and monitoring and evaluation
- Limited capacity for data collection and data analysis
- Examination malpractice and cultism
- Weak external and internal systems of communication
- Dissatisfaction with the public education system, leading to the expansion of private schools and the consequent exodus of influential stakeholders out of the state sector.[11]

These findings prompted further interventions. USAID's Northern Nigerian Education Initiative (NEI), for example, tried to expand the provision of universal basic education and delivery of education services in northern Nigeria.[12] Through the Education Sector Support Programme in Nigeria (2008–2015), Britain's Department for International Development (DfID) sought to improve the planning, financing, and delivery of basic education services and increase access, equity, and quality at the federal level and in six Nigerian states.

Yet the education machinery is not working—even according to EfD indicators of examination scores and enrollment rates. After many workshops and reports, government officers still lack a strategy to improve examination results, the main benchmark of any education project. In Nigeria, the two main examinations students take at the end of senior secondary school are the West African Examination Council's Senior Secondary Certificate Examination (WASSCE) and National Examination Council Senior School Certificate Examination (NECO SSCE).[13]

The outcomes of both WAEC and NECO have consistently painted a bleak picture. For instance, data available from the Public Affairs Department of the West African Examinations Council, WAEC, in Lagos show a consistently poor examination performance by Nigerian students, as indicated in Table 11.1.

The failure rate of almost 79% in the most-credible examination in Nigeria calls into question the efficacy of educational provisions by both the government and international agency partners.

Data on school survival, completion, and transition rates are similarly bleak. The 'survival rate'—the percentage of pupils enrolled in Primary 1 in a given

Table 11.1 Trend of Mass Failure of Students in the May/June West African Senior School Certificate Examinations (WASSCE) between 2003 and 2010

Year	% Failed	% Passed
2003	80.74	19.26
2004	81.74	18.26
2005	72.47	27.53
2006	84.44	15.56
2007	74.46	25.54
2008	86.24	13.76
2009	74.01	25.99
2010	75.06	24.94
Total	78.65	21.35

Source: Public Affairs Department of WAEC, Lagos

Table 11.2 Basic Education Population, 2006–2010

Year	Primary	Junior High School
2006	21,717,789	2,643,358
2007	20,469,395	2,998,372
2008	18,980,395	3,451,078
2009	18,818,544	3,758,093
2010	19,042,167	4,125,211

Source: Compiled from National Bureau of Statistics

school year who reach Primary 5—has fluctuated over time. Data provided by the educational authorities show that the proportion of students who survived in 2000 was 97%, but by 2009 it was only 72.3%. While an increasingly high proportion of school-age children are actually enrolling in school, more of them are dropping out over the course of their education. The Primary 6 completion rate is similarly dire. The average trend over the last five years shows almost an 11% drop.

Data on transition rates are difficult to obtain. Not only are there constant drop-outs, but cohort studies are unable to gather precise data on pupils as they progress from one level of schooling to another. However, a measure can be obtained in the absolute population of students at junior secondary school as compared with similar data on primary school pupils in the same years. This is shown in Table 11.2.

While no correlation per year is suggested, the juxtaposition of the primary and JSS populations clearly indicates a wide disparity, suggesting that far fewer children are in JSS schools than graduate from primary schools. There is a need to capture these children and determine why they remain out of school, what they do, and how to get them back.

The Paradigm Remains the Same

These failures illustrate what I call the "paradigm paradox" in development—the rhetorical commitment to a new paradigm but the continued pursuit of an old one. Under normal circumstances, the shift from one paradigm (inherited or hybridized) to a newer one (development-partner oriented, 'global') should address current problems in more effective ways, leading to growth and development. Yet despite multiple engagements in Nigerian education by development partners advocating for change from without, the results and the underlying administrative structures remain virtually the same. These interventions led to a demand for change, but paradoxically they merely reinforced the existing EfD structures rather than promoted ESD. In light of this trend, I argue that the various models and theories of development simply do not work when faced with the reality of contemporary governance in Nigeria; despite their neat categorizations of development behavior, the ground-level reality simply does not operate along their theoretical lines.

I will illustrate with a recent USAID activity in the north Nigerian state of Zamfara, one that focused on determining the total educational expenditure for a given year. Funded by an international development agency, the exercise aimed to assist state officials in determining the best ways to plan their education finances. The first problem faced was that the officials—privately—stated that they did not ask for the activity and therefore could not provide counterpart funding to sustain it, as requested by the partners. As good as the project seemed, it was not theirs and was not factored in their approved budget; they therefore could not fund it.

This refusal highlights the wider problem of shared ministerial responsibility that often goes unacknowledged in donor plans. Popular thinking promotes the myth that an educated society is the responsibility of the Ministry of Education alone. In reality, however, the Ministries of Environment, Commerce, State, Health, and others all have a stake in education. In principle, combining expertise, resources, and funding from many ministries increases the possibility of building a successful education program. In many countries, however, responsibilities are modularized and compartmentalized according to the supervising ministry. Under the education financing project referred to above, it became difficult to get non-education ministries who provided education services to come on board. They did not see why they should provide financial data to a ministry that was not theirs. The Ministry of Education, in turn, suddenly realized that it should be the sole custodian of education—no matter where it was offered—and its officials therefore wanted to re-evaluate all educational activities in other portfolios, a task that deviated from the core project. In the attempt to streamline data, in other words, the project heightened ministerial competition.

Ultimately, an agreement was worked out to launch the project. However, while officials co-operated with consultants, agreed to proposed structures, and provided the information needed, private off-record comments reflect bemusement at the year-long exercise. The comments mainly focused on the motives of the funders—and theories ranged from what Nigerians call 'spooky stuff' (that every development partner activity dealing with figures is a cover for spying) to linking the process to violent uprisings in the Middle East. In one instance, consultants were seen as spies for the Nigerian government's anti-graft agency, the Economic and Financial Crimes Commission, due to their insistence on collecting detailed expenditure data, down to the amount spent on gasoline for generators.

The use of local consultants, or 'credible outsiders,' with a national or regional reputation made it possible to overcome suspicions—even though white team leaders often prompted further 'spooky stuff theory,' such as the belief that they were tied to U.S. secret services. (Oddly, the British did not elicit such fear.) As a result, some partners reduced the presence of non-Africans in the field, relying on 'local' consultants to face Ministry officials, gather data, and report to the higher metropolitan level.

Worrying, however, were further off-record comments about the lack of synchronization between what international partner organizations saw through an EfD lens and what local officials described as 'realities on ground' that were indifferent to theoretical perspectives. The mismatch between rhetoric and practice, which extends to other initiatives as well, is revealed in at least four ways.

First, there was lack of synergy among the development partners in the education sector. In north Nigeria, for instance, more than ten development organizations descended onto schools, offices, and communities to provide 'development assistance' without coming up with a unified approach that looked at the local systems holistically. For the most part, they kept their individual programs close to their chests, giving little clue to others about what they were doing and therefore often duplicating efforts—to the bemusement of recipients.

Second, none of the development partners seemed aware of what worked or did not work in the past. There was thus a lack of historical awareness as to how the situation got to the point where international NGOs intervened in the first place. It would appear that someone came up with a concept, sold it to a funding agency, got approval, and took the first flight to Nigeria to start a project. Due to lack of clarity and continuity in government policies, Nigeria's educational system relies substantially on interventions by international aid agencies. And yet these interventions are based not on identified needs of the Nigerian education system—which do not seem to be of much concern—but on the wider global concern with EfD. This often causes a rift between what government policies set out to achieve and what international agencies do.

Third, some of the international agencies exhibited naiveté when it came to offering development assistance because their conception of what constituted a problem differed from what was seen by their target beneficiaries. This was illustrated in 2013 by an NGO that selected target states in Muslim north Nigeria for carrying out a program of 'out-of-school girl-child' education for girls 'aged 16–18,' deemed vulnerable and therefore in need of survival skills. They found it difficult to accept that in northern Nigeria, girls in that age-group are not 'girls' but married women, often in purdah matrimonial situations—and therefore are not available for 'survival skills' training. Yet they ignored the real targets of concern—pre-teen girls who were out of school and hawking food items on the streets, where they were vulnerable to all sorts of predators. This was because the original metropolitan mandate specified the higher age bracket, who it assumed would be more aware of their world.

This naiveté could also make partners miss the ways their projects were being manipulated by recipients for individual ends. Another agency in northern Nigeria insisted on implementing Conditional Cash Transfers (CCT) to families as a means of encouraging them to keep their girls in schools. Development partners failed to notice two problems. First, unrecorded observations of the CCT program indicated that the girls and their parents were motivated by the money to attend school but not to continue with their education; they almost always got married immediately after high school. They came to the cash dispensary centers for money, stayed for a required period to learn, and then left. The cash inducement alone attracted them, not the desire to learn. Ironically, those that continue their education beyond high school are those that do not need the CCTs due to higher economic status. Second, a change in state government put a stop to the program—not because it was inherently bad, but because any credit for program success would go to the previous regime, a situation the new administration could not tolerate. The project was restructured to include the children of party faithful; children whose parents were in opposition were edged out.

Fourth, the education interventions lacked sustainability. Since development partners had metropolitan funding, it was easy to travel widely, set up project offices, buy computers, pay for training, produce manuals, and print attractive reports. The partners rarely pondered what would happen when funding ended and they left the field. They seemed to expect that local managers would maintain the tempo of activities. When another agency entered the picture, it therefore did not bother to bridge the gap that existed between the previous project and the new one. In this sense, 'paradigm paradox'—a structural change that leads to stasis—resulted from both local governance and international project management.

In the end, the anticipated model of change advocated by development partners rarely led to any measurable difference in Nigerian education.

Ultimately, efforts by international agencies concentrate on educational provisions geared to improving enrollment or accountability, typical EfD preoccupations. Yet the fundamental problem of education in Nigeria is not whether students attend schools or not, but that they attend schools with poor learning outcomes, as noted in the examination results cited above.

Implications for Development Practice

Perhaps the biggest problem of implementing EfD in Nigeria is a lack of clarity about whose agenda is being served. The Nigerian government seeks to ensure that education serves development purposes by instituting programs and plans designed to improve citizen welfare (e.g., Education for All; Vision 2000, 2010, 2015, and 2020). Development partners, by contrast, seem more concerned with international benchmarks than local circumstances. For the most part, they appear to be only vaguely aware of government plans and are certainly unaware of their own ignorance of local needs. This author once had a consultant from a major development NGO request an explanation of the structure of the Nigerian educational system whose problems he was employed to synthesize! In another case, a consultant explained to trainees how an Excel spreadsheet could be used to create charts without knowing that they were seasoned computer users who had written the briefing report—complete with charts—on which his own presentation was based. Many expatriate staff fall into what Nigerians refer to as the 'squeaky clean lot'—fresh graduates from U.S. or U.K. universities who studied development and came to Africa filled with messianic zeal but ignorant of the internecine struggles for power and the raw inefficiency of the system they were trying to 'redeem.' At the very least, these examples suggest a striking disregard for local reality.

Overcoming this attitude requires a fundamentally new understanding by those engaged in development work. First, one must reject the old anthropological model of coming to a 'barren' land. For the most part, beneficiaries are aware of their problems, and most requests for partnership ultimately come down to providing funding for solutions that are locally identified. Second, interventions should be based on specific requests—a hard thing to do for a partner with good will and funding. The reality, however, is that beneficiaries need to specify a needed intervention and show their commitment to its sustainability. The partners themselves have to make subsequent engagement contingent on clear proof of the sustainability of previous interventions. Third, development partners working in the same area need to be aware of each other and how their various efforts can be harmonized and synchronized—instead of the current situation in which various partners work in the same domain without coordinating. Fourth, development partners must understand the nature of local educational provisions. A lack of awareness leads to educational plans that are universally the same, reproducing in one place what was done in another. There is also a need to base interventions on direct system analysis rather than 'anticipated development needs,' which take little consideration for local sustainability. For the most part, current 'capacity training' workshops, sensitization meetings, development teams, and other activities are sustained not by the recipients but by the funding of the development partners alone. Rarely do recipient countries build such activities into their long-term strategy budgets. It is hardly surprising, therefore, that they rarely last.

Conclusions

It would be pessimistic in the extreme to suggest that the widespread faith in educational investment as a component of economic development was an aberration. There is evidence in many studies of productivity benefits derived from educational investment.[14] How then do we resolve the paradox of a clear link between education and development and the failure of many education projects to achieve significant results?

First, we must recognize that there is no single answer to the question of how education promotes development: There are many answers depending on circumstance, developmental status, and the specification of variables. Second, the direct policy implications of macro-level research are very limited. They are constrained by dependence on historical relationships that may or may not persist, and the level of aggregation is often so high that effective and ineffective years of schooling are treated as similar. The application of findings from individual countries or groups to other countries is analytically hazardous. General and empirically verified truths about the relation between education and economic development may not hold in every circumstance.

Third, educational effects are associated with various externalities—school fees, instability due to insurgencies and political upheavals, raw poverty, creeping malaise among youth, political indifference to the plight of the poor—that lay beyond the control of particular projects. Without awareness of these externalities, project goals may be undermined.

Fourth, there are many methodological questions in the analysis of relationships between education and economic development that have only partial resolutions. For instance, there has been no convincing data showing the link between earned income and educational status in Nigeria. With a fluid economy, such absolute correlations are difficult to make.

And finally, as Hopkins and McKeown argue, sustainable development will require major changes in policy and mindset, as well as fundamental changes in our lifestyle, economy, and worldview.[15] To date, few financial resources have been dedicated to implementing education programs for sustainable development. Yet even with resources, the reform process is fraught with challenges. The initial step is to develop an awareness within the educational community and the wider public that reorienting education to achieve sustainability is essential. Unfortunately, the need to achieve sustainable development is not seen as sufficiently important to spark a major response in Nigeria. Attempts at awareness-raising are often met with cynicism from officials who fail to share the 'larger' vision held by development partners; instead, officials are typically concerned with solving immediate problems. If leaders at all levels of government are to make progress, the recognition and active involvement of the education sector is imperative.

The effort to win over the education sector to ESD is made more difficult by the fact that sustainable development is a complex, evolving concept that encompasses intricate interactions of natural and human systems. Sustainable development education, by its nature, depends on concepts and analytical tools from a variety of disciplines. For that reason, it is difficult to teach in traditional school settings where studies are divided into disciplinary frameworks. The inherent complexity is exacerbated in Africa by the introduction of a variety of educational strategies that look like experimental models because they have not been tried elsewhere. Successful national education campaigns often have simple messages, such as vaccinate your children, boil drinking water, do not drive drunk, and do not take drugs. Success in the complex arena of sustainable development education will take much longer and be more costly. The challenge to educators is to develop messages that illustrate complexity without overwhelming or confusing students.

The establishment of ESD programs, therefore, requires accountable leadership and realistic strategies. Because sustainable development education is a lifelong process, the formal, non-formal, and informal educational sectors must work together to accomplish local goals.[16] In an ideal world, the three sectors would divide the enormous task of sustainable development education by identifying target audiences as well as areas of responsibility. They would then work innovatively within their realms. This division of effort would reach a broader spectrum of people and prevent redundant effort. Many resources currently exist in the educational and administrative labor pools. Talented educators—especially in the fields of the environment, population, and development—already teach strands of sustainable development education and could easily expand their focus to include other concepts. In developing curricula, however, someone must have a sufficiently wide-ranging vision to pull together the pieces and form a complete picture of the role that individuals, communities, and nations play in a sustainable world.

Finally, our societies will need to examine how goods are manufactured and consumed; the way we use, preserve, conserve, and restore natural resources; and the way we perceive and rank social, political, and economic needs. Sustainable development will require that we learn new ways to think about problems, make decisions, and implement solutions. Education is the key to this effort. Development practitioners can play a strong role in the process only if they allow recipient partners to analyze their own educational systems, rather than coming in with neat theoretical models that do not match local conditions.

Notes

1. The EfD paradigm rests on a decades-old literature. While many early studies focused on industrialized countries, there were important contributions that compared developed and developing economies. In a study of the rates of return to educational investment in 44 countries, Psacharopoulos (1981) (cited in Fagerlind and Saha [1989]) found that primary education yields the highest social and private returns; that private returns are higher than social returns, particularly at the university level; and that all rates of return to investment in education exceed the rates of return on alternative investments in capital. He also found that developing countries' rates of return on education investments are higher than those of advanced industrialized countries at comparable levels.
2. Webster (1984); Psacharopoulos and Woodhall (1985); Fagerlind and Saha (1989).
3. Fagerlind and Saha (1989).
4. Psacharopoulos and Woodhall (1985).
5. Fagerlind and Saha (1989).
6. World Commission on Environment and Development (1987): 43.
7. Olsen (1996): 187.
8. Babikwa (2004).
9. The Good Planet Foundation (2013): 1.
10. In 1991, Decree 2 and 3 abolished the NPEC and handed the management of primary schools over to the local governments. Primary schools once more witnessed a serious downturn. Teachers' salaries went unpaid for months, and teachers embarked on strike after strike. Parents who could afford it withdrew their children and wards from public schools and enrollment dwindled drastically. The drop-out rate increased, and the incidence of street children grew. Fortunately, the government gave ear to public outcries and, through Decree 96 of 1993, reestablished the NPEC, later to become the Universal Basic Education Commission; its state counterpart, the State Primary Education Boards (SPEB), later the State Universal Basic Education Board (SUBEB); and the local government, LGEAs.
11. FME (2007): 10–11.
12. NEI was designed to strengthen state and local government systems that delivered education services for out-of-school youth, orphans, and vulnerable children. The project started as State Education Accounts (SEA) in Kano in about 2005 and ended as the Northern Education Initiative (NEI) in Sokoto in 2013.
13. Students sitting for both examinations are allowed to select up to nine subjects. Candidates are expected to pass five at credit level to gain admission to a university in Nigeria. Most courses will require that the five credit subjects include English Language and Mathematics.

14. Studies have found that:
    ■ farmers (in 18 low-income countries) with four years of primary education pro-
    duced 8% more (Lockheed et al. [1980]);
    ■ a one-year increase in schooling can increase wages by more than 10%—and has
    raised farm output and income by over 2% (Korea) and 5% (Malaysia) (World
    Bank [1991]: 52–53);
    ■ a 1% improvement in national literacy is directly associated with a two-year gain
    in life expectancy (Preston [1976]);
    ■ education is directly related to health: the higher the parents' education, the less
    likely their child will die (Cochrane et al. [1980]);
    ■ children of educated mothers are more likely to be enrolled in school and to
    attain higher education (World Bank [1986]);
    ■ women's education leads to better family health, especially for the children and
    themselves, partly because of higher family income but also due to the mother's
    increased knowledge and use of better health and nutritional practices (World
    Bank [1993]).
15. Hopkins and McKeown (1999).
16. In north Nigeria, 'non-formal education' refers to schools outside the main govern-
    ment system, such as Quranic schools, whereas 'informal education' refers to skills
    and competency training that falls outside the main education system. 'Formal
    education,' of course, designates the main government education system.

Bibliography

Agbor, S. A. (2000). The new African diaspora: Myths and realities of higher education as a
vehicle for nation building in Africa. *Proceedings of the 8th Annual African American
Adult Education Research Pre-Conference—2000 Adult Education research Conference*
(AERC). University of British Columbia. Vancouver, 1–10.

Babikwa, D. J. (2004). *Education and the Creation of Sustainable Rural Communities in
Uganda and Japan: Some Lessons for the DESD.* Paper for Post-Doctoral fellowship,
United Nations University.

Becker, G. S. (1964). *Human Capital: A Theoretical and Empirical Analysis with Special
Reference to Education.* New York: National Bureau of Economic Research.

Bowman, M. J. (1980). Education and Economic Growth: An Overview. In T. King (Ed.),
Education and Income: A Background Study for the World Development Report 1980.
Washington, DC: World Bank Staff Working Paper No 402.

Christensen, L. R., and D. W. Jorgensen. (1969). The Measurement of US Real Capital
Input 1929–67. *Review of Income and Wealth* 125: 293–320.

Cochrane, S. H., D. J. O'Hara, and J. Leslie. (1980). *The Effects of Education on Health.*
Washington, DC: The World Bank.

Denison, E. F. (1962). *The Sources of Economic Growth in the United States and the Alterna-
tives before Us.* New York: Committee for Economic Development.

Denison, E. F. (1967). *Why Growth Rates Differ: Post War Experience in Nine Western Countries.* Washington, DC: Brookings Institution.

Denison, E. F. (1979). *Accounting for Slower Economic Growth: The United States in the
1970s.* Washington, DC: The Brookings Institute.

Fagerlind, I., and L. J. Saha. (1989). *Education and National Development—A Comparative Perspective* (2nd ed.). Exeter: BPCC Wheatons Ltd.

FME, A. (2007). Education Sector Situation Analysis. Draft 5. FME. Abuja.

Foster, P. J. (1987). The Contribution of Education to Development. In G. Psacharopoulos (Ed.), *Economics of Education: Research and Studies*. Oxford: Pergamon, 93–100.

Good Planet Foundation. (2013). *Accelerating Progress to 2015*. A Report Series to the UN Special Envoy for Global Education. Washington, DC: The Good Planet Foundation.

Harbison, F. H., and C. A. Myers. (1964). *Education, Manpower and Economic Growth: Strategies of Human Resource Development*. New York: McGraw Hill.

Harrison, D. (1988). *The Sociology of Modernization and Development*. London: Unwin Hyman.

Hicks, N. L. (1987). Education and Economic Growth. In G. Psacharopoulos (Ed.), *Economics of Education: Research and Studies*. Oxford: Pergamon, 93–100.

Hough, J. (1992). *Educational Cost Benefit Analysis Overseas Development Administration Research*. Report mimeo, in DFID (1993), Education and Development: The issues and the evidence—Education Research Paper No. 06, 1993. London, Department for International Development—Education papers.

Inkeles, A., and D. H. Smith. (1974). *Becoming Modern—Individual Change in Six Developing Countries*. Cambridge: Harvard University Press.

Little, A. W. (1986). From Educating to Employing to Learning to Working. *Prospects* XIV(1): 9–31.

Lockheed, M., D. T. Jamison, and L. E. Lau. (1980). *Farmer Education and Farm Efficiency: A Survey*. Washington, DC: World Bank.

Michaelowa, K. (2000). *Returns to Education in Low Income Countries: Evidence for Africa*. Paper presented at the annual meeting of the Committee on Developing Countries of the German Economic Association (June). Hamburg Institute for International Economics.

Olsen, J. M. F. (1996). Sustainable Development: A New Challenge for Costa Rica. *SAIS Review* 16(1): 187–202.

Preston, S. (1976). *Mortality Patterns in National Populations*. New York: Academic.

Psacharopoulos, G. (1980). *Higher Education in Developing Countries—A Cost Benefit Analysis. World Bank Staff Papers #44*. Washington, DC: World Bank.

Psacharopoulos, G., K. Hinchliffe, C. Dougherty, and R. Hollistor. (1983). *Manpower Issues in Education and Investment: A Consideration of Planning Process and Techniques*. World Bank Staff Working Papers No 624.

Psacharopoulos, G., and M. Woodhall. (1985). *Education for Development: An Analysis of Investment Choices*. Oxford: Oxford University Press.

Saha, L. J. (1991). Universities and National Development—Issues and Problems in Developing Countries. *Prospects* 21(2): 248–57.

Schultz, T. W. (1961). Education and Economic Growth. In N. B. Henry (Ed.), *Social Forces Influencing American Education*. Chicago: University of Chicago Press.

Schultz, T. W. (1980). Nobel Lecture: The Economics of Being Poor. *Journal of Political Economy* 88(4): 639–52.

Schultz, T. W. (1981). *Investing In People—The Economics of Population Quality*. Berkeley, CA: University of California Press.

Webster, A. (1984). *Introduction to the Sociology of Development*. Basingstoke: Palgrave Macmillan.

World Bank. (1986). *Investing in Children*. Washington, DC: World Bank.

World Bank. (1989). *Nigeria: Primary Education Subsector Study*. Report 7389-UNI, Washington, DC: West Africa Department.

World Bank. (1991). *World Development Report: The Challenge of Development*. Washington, DC: Author.

World Bank. (1993). *World Development Report: Investing in Health*. Washington, DC: Author.

World Commission on Environment and Development. (1987). *Our Common Future*. Oxford: Oxford University Press.

Chapter 12

Fantasy, Reality, and Illusion in International Aid

Challenges NGO Workers Face in the Field

August Longino

The field of international development has seen unprecedented change in recent decades, the most notable of which may be the explosive growth of the private sector. In the 1950s and 1960s, international relief work was largely the concern of national governments, whose efforts were paralleled by a relatively small number of private, generally religious organizations. Since then, non-governmental organizations (NGOs) have risen to prominence, with over 1.5 million operating in the United States alone, and millions more overseas.[1] NGOs have become a new kind of actor on the international stage, and their characteristics vary widely. With a diverse range of goals, funding sources, and an undeveloped regulatory infrastructure, NGOs range from multi-national, billion-dollar organizations like Oxfam International (with a budget of approximately $1.3 billion in 2013) to much smaller organizations composed of only one or two staff members. In recent years, NGOs have taken on responsibilities previously reserved for state-run institutions, such as drafting international resolutions, publishing major research studies, and funding large-scale development projects.

NGOs enjoy certain advantages that state-regulated institutions do not. First, large state agencies such as USAID tend to have strictly (though often broadly) defined mandates that do not always allow for specialization or attention to detail. NGOs, on the other hand, may not be accountable to elected officials and so have the freedom to focus on issues of their own choosing, such as women's health, literacy, outdoor education, or clean water. Another difference is that NGOs are not generally subject to the same level of bureaucracy and regulation as their government counterparts. However, NGOs also face challenges that state institutions do not, the greatest of which is their financial dependence on uninformed, recalcitrant, or fickle donors. Whereas USAID uses taxpayer dollars to fund its programming, NGOs must rely on a mixture of private donations, grants, and other awards. This method of funding can create unforeseen and potentially harmful dynamics when the NGO delivering the service is held accountable to and rewarded by wealthy donors for services provided to beneficiaries in faraway countries. This is especially true if the NGO itself is the only portal through which donors receive information about those people their money is intended to help.

NGOs also serve as the point of entry for many aid workers into the world of international development, and aid workers staffing foreign projects tend to be younger than their counterparts in other professions.[2] The large number of NGOs focused on a diverse array of issues has created a growing supply of entry-level positions available to new, inexperienced aid workers, many of whom are recent college graduates. These positions allow new entrants to choose a specific area of interest, in terms of both geography and subject matter. Since many smaller NGOs have limited resources, they must take full advantage of volunteer labor and entry-level workers willing to accept a low starting salary. This can work as an advantage and a disadvantage for NGOs. Though low salaries allow for the allocation of a greater share of fund to programming, they also cause human capital problems, including high rates of employee turnover as volunteers are poached by other institutions, and an inability to hire selectively, since more-skilled workers tend to seek better-compensated jobs. As an aid worker who started field work just two days after college graduation, I experienced directly the obstacles faced by many fresh-faced, idealistic development workers confronted for the first time with the realities of their chosen profession.

My experience was with a mid-level medical relief organization, Timmy Global Health, that had an annual budget of around $1.3 million, making it representative of a broad range of similar organizations that operate around the world. Timmy Global Health describes its mission as "[e]xpanding access to healthcare; empowering students and volunteers to tackle global health challenges." To accomplish this mission, it works with local hospitals and governments to run primary care clinics that move between small underserved communities on a daily basis over the course of a one- or two-week service trip. Clinics are staffed by volunteers, including a minimum of four medical providers (physicians, nurse practitioners, or physician's assistants), two pharmacists, and two nurses, as well as a larger group of volunteers with no medical training (generally undergraduate college students). These students are part of Timmy Global Health's college "chapters": student-run organizations at many U.S. universities that run an annual week-long service trip, allowing for year-round support in Timmy Global Health service areas. These chapters assist the organization during the year by fundraising, networking, developing independent projects, and recruiting new medical professionals to come to communities. During the trips (also referred to as "medical brigades"), students do simple supervised tasks such as counting pills, measuring patients' height and weight, and recording data. This is a popular model for NGOs focused on short-term, episodic interventions because it allows for a wide-reaching volunteer support system that enables a small number of low-cost domestic and international staff to direct and coordinate large projects.[3] Students in Timmy Global Health chapters participate enthusiastically, since many of them lack experience abroad and are eager to learn about the fields of medicine and international development.

In 2010, I was one such student, participating in the Tufts University Timmy Chapter, collecting funds and distributing flyers in my spare time. The reward for this work was a week-long medical brigade to the community of Xela, Guatemala. Our chapter was composed largely of pre-medical undergraduate students hoping to do some shadowing and perhaps find inspiration for an effective medical school application essay. There were also a smaller number of students who, like me, were interested in the field of international development and eager to add real, hands-on work experience to their resumes. On my first and only brigade as a student, I served as a Spanish-English interpreter, translating between doctors and their patients, and giving detailed instructions in Spanish on how to take each medication distributed by our pharmacy. Intrigued by the work, I was excited to find that Timmy Global Health was opening a new service site in the Amazon Basin, the most remote and rugged area in which the organization had ever operated. It was also the most interesting and wild place that I could imagine, and I saw it as the perfect entry-level opportunity to show that I was capable of running a development project independently. I immediately applied for the newly open position of Medical Programs Coordinator for the Amazon Basin and was hired after two interviews in the spring of my senior year. Considering my lack of experience and demonstrated ability, the speed with which I was hired is a testament to the faith Timmy Global Health places in its students, as well as the need for workers willing to work for a starting salary of $500 per month (a middle-class income in Napo, the rural Ecuadorian province I would call home). Two days after my graduation, I was on a plane to Ecuador, brimming with confidence and completely unprepared for the challenges that awaited me there.

In my experience, and those of other young development workers new to the field, the first and biggest surprise is the stark difference between the classroom and the real world. Despite having written lengthy term papers on the barriers to development, and having examined case studies of many different projects, my schooling was of little use when practical goals needed to be accomplished. One issue was that my academic background was grounded in theory. Broad, overarching concepts of socio-economic philosophy were used to generalize and prescribe widely applicable but abstract solutions. A classic example was my study of corrupt local politicians, a problem, I had read, that was best overcome by educating local actors and engaging them in a strengthened civil society that could eventually unite to resist political parasitism. These theories were sound and well researched, but their aims were intangible. A step-by-step guide to civil society creation was nowhere to be found. My job provided me with much more immediate and practical lessons.

In order to run a medical brigade in the Amazon Basin, I needed the local government's authorization, as well as infrastructural components that only they could provide. Without the government's four-wheel drive trucks, local guides, and staff to translate between Spanish and local indigenous dialects, Timmy Global Health would be useless, regardless of how many physicians and medications we could provide. This is not to say that the local government did not also stand to gain from helping Timmy. The free medical care, referral services, and medications that we provided were of high quality, and the news that a brigade is in town spreads quickly. This made Timmy brigades a perfect populist instrument for local political parties, each of which tried to claim that they were the ones providing free healthcare to their constituents. By taking political credit for work done by Timmy Global Health, politicians reaped the benefits of our volunteers' effort. It took me some time to realize that our government partners were not wholly sincere in their generosity because, naïve as I was, I had not considered all of the motives of the parties involved. The eventual compromise was a kind of balance that, despite being commonplace in the practice of aid, is rarely discussed in the classroom. The government provided Timmy with the necessary transportation and staff to run our programming, and, in return, they were allowed to write their names on the trucks that carried volunteers, and occasionally appear with a video camera to film the work being done. I soon established certain rules: There could be no distribution of t-shirts or other political materials, there could be no appearances or speeches by political figures, and Timmy Global Health, not our government partners, would select the communities that clinics served. These rules were constantly debated and infringed on, and their enforcement was a daily struggle that affected the quality of Timmy's work in the region, requiring a calculated give-and-take that was never mentioned in my classes. In textbooks, local politicians were either corrupt "bad guys" to be confronted or avoided, or laudable "good guys" to be supported and congratulated. In practice, these black-and-white distinctions broke down almost immediately, with actors widely distributed across a spectrum of gray.

The challenges of working alongside local institutions are also often overlooked, especially when such a high value is placed on sometimes vague, idealized objectives like "Integration of Local Stakeholders" and "Empowerment through Collaboration." While these are worthy goals, essential to the sustainability of any project, the practical steps to achieving them are often neglected in academic literature. In Ecuador, local elections were particularly difficult because they often preceded a change of the party that was in charge of Patronato Provincial, the government institution with which Timmy Global Health partners. With every political change came a complete replacement of almost all Patronato employees, as the newly elected party repaid campaign favors with coveted government positions. This is common practice in Ecuador, and it often results in unskilled individuals who delivered many votes filling roles that require considerable training. In the United States, civil servants responsible for the day-to-day workings of the state do not change with the party in power. Regardless of who wins an election, the mailman and the IRS agent keep their jobs and do not require retraining. In many developing nations, however, every institution is almost completely replaced after elections with inexperienced workers who may abandon the initiatives of the previous administration, preventing programs from stabilizing or growing. This high rate of turnover, coupled with elevated levels of political polarization, made it difficult to establish protocols and working relationships with government partners. This instability affects all kinds of aid work, but the field of medical relief is particularly vulnerable. Patients' medical needs are almost always time-sensitive, meaning that the long, unexpected delays common to work in developing countries can have dire consequences—a difference of only a few hours in transportation time can mean the difference between life and death for a patient. Impressing this urgency on each wave of new employees was costly in terms of time, effort, and patient outcomes. After the third complete personnel change, I realized that the problems we were facing as a result of new, untrained employees were the real-life results my textbooks vaguely alluded to in their discussions of how detrimental populist politics can be to development work.

Aside from Patronato, the other major government office with which Timmy Global Health interacts is the Ecuadorian Ministry of Health, which has the stated mission of providing free healthcare for all citizens. Because the system is government-run, administrative posts are highly politicized, with public hospitals and clinics covered in campaign slogans for the ruling party. As in many left-leaning countries in Latin America, an Ecuadorian doctors' education is largely paid for by public funds, in exchange for service in a public hospital as well as an obligatory "rural year," during which newly graduated doctors are required to move to a remote location to serve the local population. This law has its detractors, who claim that, by taking fresh graduates, the system lets new doctors use the rural poor "as practice" before moving back to the city, creating a never-ending stream of inexperienced, unspecialized physicians in rural areas. The system is also plagued by social problems. Those with the economic and social resources to become physicians generally come from Ecuador's upper and middle classes, groups that tend to discriminate against the poor and indigenous groups that populate rural places like the Amazon Basin. In Timmy clinics, patients would often express surprise at the physical exam, explaining that many of the local doctors avoided physical contact with indigenous patients whenever possible.

Ecuador's current ruling party, "The Citizens' Revolution," maintains a political climate of patriotic socialism, which places considerable pressure on the Ministry of Health to produce positive results without relying on foreign assistance. This situation creates an interesting dynamic with local Ministry representatives. Because the Ministry of Health does not have the resources to accomplish its goals, many healthcare workers in the local Subcentros de Salud (regional health outposts) are eager to point out gaps in their coverage where Timmy Global Health can intervene, reducing the workload on already-exhausted doctors and nurses. At the local level, these interactions go smoothly, with Subcentro staff occasionally soliciting donations of medications, scrubs, and other medical supplies, and Timmy Global Health benefiting from their knowledge of local communities and pathologies. However, this collaboration is rarely celebrated or even discussed at higher administrative levels, because admitting that there is a need for foreign support (especially from the United States) could be politically ruinous. Part of my job was to provide senior Ministry executives with plausible deniability by learning the schedule of supervisory visits and moving Timmy Global Health physicians to a different area when necessary. Of course, because we featured heavily in Patronato's radio and television campaigns, we remained the Ministry's worst-kept secret; nonetheless, physical appearances mattered, another example of the kind of gray-zone negotiation that is often required to operate effectively on development projects.

Aside from these institutional quandaries, there was the challenge of daily living in an unfamiliar and culturally complex environment. Social integration is a time consuming, emotionally difficult process that many new aid workers find challenging. Where a more experienced employee with a number of overseas stints might have more success, new aid workers often waste a great deal of time and effort simply because they do not have the cultural insight to know how best to achieve their goals. It is not uncommon for new in-country staff to arrive in the field, only to leave shortly thereafter, forcing the supervising organization to scramble to find a replacement. These productivity losses are part of the price that NGOs pay by having a labor force that is disproportionately young and inexperienced. Unfortunately, it is also common for workers to leave the field of development after gaining sufficient experience to be hired by the more lucrative private sector, where their international skills are put to use by multinational companies. This cycle removes valuable expertise from the pool of human capital available to NGOs.

In the health sector, inexperience is limiting in a variety of ways. When I arrived, I was largely ignorant of information that I now know is essential to the work I was asked to perform. My rudimentary understanding of local culture was a barrier to successful communication with patients. In many cases, I was put in the position of convincing—often begging—a patient to leave his or her small village in the Amazon in order to travel many hours to the mountainous capital city of Quito in order to undergo an important operation. For an indigenous, Quechua-speaking patient that has never traveled more than a dozen miles from his or her front door, Quito might as well be a different planet. Far from family, populated by strange people that speak a different language, and rumored to be freezing cold, a trip to Quito to undergo surgery (itself a poorly understood concept) was a terrifying prospect. Over time I got better at addressing fears like these, but the social barriers to health remained formidable.

Another problem was my lack of medical knowledge. I had been hired as a Medical Programs Director, whose responsibilities included medical translation for doctors, explaining World Health Organization protocols for tropical diseases to American physicians, and, most importantly, organizing the follow-up care that patients received at local hospitals between brigades. My degrees were in International Development and Spanish—I was in no way prepared for the complex medical questions addressed to me by American and Ecuadorian medical professionals and patients. I was also in charge of Timmy Global Health's pharmacy, which contained a wide range of medications, from oral and IV antibiotics to topical creams to drugs used to combat chronic hypertension and diabetes. I spent long hours doing internet research, and volunteer physicians and pharmacists were instrumental in my trial-by-fire medical training. Nevertheless, there is no doubt that my lack of medical knowledge was a detriment to Timmy Global Health's programming in the Amazon Basin.

I had traveled extensively in Latin America as a child and studied abroad in Chile in college. Neither of these structured experiences prepared me to be an independent, professional adult in a largely indigenous area of rural Ecuador. In the months leading up to my departure, I did all I could to educate myself about the place that would become my home for the next two years. When it comes to learning about a foreign country, there are any number of resources available to the tourist, the backpacker, or the traveling businessperson, but almost none for the aspiring aid worker. Comprehensive guidebooks listed Ecuadorian hostels and boating tours for all tastes and budgets, but even the most detailed of these dedicated only a few pages to cultural history or local living. In order to find a social analysis with insights into more than bargaining strategies, I turned to the many anthropological papers published on Ecuadorian people. These were as numerous (if not more so) than the travelers' guides, but, where the guidebooks were too superficial, the anthropological texts were often overly specific and esoteric. A historical comparison of Western and indigenous roofing techniques was not going to help me find a place to live.

The kind of information that a newly arrived aid worker needs lies between these two extremes. I was interested first and foremost in finding a home (a surprisingly difficult proposition in Napo, Ecuador), figuring out whom to talk to when the power went out, and how to solve the ever-present problem of security in a country with stark income inequality and where all Americans are believed to be wealthy. Outside these practical concerns, I found that I was badly in need of a lesson in local protocol and indigenous customs. Fortunately, local Ecuadorian Timmy Global Health staff had experience educating new arrivals on some of the finer points of regional etiquette: Eat at least some of whatever is offered to you; never respond to a request with "no" ("not at the moment" is acceptable); it is the responsibility of the homeowner to secure the house (if a door is locked, then theft is the fault of the thief, a criminal; if a door is left unlocked, theft is the fault of the owner, a fool). Most importantly, they were able to help me understand the strangeness of my position as a gringo aid worker and the curious paradox my presence created for my neighbors: "A young man from America has come to Ecuador, but anyone with any sense is trying to travel in the opposite direction: from Ecuador to America. He says he is here to help, but he seems clueless about some of the most basic realities—he does not even know who to talk to when the power goes out!" In order to be taken seriously by my colleagues and neighbors, I needed to overcome two sets of stereotypes. The first were my own. Even (perhaps especially) as a college-educated, self-aware student of development, it took time for me to see the people around me as individuals, rather than as the caricatures I had read about for years. The second set was about Americans. In the Napo region, Americans tended to fall into one of three categories: oil workers, tourists, or missionaries. My role as a government negotiator, provider of health services, and guide for volunteer medical providers fell outside these boundaries, leaving it up to me to explain my position and my identity.

My odd position in society is best described by my unorthodox security system. As an American living in a small, poor neighborhood on the outskirts of town, I could not help but stick out. Not only was I a foot taller than everyone in my town, but my job required frequent comings and goings by government officials and other Americans in fancy trucks full of medicine and equipment. All of this drew attention to my presence and made me an object of fascination for local children and adults, as well as a target for thieves, burglars, and pickpockets. After the second break-in, I knew I had to find a low-cost but effective way to protect my house while I was away on brigade. My first instinct was to hire a security guard, an idea my friends and neighbors found laughable and very American. They reasoned, correctly, that posting a guard would only encourage theft by showing that I must be protecting something of tremendous value, that the security guard would eventually conspire to rob me himself, and that the cost of such an investment would vastly outweigh any benefit. A solution occurred to me during one of the informal evening English classes I taught to neighborhood children. The other houses in the neighborhood were almost never robbed. This was partly because they were not associated with wealth, as I was, but it was also because as long-time, "legitimate" community members, their familial and social ties protected them from the thieves who found my house such an exotic and inviting prize. As an outsider, I was no one's relative, close friend, or godparent. In short, I had insufficient social capital to guarantee my security. In order to solve this problem, I needed to find a way to contribute locally and visibly. I started with the most important part of any community: the children. Disguising my survey questions as English lessons, I asked my students about what our district lacked and told them to quiz their parents. After about two weeks of debate, my security system began to take shape, in the form of a large, homemade chicken coop in my front yard. The mechanism was simple. I would purchase the necessary inputs: wood, wire, chicks, and cornmeal; the local children would have the responsibility of feeding and caring for the chickens, and keeping an eye on my house in my absence. In return for this service, we would sell some of the chickens, and the proceeds would go to the children's families. We would also butcher some of the hens ourselves, and deliver plucked and prepared birds to the students' parents. Older children were given supervisory responsibility over younger ones, who delighted in the day-to-day tasks of gathering eggs and scattering feed. And though the process was not as idyllic as it might sound, it did work. Parents became invested in my presence, even if only as a way to keep their kids occupied after school. My gifts of food were culturally appropriate and were reciprocated many times over. In coming months, I occasionally came home to reports that a watchful neighbor had run off some suspicious stranger. Interactions like these served to break down misconceptions held both by me, an unconsciously aloof gringo, and my neighbors, initially untrusting of a newcomer in their town.

As I became more comfortable with my life in Ecuador, the pressures I noticed most began to change. No longer worried about issues like my personal safety or well-being, I set my sights on professional goals. Gradually, I began to realize the seriousness of a much-discussed problem in the world of international development: the gap between fieldwork and funding. Timmy Global Health is a small NGO that secures funding mainly through private donations, a common model for medical relief organizations. This is what fundamentally differentiates development work from other goal-oriented professions like business or government. Compensation is not directly linked to service—the client who receives a service gets it for free, because it is paid for by a third party: the donor. This disconnect effectively takes power away from the person being served and gives it to the person doing the compensating. In a for-profit business model, these two roles are filled by the same person: the customer. Because the customers pay for services they value, they ultimately have some control over which services are provided. In the development world, the donors become a paying intermediary for the underserved people receiving the services.

As an agent in the field, I would often see needs that fell within the scope of Timmy Global Health's mission. A common example was a child whose life could be saved or drastically improved by a costly surgery that Timmy could help pay for. Timmy's limited budget could not cover all these situations, so part of my job was helping to choose which cases to fund. I would write a report detailing the expense involved, the likely outcomes, and a cost-benefit analysis from the perspective of the patient; I then sent it to the main office in Indianapolis where it was evaluated, with a final decision handed down in the form of a yes or no. How many of these cases I was allowed to act on depended entirely on the generosity of Timmy's donor base. Often I would write a small promotional piece for the Timmy website, with an accompanying photo, beseeching visitors to fund this or that patient. After a successful operation, I would write a triumphant post with happy photos and a testimonial by a grateful family.

There is nothing immediately wrong with this picture. After all, good work is done, a life is saved, and the donor has made the world a better place. What started to bother me was that I was never asked to write about operations that failed. And operations did fail, for a variety of reasons, including surgical complications, unsanitary housing conditions, or inattention on the part of Timmy Global Health staff like me. What I came to understand was that except for a self-imposed sense of duty, and occasional reports to the U.S. office, I was almost never held accountable for any negative outcomes of my work, and certainly not by the people I was serving. Where elected officials have voters, or businesses have stockholders, many development organizations have only their powerless underserved populations, indirectly represented by well-intentioned but distant donors.

This reality was driven home to me whenever I tried to get funding for larger, more systemic projects like local health outposts or patient transportation infrastructure. My boss, Timmy Global Health's Executive Director, often understood the need, but, above a certain amount, expenses had to be approved by a Board of Directors composed of individuals that were themselves mostly wealthy donors, not aid workers. At first I was surprised by the amount of cajoling necessary to sway the board, but I came to understand that donors have a different view from fieldworkers. A board member might feel that a 4×4 truck for moving patients from the countryside to a city hospital has a less direct effect than allotting money for more surgeries, which seem to reliably result in grateful testimonial blog posts. The aid worker in the field can see that those blog posts are coming disproportionately from villages with access to bus routes and that the logistical apparatus for moving remote patients to hospitals breaks down due to complications with the local government partner responsible for transportation. The clearest but least-expressed view belongs to the supposed beneficiary, the patient, who waits and waits for a truck to take him or her to the hospital. Sometimes, it never comes.

If the NGO were a for-profit company, this would never stand. The customer is always right, and whoever was responsible for the negative experience would be fired. In the aid world, this logic does not apply. Perhaps if the board members knew about the transportation problem, things would be different. But the board is composed of administrators and donors who have limited time to read and understand the subtleties of programming in the many different countries they serve. This is the same reason that my posts soliciting help for patients had to be short: Most donors do not have the time to read an in-depth analysis of development dollars. They want a one-click guarantee that they will create a tangible improvement in the world, a message that is efficiently conveyed by two short paragraphs with italicized quotes and a patient photograph.

This problem has led to a series of lectures and publications lamenting the prevalence of mediocre, ineffective aid (nicely summarized in a 2011 TED talk by David Damberger). The response has taken two major forms. The first is an effort to increase accountability to and involvement with the beneficiaries themselves, which has led to a more sophisticated view of patients and partners as "local stakeholders." This is an effort to give that patient some power to make their situation known and even do something about it. This trend plays into the second part of the paradigm shift, which is a push to make more detailed data available to donors in a way that is easily digestible, in hopes of encouraging more informed decisions. This has resulted in donor-funded NGOs generating publicly available budgets and quarterly reports, just like their counterparts in business.

One of the largest challenges to this new orthodoxy has been determining which data are significant, and then collecting them. I have some experience with this issue in the field of rural healthcare provision. A large part of my job in Ecuador was helping to computerize our system of paper records, shifting our mobile clinics from paper charts to a new Electronic Health Record (EHR). This effort began when a group of young, charitable software engineers from Microsoft saw an opportunity to move Timmy Global Health into the modern age. They created an EHR for Timmy that was specifically designed for the challenges of the developing world. With only a generator, a laptop, and some tablets, Timmy clinics were suddenly generating secure, HIPAA-compliant patient data that we could use for everything from public health research to medicine inventories to referral rates. This new system (dubbed TimmyCare), and others like it, are changing the face of development aid. With large amounts of readily available information, it is becoming easier and easier to demonstrate needs, explain interventions, and, most importantly, link those interventions to outcomes. Of course, this solution has created new problems. Until relatively recently, data management and quantitative research skills have not been as essential to the small-time NGO as a charismatic executive director or a well-connected board of directors; this new kind of talent is slow to enter the field. But for the moment, data-driven decision-making is gradually changing that reality.

As in many disciplines, new ideas in development often come from workers who are confronted with problems to solve. The new wave of young employees, inexperienced though they might be, is changing the field of international aid very quickly. From the 1940s to the 1970s, when development was mainly the responsibility of governments, funds tended to be dedicated to large, state-built infrastructure projects or state-run health interventions. As NGOs entered the field starting in the 1970s, along with their young, innovative, entrepreneurial workers, the type and rhythm of activities changed. Now, new trends emerge all the time, as young professionals carefully assess the pros and cons of novel interventions. One example of this phenomenon is microcredit, which began in the 1970s and was enthusiastically adopted in the 1990s as a neoliberal, cure-all for poverty.

The application of modern research methods to aid work may also be due partly to the rise of NGOs and their younger workforces, all of whom have an incentive to demonstrate that their interventions are the most effective. At Timmy Global Health, and in the field of medical aid in general, new indicators—specific quantitative measures of service that can be used to draw conclusions about the quality of an intervention—are extremely important, because the services provided are logistically complex. In order for patients to complete the referral process, they must be diagnosed in the field, their information must be accurately recorded, and government drivers have to coordinate with the health promoter and the families to take the patients to Quito, where appointments have to be arranged, attended, and paid for. Sometimes Quechua-Spanish translators are necessary if the doctors and patients are to understand one another. Depending on the outcome of the consultation, follow-up appointments may be required, in which case this process has to be repeated. Each of these events is an opportunity for the system to break down, and, without very specific knowledge of where problems occur, it can be difficult to assess why patients are not receiving the care they need. In order to get a clear picture of this chain of events, Timmy Global Health has multiple indicators to evaluate quality: the fraction of patients that get picked up from their villages, the fraction of those patients that sees a doctor in the city, and the fraction of patients that report success in any further care needed. Collecting and analyzing this data by hand consumes a large amount of labor and time, which is why a new generation of aid workers is using technological tools like TimmyCare not only to help collect but to analyze large datasets in order to improve the care they provide.

Young college graduates are more involved in international aid today than ever before. Some argue that this is the logical result of a globalized media that shows the plight of the world's poor more clearly than it has been shown in the past. Others say the movement has more to do with an economic recession in the developed world, which is pushing over-educated and under-employed young jobseekers into previously unexplored niches. Whatever the reason, recent graduates hoping to find a development job with a mid-sized NGO should know what they are getting into. The ever-shifting nature of the field dictates that by the time they read these words, a new set of ideas will already have taken hold. What most likely will not have changed are the very real challenges of sociocultural integration and reconciliation of classroom instruction with real-world complexity. Even more certain is the fact that the field of development aid has benefited from the innovative ideas of young, multi-disciplinary workers, as demonstrated by projects like TimmyCare.

Notes

1. On the first figure, see www.humanrights.gov/dyn/2016/01/fact-sheet-non-gov ernmental-organizations-ngos-in-the-united-states/. On the second, see www.cid. org.nz/news/25-facts-and-stats-about-ngos-worldwide/.
2. This is in part because older, more experienced aid workers are often hired away by for-profit businesses, where their expertise in foreign affairs remains a valuable asset.
3. Global Brigades and Shoulder to Shoulder are similar organizations.

Index

Printed in the United States
by Baker & Taylor Publisher Services